PROGRAMMING ON PURPOSE

PURPOSE

III

Essays on Software Technology

P.J. Plauger

PTR Prentice Hall
Englewood Cliffs, New Jersey 07632

Acquisitions editor: Paul Becker
Editorial assistant: Noreen Regina
Cover design director: Eloise Starkweather
Cover designer: Lundgren Graphics
Manufacturing buyer: Mary E. McCartney

 Published by PTR Prentice-Hall, Inc.
A Simon & Schuster Company
Englewood Cliffs, New Jersey 07632

The publisher offers discounts on this book when ordered in
bulk quantities. For more information, contact Corporate Sales Department,
PTR Prentice Hall, 113 Sylvan Avenue, Englewood Cliffs, NJ 07632.
Phone: 201-592-2863; FAX: 201-592-2249.

Printed in the United States of America
10 9 8 7 6 5 4 3 2 1

ISBN   0-13-328113-2

Prentice-Hall International (UK) Limited, *London*
Prentice-Hall of Australia, Pty. Limited, *Sydney*
Prentice-Hall Canada Inc., *Toronto*
Prentice-Hall Hispanoamericana, S.A., *Mexico*
Prentice-Hall of India Private Limited, *New Delhi*
Prentice-Hall of Japan, Inc., *Tokyo*
Simon & Schuster Asia Pte. Ltd., *Singapore*
Editora Prentice-Hall do Brazil, Ltda., *Rio de Janeiro*

In memory of Isaac Asimov,
who taught us
that complexity need not be obscure
and that rationality need not be cold

PERMISSIONS

The essays in this book originally appeared as installments
of the monthly column "Programming on Purpose" by P.J. Plauger
in the magazine *Computer Language,* published by Miller Freeman Inc.
All are reprinted by permission of the author.

TRADEMARKS

TYPOGRAPHY

This book was typeset in Palatino, Avant Garde,
Bitstream Cloister, and Courier bold by the author
using a Compaq SLT/386s-20 computer running
Ventura Publisher 4.0.1 and Corel Draw 2.01L
under Microsoft Windows 3.1.

Table of Contents

Preface

I began a journey in July, 1986, that continues to this day. That month marks the first installment of my column "Programming on Purpose" in the magazine *Computer Language*. Many years and many issues later, I find myself still writing those monthly columns. And, *mirabile dictu*, I have yet to miss an issue.

Do something every month for six or more years and material accumulates. I have been asked repeatedly by readers to make some of that accumulated material more widely available. For many years my excuse was that I was too busy to do so. I was president of my own software company, Whitesmiths, Ltd. Then I sold the company to become a full-time writer. Packaging these essays has at last risen to the top of the queue.

This particular collection concerns itself with the technology of writing computer software. That can span many disciplines. You will find essays on computer arithmetic and approximating math functions, on human perception and artificial intelligence, on encrypting data and clarifying documentation. If a programmer may need to know it to do a job, it's fair game here. You will find here a useful sampler of topics not always covered in conventional computer science courses.

Thus, this collection can serve as supplemental reading for an intermediate or advanced course in programming methods, such as data structures or algorithms. For "remedial software engineering," it can be quite useful. The independent reader can get a taste of many topics. Some are fundamental to every day programming. Some are at the cutting edge. All are valuable to the practicing software engineer.

I follow each essay with a brief Afterword. That gives me the opportunity to fill in historical context where necessary. It also lets me excuse away the worst naivetes. I chose to present these notes as Afterwords rather than Forewords so as not to bias the reader up front. Mostly, the essays speak for themselves.

Other collections from "Programming on Purpose" deal with other themes. Besides programming technology, I have written essays on (among other things): software design, software standards development, the business of software, and the people who love and write computer software. Some essays are humorous, some are deadly serious. A few are gems, but I like to think that all are worth reading. If you enjoy what you find here, please consider the other collections as well.

The magazine business sees considerable turnover of editorial staff. Miller Freeman, the publisher of *Computer Language,* is no exception. I have thus enjoyed the services of many editors over the years. All have worked hard to rescue my prose from its more florid excursions. They have nevertheless permitted me to retain a certain colloquial illiteracy that I find comfortable. I thank all the people at Miller Freeman who, over the years, have helped make these essays more readable. You should too.

Two people in particular deserve oak-leaf clusters. Regina Starr Ridley, now a publisher at Miller Freeman, was one of my earliest editors. And Nicole Freeman, now a managing editor there, has cheerfully haunted my career in many editorial guises. I am happy to acknowledge their continuing assistance in making "Programming on Purpose" better. I am also happy to count both as good friends.

Having given credit where it is due, I must issue a warning. I re-edited these essays from the original machine readable. I certainly strove to recapture the spirit of *Computer Language* edits, but I make no pretense at following them to the letter. If any have lost ground as a result, you can blame me.

P.J. Plauger
Concord, Massachusetts

1 You Must Be Joking

This being the April Fool's issue, I felt a strong obligation to provide something specious, dry, and puckish by way of an essay. I flinched, however, at one frightening possibility — suppose nobody noticed? (Have you ever wondered why professional people so seldom go on strike? Same reason.)

As a safer course, I decided to take this opportunity to celebrate in print some of the design and engineering gaffes that I have run afoul of over the years. In all cases, these are fundamental decisions that, once I understood that they were deliberate and premeditated, elicited the thunderstruck remark, "You must be joking!" These are also decisions that have cost me and other practitioners of the programming trade countless hours of productivity, either because of the high error rates they lead to or because of the energy that must be dedicated to doing battle with their consequences. We're talking the April Fool's Hall of Fame for data processing, here.

In no particular order, here are some of my most unhousebroken pet peeves.

First is "the NUXI problem." I guess DEC gets principal credit for this one, but I'm not sure. It seems that, once upon a time (in the early 1960s), a company called IBM married the disparate technologies of scientific and commercial computing into one cohesive family of machines called System/360. Its upgraded form, System/370, still dominates mainframe computing, in case you hadn't noticed. Never mind all the mistakes they made as pioneers, the fact is that IBM succeeded in many important ways. System/370 also influenced many subsequent machine architectures. Several often imitated features are:

1) eight-bit bytes
2) twos-complement integer arithmetic on one-, two-, and four-byte integers
3) byte-level addressing, using the lowest-addressed byte as the address of a multibyte datum

Yes, I know there are still significant architectures in use today that differ in one or more of those attributes, but there are also gazillions of lines of code (written in FORTRAN, Pascal, and C among other languages) that work right only if all those attributes are as stated. And if you list the best selling computers of all sizes, this class tops the list.

When DEC introduced the PDP-11, it had all these attributes. It differed from System/370 in one important way, however. Whereas on System/370, a two-byte integer had its more significant byte at the lower byte address, the PDP-11 put its *less* significant byte there. If you write 0 for the less significant byte, and 1 for the other, then System/370 is a *big-endian* with integers stored as **10**, and PDP-11 is a *little-endian* with integers stored as **01**.

My first tip off that something fishy was going on was when I ran across the **SWAB** (for "swap bytes") instruction in the original PDP-11 manual. It struck me as silly to dedicate a precious instruction merely to optimizing a left rotate by eight bits. Surely that didn't happen all that often. Then I reread the description of data formats, slapped my forehead, and expostulated (in the general direction of Maynard, Mass.), "You must be joking!"

The only reason I can contrive, to this day, for trotting up a new way of ordering bytes is that you can locate the smaller integer (one-byte) within the larger (two-byte) without incrementing the address. In sixteen years of living with little-endian architectures, I have encountered any number of bugs encouraged by this latitude, but never a case where it truly makes life better.

Far worse, the introduction of variant byte orders has created a whole bestiary of difficulties in moving multibyte data among machines, and in writing programs that run on diverse instruction sets. We early users of the PDP-11 quickly found uses for that **SWAB** instruction, in all the ad hoc translation programs we had to contrive to get existing data (and cross-assembled programs) onto the PDP-11 from other machines. And we slowly learned all the subtle ways that byte-order dependencies can creep into code, particularly in the hands of programmers innocent in the evil ways of hardware designers.

My favorite name for this syndrome is the NUXI problem. I believe Dennis Ritchie coined the term as a way of describing the putative effect on UNIX when moved between architectures with insufficient forethought. It gets byte-swapped, or NUXIed if you wish. (NUXI is *not* a trademark of TAT&.)

The real killer, however, lies not in that simple **SWAB** kludge that came with the PDP-11, but in all the variant byte orders that have come afterward. There are only two ways you can order two bytes, **10** and **01**. But with four or more bytes you can get pretty creative. For long integers, I know of machines that use **0123** (VAX), **3210** (System/370, MC68000), and **2301** (PDP-11).

PDP-11 and VAX floating point somehow ended up with **67452301**. Intel and Motorola both use IEEE floating-point format, but the former is **01234567** and the latter is **76543210**. The NSC32016 uses **0123** for integers in data space, and **3210** for constants embedded in the instruction stream! And if you think that's bad, I know of a significant new comer that's even more exciting. But I am constrained by nondisclosure from telling you what the machine is or how the designers could contrive yet another variation on this overworked theme.

Still another sad side effect of this arbitrary variation in byte ordering haunts the design of UNIX itself. As a portable operating system, UNIX is potentially capable of enforcing a standard format for disk-based file systems across multiple architectures. It's always the same code manipulating the control information of a file system, regardless of the machine architecture you're running on. Unfortunately, that control information (called inodes, super blocks, and free lists in UNIX-ese) involves lots of multibyte data, and that data is read and written by the UNIX resident in native byte order for the host machine. What this means is that you can have two machines running identical releases of UNIX and equipped with identical disk (or diskette) drives, but you can't make a file system on one machine and read it on the other if the CPUs support different native byte orders.

I am told that this behavior was the result of an intentional decision made in the early days of porting UNIX about. I was never privy to the reasons behind the decision, but there are many small ways in which UNIX seems to presume that file systems are the private property of the machine that first made them, not to be involved in interstate commerce. You can guess my reaction when I heard of this decision.

If performance was a consideration, then it was a misplaced concern. The Idris operating system has always supported a standard byte order for file systems, regardless of host. It just swaps bytes about as necessary as control information moves in and out of memory. We have never measured a significant performance degradation from this extra work. On the other hand, having truly interchangeable file systems has been invaluable in moving data among diverse Idris machines (and in moving Idris to new machines, for that matter).

I have railed too often in the past about the ghettoization of the UNIX community to bore you further with this particular topic. Let me just end with a whimsical sigh that the NUXI problem bites in so many subtle ways.

The next gripe I'll call "militant segmentism." Intel gets credit for this one. Picking on the architecture of the Intel 8086 family is like shooting fish in a barrel, but I'm not going after the obvious shortcomings here. There were strong market forces pulling this design in several directions. (See **Pla87**.) Those forces explain a number of the peculiarities of the 8086, even if they don't fully excuse them. What bugs me the most is the several small decisions that prevent us implementors from glossing over a Balkanized address space.

The Intel 8086 is a segmented architecture. That means that a program's memory is conceptually chopped up into hundreds, or even thousands, of contiguous chunks. Each chunk conceptually is just big enough to hold one function or data object. With the kind of hardware access checking supported by the 80286 and 80386 family members, your program should be pretty quick to discover many of the bad jumps or bad data pointers that otherwise plague debugging and lower program reliability. Those two "conceptually"s warn you, however, that few if any implementors push program segmentation to this logical extreme. In point of fact, most programmers and all compilers stuff functions and data objects willy nilly into just a few segments. The checking, when available, is largely subverted.

What bugs programmers most, in fact, is the relatively small size of those segments. You can't support a group of functions or a data object larger than 64 kilobytes as a single segment. The advantage of this size limitation is that within a segment you can address all bytes with a two-byte (near) pointer. Once the function group gets large, you must use four-byte (far) pointers to address the individual functions and intersegment calls to enter them. Once a data object gets large, you must use a far pointer to address it and perform truly horrendous arithmetic to step through it.

Since there is a significant increase in code space and execution time once you start trafficking in far pointers, you naturally avoid them as long as possible. This gets you to fretting about code and data sizes, diverting energy in the solution away from just solving the original problem. Or to mixing near and far pointers, imposing structure and complexity on the solution that is not intrinsic in the original problem. However you look at it, the architecture gets in the way.

A particular nuisance that plagues us compiler vendors is that we must ship the same support libraries compiled in a number of different ways, so the customer can have a library consistent with any of several choices of pointer sizes. Half the libraries could have been eliminated had Intel made one small decision differently.

When the 8086 executes an intrasegment call, it pushes the instruction pointer (IP) on the stack as a near pointer and jumps to the called function. An intrasegment return instruction pops the IP to continue execution in the caller just past the call. For an intersegment call, however, the machine must push both the IP and the code segment register (CS) as a far pointer. The call jumps by loading new values into both IP and CS. To get back, there is an intersegment return to pop both CS and IP. Since the two calling sequences are so different, the caller had better agree with the callee, lest madness ensue.

Now, my first reaction on reading the 8086 manual was to say, "Oh, I see. You can merge the two models with a simple trick." The trick was to provide two entry points for each function, one with a far name and one with a near one, as in:

```
NEAR_func:
    push    cs
FAR_func:
```

You can then perform an intersegment (far) return unconditionally. At the cost of an extra push and pop of CS, the near function is merged with its far equivalent.

Unfortunately, this doesn't work. Why? Because an intersegment call pushes CS on the stack *before* it pushes IP. And the code needed to pick up IP, push CS, then push IP again is a bit harder to shrug off — particularly if your calling sequence doesn't permit you to clobber any registers before they are pushed on the stack. If there is any fundamental reason why CS and IP couldn't have been stacked in the other order, it is beyond me. When I saw my beautiful trick go up in smoke, I faced the general direction of Aloha, Oregon and said, "You must be joking."

Now let's look at data pointers. If you want to poke about within a data object larger than 64 kilobytes, you have to grit your teeth a lot while writing the code. To access the object, you must load the far pointer into a segment register and an index register. There are nice instructions for doing this. But once you put it there, you can't do arithmetic on the full pointer, since you can't add a carry out of the offset part to a segment register. So you shuffle the segment register to a data register to do the arithmetic, then put it back. Sigh.

Even in a data register, a segment value is a tough beast to do arithmetic on. For an 8086, 80186, or 8088, a carry out of the offset requires that you add 4096 (!) to the segment, to get to the next contiguous byte in memory. You also have a choice of 4096 ways to represent the address of any particular byte in memory, so comparing two pointers just for equality requires either:

- that you perform a nontrivial calculation for the comparison
- that you put both pointers in canonical form before each comparison
- that you keep all pointers in canonical form at all times

None of these choices leads to compact code.

Okay, I'm willing to forgive the original design of the 8086 for being shortsighted, for the reasons given in an earlier article (**Pla87** again). But with the 80286, Intel had a second chance. For this chip, and the later 80386, the segment portion no longer has a fixed numerical relationship to the offset portion of a pointer. Depending upon how the operating system loads up the segment descriptor tables, you can map segment numbers to physical addresses almost any way you'd like. Almost.

My first reaction on reading the 286 manual (later renamed the 80286) was to say, "Oh, I see. You can merge adjacent segments to make an object larger than 64 kilobytes with a simple trick." The trick was to assign segment number *N* to the first 64 kilobytes of the data object, then segment number *N+1* to the next chunk, and so on for as long as necessary. With this preparation, pointer arithmetic is almost indistinguishable from long-integer arithmetic, just like on machines with large flat address spaces. It is still not as easy as one would like, but it's reasonable.

Unfortunately, this doesn't work. Why? Because two bits of the segment value are used to specify requested access, not select a segment descriptor. A third bit selects which table (local or global) contains the segment descriptor. And these happen to be the three *least* significant bits of the value. So you're back to turning a simple carry from the offset into an add of eight (or possibly four) to the segment, thereby destroying any simple flattening of the address space. If there is any fundamental reason why these bits couldn't have been put in the high part of the value, it is beyond me. When I saw my beautiful trick go up in smoke — well, you get the drift.

I'm all in favor of segmented architectures, by the way, so long as either

- the segments are large enough to stay out of my way
- I can pave over the segmentation from time to time

The attitude that says this is not necessary I call *militant segmentism.* I believe that it led to the early demise of the Zilog Z8000 (which had the jump on the Intel 8086 and the Motorola 68000), and the stillbirth of the Intel 432. Both of these were segmented architectures designed in such a way, for no good reason that I can see, that their 64-kilobyte segments could not be merged. The Intel 8086 family has a strong toehold (for obvious reasons), so I don't expect it to fade from the scene the same way. And the 80386 may have solved the small segment problem. But meanwhile there are lots of kiloprogrammer hours diverted from the real problems at hand.

Now let's talk about arrays in C. This one goes to Dennis Ritchie, so I'll keep it short. (It's a lot easier to zing a diffuse corporate entity than a single individual who has clearly done so many things right.) There are several things that people knock about the C language — its terseness, its lack of checking, its bizarre declaration syntax. All of these have been blamed, with some degree of justification, for higher error rates among C programmers. But there is one aspect that I think rivals all of the above, and is almost never mentioned as a problem area. C programmers can't tell the difference between pointers and arrays.

It is fundamental to the design of C that nearly all references to arrays within an expression are converted to pointer values. Thus, given the declaration:

```
int arr[10];
```

the expression:

```
arr[2]
```

selects the third (counting from zero) element of the array.

In a language like FORTRAN, this is obvious. In C, it depends upon several subtleties. First, the subscript operator is replaced by its equivalent:

```
*(arr + 2)
```

Then, because C is a language of (mostly) scalar expressions, the term **arr** is replaced by the value of the pointer to the first (number zero) element of the array, and the type of the term is changed to *pointer to int* because **arr** is an array of *int*s. Finally, the **2** is scaled by the size of *int* data objects on the target machine, so the pointer addition gets you to the proper *int* within the array when the indirection is performed.

All of that is explained, in some form, early in the career of every C programmer. The conversion of arrays to pointers in expressions happens so often and so effortlessly that programmers quickly learn to write **p[i]** (where **p** is a pointer type) as freely as **a[i]**. And they learn to declare array arguments such as:

```
int f(a)
    char a[10];
    {.....}
```

knowing that C will pass a pointer to the array, rather than copy the whole array contents. That's the good news.

The bad news is that skilled and intelligent C programmers come to me regularly with bugs caused by declaring a pointer data object where they really needed an entire array, or contrariwise. Even worse, several compilers in common use now convert arrays to pointer values so quickly that useful expressions such as **&a** are outlawed. (Guess what I said when I tripped over that one in the UNIX C compiler?) The discussions on this topic that I have enjoyed in X3J11 Standards meetings have been heated, circular, and frustrating. For skilled C programmers to see array names as other than some form of pointer constants can often border on the impossible.

With 20-20 hindsight, I think that Ritchie should have restricted the implicit conversion of arrays to pointers to just the subscript operator. Of course, you would have to write **f(&a[0])** in places where C programmers gleefully write **f(a)**, but I find that a small price to pay for the clarity of understanding that would (might) ensue. It would also have opened the door for making arrays first-class objects that you could pass as arguments and assign, just like structures and unions are these days.

It is often the case that the fundamental strengths of a design also contain the seeds of its fundamental weakness. I believe that, in the case of C, this fundamental approach to keeping expressions scalar in the early days is more of a limitation on the language than anything else that has been cited.

Now for the apologia. Having gotten all this off my chest, I feel more like Andy Rooney than Clive Barnes, but what the heck it's April. On a more serious note, I would like to confess that I have designed more than one computer architecture (for pay) and more than one programming language (ditto). I can't say that I've done any better than the commercial successes I've just taken several swipes at.

So before you start writing irate letters because I zinged your favorite chip/language/designer, please note that I at least have the decency to be humble about my criticism, if not contrite. □

Afterword: This was the first in a series of annual April Fool's specials. My original intent was to trot out a fresh handful of design gaffes (as I saw them) every year. That didn't happen. Instead, I used April Fool's Day as an excuse to tackle a variety of off the wall subjects, humorous and otherwise. The others follow in this collection.

*I believe our business desperately needs criticism such as this. Edsger Dijkstra once spoke about reviewing computer architectures, but drew back from doing so. I wish that he had. C.A.R. Hoare spoke out against Ada in his Turing Award Lecture (**Hoa81**), but I disagree with his conclusions. Ah well. The problem with critics is that they often fail to reinforce our prejudices.*

2 Computer Arithmetic

Computer arithmetic occurs in many forms. Chances are your favorite programming language, or computer architecture, supports only a few varieties. Chances are you have learned just enough of the properties of these varieties of arithmetic to (mostly) get by.

There are times, however, when you have considerable latitude in choosing a numeric data representation, and hence the rules for doing arithmetic on that data. You should know enough to choose wisely, and not just accept the native arithmetic of your current host architecture. There are even more times when you obtain arithmetic results that are surprising. You should know enough to avoid the worst surprises, and to recognize the lesser anomalies when they rise up and bite.

This essay is an overview of the principal forms of arithmetic supported by modern computers. It ranges from the basic, and fairly widely known, to the esoteric, and fairly widely overlooked. Most programmers, in my experience, learn this stuff in patches. Here is my attempt at pasting some of those patches together and putting them all in one place.

I begin with integer arithmetic, because the only arithmetic that most computer hardware actually performs is to add together two binary integers of some predetermined length. Arithmetic is by far the easiest to perform if numbers are represented in a *positional encoding*. That is, the least-significant (rightmost) bit carries a numeric weight of 1, the next least-significant bit carries a weight of 2, the next 4, and so on with higher powers of 2. Using four bits, you can write sixteen different numbers, the first of which are:

0000	0	0100	4
0001	1	0101	5
0010	2	0110	6
0011	3	0111	7

And so forth. Lest you think this is the only way to fly, I can tell you that there are other ways to encode numbers:

- You can use groups of four bits to encode decimal digits, in a representation called *binary-coded decimal*, or BCD. This is a positional encoding, but not binary weighted. It is still widely used where the cost of conversion to human-readable form is comparable to the cost of performing computations. You sort of meet both needs halfway.

- You can represent numbers in *Gray code*, which ensures that any two adjacent values differ in their representations in only one bit. This is a binary positional encoding, but not weighted. Gray code is very useful in mechanical position transducers, because of its tolerance for alignment errors. Some sample values are:

0000	0	0110	4
0001	1	0111	5
0011	2	0101	6
0010	3	0100	7

- You can use groups of bits to represent the digits in a Roman numeral. This is a partly positional, weighted encoding that is not binary. It is useful for making dates that are hard to read on cornerstones of buildings.

Binary and BCD are the only sensible representations for performing arithmetic conveniently. The other representations have more specialized uses. Let's focus on binary arithmetic for now.

The result of a binary addition is a binary integer with one more digit (bit) than the two operands. (Why?) The extra bit is called a *carry*, which is usually retained in a place separate from the rest of the sum. That way, the sum will fit in the same size storage as the operands, and the carry can be held in a place more convenient for testing.

If you simply ignore the carry bit, the sum represents the low-order bits of the full result. When you add one to the largest number you can represent, the result wraps around to zero. This is called *modulus arithmetic*.

You use modulus arithmetic every day for telling time on a clock face. Ten o'clock plus three hours is one o'clock, or thirteen modulo twelve. You don't worry about overflow, because all times are representable somewhere on the face of a clock. What you do, in fact, is maintain extra bits of information separately, such as whether it's a.m. or p.m., or what date goes with the clock time. Days of the week are also a form of modulus arithmetic, modulo seven, as are compass angles, modulo 360.

If you treat the carry bit as an overflow indication, the sum represents a positive counting number. When you add one to the largest number you can represent, the result is erroneous. This is called *unsigned arithmetic.*

You use unsigned arithmetic every day for measuring the distance your car has traveled. The odometer on your car's dashboard maintains five or six digits of the total number of miles, or kilometers, that your car has traveled. You don't worry too much about overflow, because it's easy enough to keep track of the lost bits of information. All you have to do is look at the rust on the rocker panels to know that 00015 does not signify a mere fifteen miles traveled. You do worry, however, when your stock market tracking software tells you the market dropped 08 points, on a day when it dropped 508 points. In the absence of additional information, that may lead you to make suboptimal investment decisions.

If you want to do arithmetic on negative integers as well, you generally rely on one of three approaches. In all three approaches, you treat all numbers whose most-significant bit is set as negative integers. What value you assign to a given representation of a negative number varies considerably, however.

To negate a number with the first approach, complement (toggle) all of its bits and add one. Some sample negative numbers are:

```
1111    -1
1110    -2
1101    -3
1100    -4
```

To algebraically add two numbers, add them as unsigned integers and discard any carry. This approach is called *twos-complement arithmetic*. Its biggest wart is that there is one more negative number than there are positive numbers.

To negate a number with the second approach, you just complement all of its bits. Some sample negative numbers are:

```
1110    -1
1101    -2
1100    -3
1011    -4
```

To algebraically add two numbers, add them as unsigned integers and add any carry back to the least-significant bit of the result. (You cannot get a second carry from this "end-around carry." Why?) This approach is called *ones-complement arithmetic*. It requires different addition rules from unsigned arithmetic, and it has a negative zero. While negative zero participates properly in arithmetic, it can make comparisons more difficult.

To negate a number with the third approach, you just complement the most significant bit. Some sample negative numbers are:

```
1001    -1
1010    -2
1011    -3
1100    -4
```

To algebraically add two numbers, you must first convert each negative operand to a ones-complement or a twos-complement form, add by the appropriate rules, then convert a negative result back. This approach is called *signed-magnitude arithmetic*. It also has a negative zero, just like ones-complement arithmetic. And unless you need the positive form of the number most of the time, it is less convenient for performing arithmetic.

Of the three approaches, twos-complement arithmetic is by far the most widely used today. Perhaps its greatest advantage is that you perform addition, subtraction, and sometimes even multiplication by the same rules regardless of whether you want a modulus, unsigned, or signed result. You can summarize the result of each arithmetic operation with just four bits of additional information, in what is usually called a *condition code:*

- whether the result is zero
- whether the result has its sign bit set
- whether the result has suffered a signed overflow
- whether the result has suffered an unsigned overflow (carry)

Given a rich enough set of test and branch instructions, you can test for any combination of negative (if signed), zero, or positive nonzero results. You can test either the stored result or the full computed result. And you can test correctly either for modulus, unsigned, or signed results.

Modulus arithmetic, with carry testing, is just what you need to perform multiple-precision arithmetic. You can chain together fixed-size binary integers to make arbitrarily large arithmetic operands, much the way you write multidigit numbers when you perform arithmetic by hand. Since modulus arithmetic coexists so peacefully with twos-complement, a manufacturer can provide both useful forms with fewer instructions than if some other representation for negative numbers were chosen. Little wonder that twos-complement arithmetic is so widely used today.

There are, of course, some drawbacks to twos-complement arithmetic:

- You can negate a number and cause an overflow, since there is one more negative value than there are positive values. The code **1000**, for **-8**, becomes **1000** again when you negate it. This often surprise people, who can fail to plan for it.
- You still need different operations for signed and unsigned divide. And if you want to multiply two operands to get the full result at twice the precision, you need different operations for signed and unsigned multiply.
- You can double an integer by shifting all of its bits left and inserting a zero on the right. You can do this repeatedly to multiply a number by any power of two. If you try to halve an integer by shifting it one bit position to the right, however, you encounter a difficulty and a surprise. The difficulty is that you must copy the sign bit into itself, rather than insert a zero, to get (almost) the right negative result. This requires a different right shift from unsigned arithmetic. The surprise is that negative numbers do not truncate toward zero the way you expect. If you shift any one bits off the right end, the result is more negative by one than you probably want. Many an innocent programmer has been burned by this behavior. Some examples of right-shifted values are:

```
1111   -1 => 1111   -1
1101   -3 => 1110   -2
1011   -5 => 1101   -3
```

Actually, the most insidious problem caused by twos-complement arithmetic stems from its ability to cohabit with modulus and unsigned arithmetic. Because the same instruction can be used for three different kinds of addition, the computer cannot know which flavor you intend at any given time. If it were to trap on signed overflow, that might interfere with a perfectly valid unsigned addition. If it were to trap on unsigned overflow, that might interfere with a perfectly valid modulus addition.

So what most computers do these days is simply nothing. They set the condition code for all possible interpretations of the result, then leave it to the programmer to take appropriate action. Most assembly-language programmers, and most high-level language translators, ignore potential overflows.

Programmers have learned that they can get away with murder when it comes to integer arithmetic. Even if you declare your operands to be signed integers, you can go ahead and treat them as unsigned or modulus operands and you will still get the right answer more often than not.

Like all mammals, you learn to avoid fire by getting your fingers burned, or by getting slapped by your mother at judicious times. Reading a few pious platitudes that are demonstrably unenforced does not have the same educational effect. As a result, we have produced a generation of programmers who view integer overflow as something somewhat less bothersome than a mosquito bite.

At one meeting of X3J11, the committee standardizing C, there was considerable sentiment that translators should be free to regroup arithmetic expressions even if the regrouping introduced integer overflows that would not otherwise occur. Many people feared the loss of optimization opportunities more than they feared the loss of programmer control over how expressions are evaluated. In the end, the committee elected to honor grouping and disallow the introduction of spurious overflows, but in doing so they went against an attitude that has prevailed since the earliest days of C.

C is actually a cleaner language than many people think, at least in the area of integer arithmetic. What C calls unsigned arithmetic is actually modulus arithmetic, but it does distinguish between modulus and signed arithmetic. An overflow in signed arithmetic is classified as "undefined behavior," which gives an implementation license to check for it and trap it. If integer overflow trapping is rarely enabled, you must blame implementations more than the language itself.

Standard C is also defined in such a way that an implementation may use any of the three encodings for signed integers that I outlined above. At least in principle. My suspicion is that many C programs, like programs in general, are sufficiently lax about mixing modulus, unsigned, and signed arithmetic that they are not likely to work unchanged on machines that support other than twos-complement arithmetic with quiet wraparound on overflow. It will be interesting to see the experience of those vendors who, for whatever good reason, elect to support Standard C on hardware that does not use twos-complement arithmetic.

If you want to represent fractional values as well as integers, you must tackle an additional set of problems. The simplest thing to do is simply decree that the rightmost N bits of each representation are fraction bits. That is, there is an implied binary point (analogous to a decimal point) immediately to the left of the Nth least-significant bit. Or to put it yet another way, the true value is the apparent integer value divided by two raised to the Nth power.

This representation is called *fixed point*. Integers are simply a special case of fixed point, with the binary point immediately to the right of the least-significant bit. If you've ever written a program that deals in dollar amounts as an integer number of pennies, then you've used a fixed-point (decimal) representation.

Assuming for the moment that all of the values that participate in arithmetic expressions together have the same number of binary places, then addition and subtraction take care of themselves. Your major concern is deciding where to place the binary point. If you devote too few bits to representing the fraction, you lose the ability to represent small numbers precisely. If you devote too few bits to representing the integer part, you lose the ability to represent large numbers well.

For the usual case that all of your operands have the same fixed number of bits, you must trade off these two numbers carefully. And you must trade them off differently for each program you write. You may even have to trade them off differently for each range of input cases you wish to handle. So while fixed-point arithmetic gives you the ability to represent fractional values for about the cost of integer arithmetic, your intellectual investment in designing a correct program can be high.

There are a few other problems. While addition and subtraction are the same as for integer arithmetic, you must handle multiplication with special care. Form the integer product of two fixed-point numbers and you have a result with twice the fraction bits of the two operands. You have to shift the result right N bits (taking care to fix up negative numbers in twos-complement, as described above). And unless you can capture a double-precision product long enough to shift it back into proper alignment, you must reserve N additional integer bits to avoid intermediate overflow.

Alternatively, you can preshift one operand to discard its fraction bits. Do this, however, and you really sacrifice precision. For 1.5 times 1.5, you get a product of 1.5 instead of 2.25. Not acceptable.

You face similar issues with fixed-point divides. The only easy thing to do is convert the dividend to double precision (if you can), then preshift it left N bits. There are enough headaches with signed divides on many computers that you are better off working with positive operands and negating the result as necessary. Even then, the fraction you get is truncated. If you want a rounded result, you must develop an extra fraction bit, by preshifting $N+1$ bits, to determine which way to round.

I have probably coded considerably more fixed-point arithmetic than the average programmer, yet I still find myself botching this stuff with regularity. Opportunities for error abound. Little wonder that fixed point arithmetic is largely unused.

There is, of course, a better alternative. Rather than tailor a fixed-point representation for each application you tackle, you can use a more generic representation. Say you represent each operand as a pair of numbers, a signed integer value as before, plus a scale factor. The scale factor indicates where to locate the binary point. The point need not be located among the bits of the signed-integer value. A large positive scale factor indicates a large integer operand, a large negative scale factor indicates a small fractional operand.

This representation is called *floating point*. The binary point floats under control of the scale factor. You can represent a wide range of values and retain a fixed number of bits of precision regardless of magnitude. Floating-point arithmetic is complicated and hard to get right, but it can be used just about everywhere you might feel a need for fixed point. It is the sort of thing that a few experts can implement and many other programmers can use repeatedly.

Floating-point arithmetic is a study in tradeoffs. You trade off a few bits that could be used to represent value for flexibility in how the value is scaled. You trade off control of absolute errors in how well you represent values for rather good control of relative errors. You trade off considerable additional complexity for wider utility.

The vast majority of programmers have accepted these tradeoffs gladly. Hardware vendors accept them more reluctantly. It takes about as much microcode to implement floating-point add, subtract, multiply, divide, and compare as it does all of the other instructions combined in a typical mini- or microcomputer.

Microcode costs money, if not in hardware then in lower chip yields due to added complexity. As a result, floating-point instructions are standard equipment only in mainframes, superminis, or top-of-the-line microprocessors. They are implemented as plug-in options for minis and as coprocessor chips for mid-line microcomputers. They are implemented in software just about everywhere that floating-point hardware support is not available.

There is no question that floating-point arithmetic fills an important need for many computer programs. Unfortunately, many programmers tend to view it as a panacea for all computational ills. The list of difficulties I have just enumerated for integer and fixed-point arithmetic pales in comparison to the ways you can get in trouble with floating point. Sooner or later, you get burned.

Programmers who get burned a few times by floating-point idiosyncrasies often overreact. They develop a fear of floating point that is as misplaced as their original innocent delight. The truth, as always, lies somewhere in between. There's lots more to be said about floating-point arithmetic. I will cover some of that in the next essay. (See **Essay 3: Floating-Point Arithmetic**.) □

Afterword: I put off writing this essay more than once. It struck me as such an elementary topic that I was afraid to insult my readers. Then I saw what happened in discussions of computer arithmetic at C standards meetings. It was clear that we all had a lot to learn about what we thought was obvious. So I wrote this essay to capture the basics of computer integer arithmetic. Now I'm not sorry I did.

3 Floating-Point Arithmetic

$\mathbb{I}$n the previous essay, I talked about various aspects of computer arithmetic. (See **Essay 2: Computer Arithmetic**.) How signed integers are represented has a strong influence on how easy it is for you to mix signed arithmetic with unsigned and modulus arithmetic, how easy it is for you to perform fixed-point (fractional) and multi-precision arithmetic, and how cavalier you tend to be about overflows. I ended with a brief introduction to floating-point arithmetic.

This essay extends that discussion. If you believe that using floating-point arithmetic lets you avoid all computational problems, my goal is to dissuade you of that fantasy. If you believe, on the other hand, that floating-point arithmetic is completely untrustworthy, my goal is to dissuade you of that pessimism. Floating-point arithmetic is one of the tools that you, as a professional programmer, should know when to use and how to use to best advantage. Let's begin with the basics. However it is represented, a floating-point number has two varying components:

- a signed-value part, which represents the most-significant digits of the actual value

- a signed-exponent part, which tells how to scale the signed-value part up or down to get the actual value.

There are also several non-varying components:

- the implied base and fixed scale factor used to represent the signed-value part

- the implied base and bias used to represent the signed-exponent part

- the implied base, raised to the power represented by the signed-exponent part, to make the varying scale factor for the signed-value part

As an example, the IEEE 754 standard for floating-point arithmetic (**IEE85**) specifies several formats for representing floating-point numbers. The smallest of these calls for:

- a 25-bit binary signed-value part, which represents a signed-magnitude integer with a fixed scale factor of 2^{-24}. All signed-value parts represent fractions strictly less than 1.0.

- an 8-bit binary exponent, which represents as an unsigned integer, biased by adding 126. Values less than 126 represent negative signed exponents.

- an implied base of 2

I won't thrill you with all of the perverse combinations of 2s, 10s, and 16s that have been used over the years for these implied bases. Instead, I will restrict the remaining discussion to representations like this one, where all of these implied bases have the value 2. That is, the signed-value part and signed-exponent part are both binary numbers, and the exponent tells you how far to shift the value left or right to get the actual value. There are only a few surprises introduced when you deal in bases other than 2. I will mention some of them in passing.

The designer of a floating-point number format faces a number of difficult tradeoffs. Perhaps the most important is the number of bits to allocate for the signed-value part. That determines the precision with which you can represent the magnitude of all the values you wish to manipulate. Too few bits and you can't maintain enough precision for your final computed results to be meaningful. Too many bits and you consume excessive amounts of storage for intermediate results. Also, arithmetic costs you more in hardware complexity and/or execution time.

I have seen a number of digital-filtering applications, involving speech or picture processing, where four or five decimal digits of precision suffice and computational speed is of the essence. I have met few numerical analysts who are content with fewer than ten decimal digits of precision for the computations they wish to perform. I have encountered few occasions where more than about 20 decimal digits of precision were justified.

It is no surprise, given these observations, to find that floating-point arithmetic is generally offered at two precisions. Normal precision provides about six decimal digits of precision and occupies a total of 32 bits, exponent and all. Double precision provides about 16 decimal digits of precision and occupies a total of 64 bits. "Double" is an obvious misnomer if the precision more than doubles when you double the number of bits. The anomaly stems from the common practice of allocating most, if not all, of the extra bits to the signed-value part, which more than doubles in size.

The number of bits that the designer allocates for the signed-exponent part determines the range of values that you can represent. Too few bits and you keep hitting the stops with very large or very small results. Too many bits and you either consume excessive amounts of storage for intermediate results, or you reduce the precision that you can represent.

The smallest range of values that people seem willing to tolerate is from 10^{-38} to 10^{+38}. This corresponds to an 8-bit exponent, as for the IEEE short format shown above. I have never seen a range large enough to make everybody happy, but the largest I have seen implemented lets you represent numbers as big as $10^{10,000}$. This corresponds to a 16-bit exponent, which is the size used in the IEEE extended-precision format.

If you want to write programs that perform floating-point arithmetic and which are as portable as possible across a variety of machines, you need to keep these ranges in mind. It's pretty safe to assume:

- a choice of two precisions, one about 6 decimal digits and one about 16
- a decimal exponent range from about 10^{-38} to 10^{+38}

Beyond that, the less you know about the underlying format, the more likely you will not take advantage of that knowledge.

You do need to be aware of some of the ways in which format decisions can affect your results, however, if only to avoid algorithms (or environments) that will cause trouble. One important issue, for instance, is whether all floating-point numbers must be *normalized*. The encoding I have described so far allows for multiple ways of representing the same value, at least in many cases. Consider a four-bit signed value part, for simplicity, with three bits to the right of the binary point. There are three different ways to represent the value 1.0:

```
0.100 x 2¹
0.010 x 2²
0.001 x 2³
```

Of these, only the first maintains the full three bits of precision. It is the form always chosen for the normalized representation — the binary fraction must be in the semi-closed interval [1/2, 1). (This notation tells you that the range includes 1/2, but stops short of including 1.)

Why is normalization so important? Well, for one thing, it's much harder to compare two floating-point numbers if either or both need not be normalized. You can't just assume that the one with the larger signed-exponent part is the larger number, because leading zeros in the fraction might more than make up the difference in determining the actual value. You must either prenormalize all numbers before you compare them, or be content with getting the wrong answer when you compare unnormalized numbers.

But there is a more important reason why you want to stick with normalized operands. Consider the following subtraction, which I write as decimal fractions to avoid overtaxing your imagination:

```
 0.123456 x 10⁰
-0.123000 x 10⁰
 0.000456 x 10⁰
```

This result has lost three decimal digits of significance, to be sure. You might think that the most honest thing to do would be to leave it in this form for future computations to record the true retained significance. But if you then add, say:

```
 0.000456 x 10⁰
+0.111234 x 10⁻³
```

you must prescale the smaller operand and retain only six digits of the result, to get:

$$\begin{array}{ll} 0.000456 & \times\ 10^0 \\ +0.000111234 & \times\ 10^0 \\ \hline 0.000567 & \times\ 10^0 \end{array}$$

This is hardly the best internal representation of the result. Had you *post normalized* the result of the first subtraction, however, you would get 0.456000×10^{-3} for the intermediate result. And the final result would have been much better represented as 0.567234×10^{-3}.

There is a subtle but important distinction between the accuracy of a result and the best internal representation of that result. Both are described in terms of the number of significant digits, but it often takes more bits of the latter to do right by the former.

What you need to know is that unnormalized floating-point arithmetic is bad news. Very seldom does modern computer hardware generate an unnormalized result, unless you go out of your way to ask for it. But I still encounter from time to time a program that throws together unnormalized floating-point numbers, using machine-specific ad hoc code, because normalizing the numbers is tedious and/or time consuming. Usually, these values get cleaned up early enough as arithmetic results get postnormalized. But sometimes they trash precision in surprising ways.

If you play games with unnormalized floating point numbers, make sure you know what you're doing.

There are some floating-point representations where you can't even write an unnormalized number. I emphasized earlier how precious bits are, and how a designer must trade off total bits against the sizes of the two parts of a floating-point number. Then I went on to say that you want to restrict yourself to using only normalized representations. But for a binary representation, this means that there is one bit (the 1/2-weighted bit in the fraction, typically) that is always set. If a bit must always be set, it is not conveying useful information. It is wasting space.

A common practice, therefore, is to suppress this bit in the stored representation of floating-point numbers. When you unpack the representation into its two component parts to perform arithmetic, you insert this *hidden bit* once again. You may have noticed that the description I gave earlier of short-format IEEE floating point numbers required 33 bits. They can be represented in 32 bits by hiding the most-significant bit of a normalized signed-value part.

Employing a hidden bit does cause a minor difficulty. How do you represent the value zero? Zero is a wart in floating-point arithmetic, but it is an important one. You can't simply approximate it by 10^{-300}, or some other tiny but finite value. Sooner or later, that approach leads to trouble.

If you don't use the hidden-bit trick, then any zero signed-value part can represent the value zero. (You pick one preferred signed exponent-part value, usually zero, to use for writing a normalized zero.) If you do use the hidden bit, then you can't write a signed-value part that has the value zero.

The usual approach is to reserve one value of the signed-exponent part as a code that the actual value is not obtained by the usual rules. Instead of representing a binary exponent of –126, for instance, a signed-exponent part with value zero in IEEE short form means that a signed-fraction part of zero represents the actual value zero. (IEEE extends this technique, of giving special meaning to certain values, in all sorts of directions that I can't begin to describe here.)

There is one other trick for saving representation bits that you should be aware of. On System/370, the implied base is 16. This means that you have to shift the signed-value part by four binary places every time you change the signed exponent-part by a count of one. A normalized signed value part lies in the interval [1/16, 1). The hidden-bit trick can't be used, because no one bit must always be set. But you can look at this encoding as a way of suppressing the low two bits of the signed-exponent part. A 7-bit signed exponent, base 16, gives you the same range of representable values as a 9-bit signed exponent, base 2.

What it costs you is a degree of uncertainty in how much precision you have for representing values. If the normalized signed-value part happens to fall in the interval [1/2, 1), then a 32-bit floating point number retains 24 bits of precision. If it happens to fall in the interval [1/16, 1/8), however, it retains only 21 bits. This encoding has been aptly dubbed *wobbly precision*. It gives numerical analysts headaches when they attempt any serious error analysis.

What it means to you is that you should assume you have only 21 bits of precision (or 53 for double precision) when you perform floating-point arithmetic on System/370.

When I discussed fixed-point arithmetic in the previous essay, I talked quite a bit about overflow. Overflow occurs when the result of a computation is too large to be represented by the encoding you have chosen for stored results. For a variety of good, and not so good, reasons, a common practice with fixed-point overflow is to retain only the low bits of the correct result. The value effectively wraps around, like an automobile odometer, from very large to very small values.

Floating-point overflow is not so lightly handled. You get a floating-point overflow when you cannot represent a signed-exponent part large enough to correctly represent the actual value. When this happens, there are a variety of recovery strategies that you can imagine:

- You can let the signed-exponent part wrap around, much like in fixed point arithmetic, yielding a tiny garbage result.
- You can replace the result with the largest representable value, yielding garbage which is arguably more representative of the actual result.
- You can raise an exception, so that program execution either terminates or resumes under control of a user-supplied exception handler designed to do something constructive in the face of floating-point overflows.
- You can replace the result with some special code that indicates the value is untrustworthy. This code propagates through subsequent arithmetic, so that you can detect the untrustworthy result later in the calculation.

As you might expect, all of these strategies have been tried at one time or another. Most are still in use in popular architectures today. I have sorted them in increasing order of sophistication. Naturally, none are of much use if your program contrives to ignore the warnings being sent your way.

Floating-point arithmetic can also suffer underflow, unlike fixed-point arithmetic. You get a floating-point underflow when you cannot represent a signed-exponent part small enough to correctly represent the actual value. When this happens, there are a variety of recovery strategies:

- You can let the signed exponent part wrap around, much like in fixed-point arithmetic, yielding a huge garbage result.
- You can replace the result with zero.
- You can raise an exception.

Again, all of these strategies have been tried, and most are still in use today. And again, I have sorted them in increasing order of sophistication. What makes underflow more pernicious than overflow is that many people consider zero quite an adequate fixup value for a result that has underflowed, while most people have a proper fear of any substitute for a result that is too large. It is not until you get an unexpected zero divide that you realize the important difference between zero and almost nothing. (See my article "Programming on Purpose: Handling Exceptions," *Computer Language*, January 1987.)

If you want to write truly portable and robust code that uses floating-point arithmetic, there is only one strategy that I have found effective in dealing with floating-point overflow. Don't let it happen. You can often get away with *zero fixup* for underflow, but you can and should avoid even that. You might run across an implementation that insists on printing a nasty message for every underflow.

It's much easier than you think to analyze a computation sufficiently to see whether exponents can ever get too large or too small. At the worst, you may have to identify a handful of places where overflow will occur if it's ever going to occur in your program. In these cases, I make use of a primitive function that I call **_prod**. You use it in expressions that look like:

```
z = _prod(x, y, "scale factor too big");
```

What **_prod** does is form the product of **x** and **y** safely — in such a way that the function does not lose control to an exception handler if the hardware can trap floating-point overflows. If no overflow occurs, then it returns the product as the value of the function. Otherwise, it calls a portable exception handler (called **_range**) with the third argument as a message string. I can then choose either to have the program terminate with a more or less meaningful message, or to return control to the proper part of the program. (C has a primitive non-local **GOTO** capability to process exceptions, using the library functions **setjmp** and **longjmp**.) I have yet to find a need to interface with arbitrary exception handling machinery, given **_prod**.

The function **_prod** is, of course, machine dependent. At least in principle. In practice, it is written in terms of two lower-level functions that are indeed machine dependent. One of these unpacks a floating-point number into its component parts, the other repacks them. There are two other important machine-dependent functions. One of these splits a floating-point number into an integer and a fraction, the other does a more sophisticated version of the same job with a scale factor. (The Standard C library has reasonable approximations to these functions, called **fmod**, **frexp**, **ldexp**, and **modf**.)

What these lower-level primitives let you do is to treat many floating-point operations semi-numerically. You rip an operand apart, perform simple logic or fixed-point arithmetic on its pieces, then paste the final result together. In between, you perform far fewer floating-point operations than you might imagine. And the fewer operations you perform in that domain, the fewer opportunities you have for unexpected overflow, underflow, or loss of significance. (See **Essay 5: Safe Math**.)

There are other things you can find to worry about with floating-point arithmetic that I have not chosen to discuss here. How your implementation rounds or truncates results can make a real difference in how much precision and accuracy you retain. Things like guard digits, rounding digits, and sticky bits are fun to describe. (See **Pla91**.) But unless you plan to write your own floating-point arithmetic routines — heaven forfend — you are at the mercy of whatever machinery is provided for you. The good news is that the current level of sophistication in this arena is quite high. I don't know of any floating-point arithmetic on computers in wide use today that is truly bad.

If you want to learn more, however, the ultimate reference is Pat Sterbenz, *Floating-Point Computation* (**Ste72**). R.W. Hamming best characterized this book by saying, "Nobody should ever have to know that much about floating-point arithmetic. But I'm afraid sometimes you might." □

Afterword: The problem with floating-point arithmetic is that it works so well. You are easily lulled into believing that it solves all numeric representation issues. Then you get burned and often overreact. I wrote this essay to help people stay more in a sane middle ground. Knowing the design tradeoffs makes most people more tolerant. Knowing the dangers makes some people more cautious. Seldom do you need more sophistication to safely do business with floating-point arithmetic.

4 The Central Folly

𝕴 learned a long time ago how to buy a television set. Sure, you worry about how the picture looks on the demo set. And sure, you check that it has all the gadgets you want. If you're sufficiently fastidious, you might paw through recent issues of *Consumer Reports* to reinforce your current prejudice. And if you care anything about decor, you might even note whether the cabinet clashes with your beer-can collection. But that's not where the real action is.

What I learned to do, after I had convinced myself a given model was a likely candidate, was to turn it around. On the back of nearly every television set ever made is at least one mysterious knob. It may be as modest as a screwdriver hole giving you access to some inner trimpot. It may be as grandiose as a knurled plastic gismo that more or less matches the knobs on the front. But that knob is there all right.

The knob invariably has some arcane label. BUZZ is a nice blend of the familiar and the ominous. FOCUS and VERT LIN are somewhat shopworn, but still dependable entrants. AGC SYNC STABILITY is one of my all-time favorites. Whatever the label says, you can be sure that it's not something that you really want to adjust. You'd be quite content for the television set to give you its best shot at controlling the parameter in question and not solicit your input on the subject.

There is a well known principle in drama that I like to think of as the Pistol Principle. If you, the playwright, cause an actor to call attention to a pistol in the top left-hand drawer of a Louis XIV desk sometime during Act I, then you'd better make sure that pistol gets used before the end of the last act. Otherwise, you are guilty of intellectual clutter.

You can bet that whoever designed the television set you are about to buy was just as sensitive to clutter as the most fastidious playwright. The designer is not competing in the marketplace of ideas, to be sure, but in the much tougher arena of consumer electronics. Those folks count tenths of a cent (or yen, these days) when pricing the cost of parts and assembly, even for a product that will retail in the hundreds of dollars. If there is a knob on the back of your soon-to-be television set, it is there for a reason.

What the knob tells you is that the designer had to compromise. Some part of the circuitry proved to be a little unstable, if not when the set was new then after it had baked in for a few thousand hours. The designer might have added more (or higher quality) components at a critical point, and gone over the 17.3 cent budget for that subassembly. Or the designer might have started over from scratch, to avoid the fundamental problems leading to the instability, and risked delivering the design late (with a different instability). Or the designer could simply bring a knob out to the back, for that fine day when you discover you have to tweak the AGC SYNC STABILITY to watch channel 13.

Guess which is the cheapest alternative.

I was pleasantly surprised to learn that I could evaluate computer programming languages by much the same rules as television sets. No, programming languages don't have knobs on the back. But they do have the moral equivalent thereof.

Every programming language comes with a reference manual, at least, and one or more tutorials, at best. That documentation should tell you all you need to know about the language to put it to use. If it doesn't tell you enough, you're reduced to performing experiments on the current translator you happen to own. Or you switch to another language. If it tells you too much, you are too overwhelmed to get your bearings. Programming languages are among the most complex creations that a single person has to do battle with these days. The last thing you need, when mastering a language, is extraneous detail.

Intellectual clutter in a programming language is just as fatal as over engineered circuitry in mass-market electronic appliances. It can price you out of the market. You can bet that an earnest language documentor tells you only what you need to know. The knobs are kept to a minimum.

So when I evaluate a programming language, I look for the extra knobs sticking out the back. When I see pages and pages of discussion about how to deal with something that I don't care about, I've found the knob. If I can't relate the discussion to the problem I want to solve, then I know I'm being asked to work around a design compromise in the language. Sooner or later, I'm going to have to learn how to tweak that mysterious knob to get the results I want.

The mere presence of a lengthy and arcane discussion in a language tutorial tells me that the designer couldn't eliminate the compromise. The language was in danger of becoming even more complex, or of being late to market due to redesign. The cheapest way out was to try to explain the compromise, rather than eliminate it.

I call this compromise "the central folly." It lies at the heart of the language design, and it is arguably a fundamental mistake. Someone made a conjecture, early on in the design process, and had to stick to it. And later came to regret it.

With that lengthy preamble, I am now ready to introduce my (second) annual April Fool's essay. By long-standing tradition, I take this opportunity to savage other designers, in the thin disguise of good clean fun. My topic this time, as you must have guessed by now, is computer programming languages. And I intend to snipe at three of the biggest ducks in the bay — PL/I, Algol 68, and Ada. Are you ready?

𝕴 have this vision of how PL/I came into being. No, I don't really know its exact history, so I won't pretend to anything other than fantasy. Anyway, I imagine a committee forming in the early 1960s, under the benign guidance of IBM. On that committee are numerous FORTRAN and COBOL programmers. All are determined to make a new language worthy of System/360, one that will combine the best points of the most popular scientific programming language and the most popular business programming language. Each is willing to compromise on many broad design issues, provided his or her three favorite features go in as well.

I am convinced that PL/I was designed by a committee of users. I suspect that the only serious arguments they had while piling on all the features they could imagine was whether there was room for three kitchen sinks or four.

PL/I supports every data type you can imagine, and then some. For encoded values, you can choose any combination of:

- binary or decimal base
- fixed-point integers, fixed point with a scale factor, or floating point
- real or complex
- various precisions

You can also specify character strings, with or without an editing picture, and bit strings. In the early days, you could even perform arithmetic in pounds, shillings, and pence! (PL/I dropped Sterling fixed-point constants only after the British empire did.)

It was an interesting conjecture that you needed all of those data types supported directly in the language, if you were going to capture the hearts and minds of all of those FORTRAN and COBOL programmers. But that interacted with another conjecture to cause a few problems.

𝕿he other conjecture was that the language must be blindly subsettable. After pouring in features from two distinct cultures, the designers then wanted each culture to be able to use PL/I without learning about the other. Permeating the language design is the attitude, "What you don't know shouldn't hurt you." Every option should have a default. If you fail to specify it, the translator will guess what you probably intended.

One aspect of this conjecture is that keywords are not reserved names in PL/I. (FORTRAN has no reserved names, COBOL has tons of them.) If you write a keyword in a context where it is not expected, the translator will guess that you intend it to be an ordinary name. That attitude permits barbarisms such as:

```
IF IF = THEN
   THEN THEN = ELSE
   ELSE ELSE = IF
```

which ascribes two distinct meanings to each of **IF, THEN, ELSE**, and the = operator. But what the heck. Any tool can be abused.

Another aspect of this conjecture is that you can write an expression with nearly any combination of data types. Many FORTRAN programmers enjoyed being able to mix integer and floating-point types, and let the translator guess how to combine them sensibly. Why not bring this luxury to the richer world of PL/I data types? The result is that the language explainers had to write pages and pages describing what happens when you combine **REAL FLOAT DECIMAL** operands with bit strings and Sterling fixed-point constants.

There's the knob on the back of the set.

Life is interesting enough with FORTRAN. If you convert a **REAL** to an **INTEGER**, implicitly by assignment, the translator guesses that you want to truncate the result toward zero. Rounding is often a better idea. If you convert an **INTEGER** to a **REAL**, the translator guesses that any low-order bits lost in the process are not worth mentioning. Reporting a loss of significance can sometimes be important. Nevertheless, the number of questionable conversions in FORTRAN is small and easily learned. The conscientious programmer learns when to be careful, or to use the explicit conversion functions.

PL/I, however, offers boundless opportunities for the translator to think up questionable conversions. My favorite eyebrow raisers usually involve some sequence that takes you from a **DECIMAL** form, through a bit string, to a single bit that you want to test. Picking up a meaningless leading zero bit along the way, that you eventually test instead of the good stuff, is frighteningly easy.

Things would not be so bad were programmers educated to write explicit conversions, but such is not the case. Part of the culture of PL/I, as I have seen it practiced, is that real programmers never write anything that doesn't have to be specified. (Imagine taking your favorite large Pascal or C program, erasing all of the conversion functions and/or type casts, and expecting the translator to guess how to put them back.) Getting the expressions right in the first place is hard enough, but maintaining PL/I, to me, often resembles tweaking a knob whose effect I don't understand.

My vision of the origins of Algol 68 also begins in the early 1960s. Again I see a committee, this time composed of numerous language theorists. All share a love for the elegant orthogonality of Algol 60 and a zeal for making a successor that will be even more elegant and even more orthogonal. All have lots of interesting ideas about how to specify a programming language. Here, the major concern is whether the language must have a kitchen sink, per se, or whether you can construct one from underlying primitives.

I understand that the working goal of the committee was to make a language called Algol 64. At least through the end of 1964. The fact that it was eventually called Algol 68 tells us that theoreticians are not immune to schedule overruns either. But what the heck. We're all human, and committees move slowly.

The cute thing about Algol 68 was that the committee ended up inventing a language to describe the language that describes the language. Algol 68 itself has a grammar with an infinite number of productions. (Try writing *that* on a four-sided reference card.) You need a meta-grammar to produce all of the productions that produce all of the valid sentences of the language. Why the committee felt it necessary to retread the English language to describe the meta-grammar, however, is beyond me.

Digging through pages of jargon about "softly deproceduring" and "stirmly hipping to void" is off-putting in the extreme. It is a real barrier to understanding. True, you occasionally unearth a real gem such as, "An assignation is the commonest form of confrontation." But it's not worth sapping through all of the mud along the way. There should probably be a law against quoting Lewis Carroll or W.S. Gilbert in a computer-language reference manual.

Algol 68 lets you declare all sorts of pointer types, a luxury to which we have grown accustomed with Pascal and C. They are called "reference variables" in Algol 68. Accessing a variable via a pointer is called *dereferencing*. Calling a function, given its name or a pointer to it, is called *deproceduring*. All fine and good.

The designers made an interesting conjecture early on, however. They concluded that if you merely mention the name of any variable in an expression, the translator should know what to do with it. If a variable points to another variable, you probably want to dereference it to get the contents of that other variable. You only want to copy it *as a reference variable* if you are assigning it to another reference variable of the same type. Similarly, if a variable names a procedure that has no arguments, then you probably want to deprocedure it, or call it, when you mention it in an expression. And that's always the case. Except when you don't.

Sure, you can also decorate the names with operators to say what you mean. But you don't have to. Instead, the description of Algol 68 contains pages of explanation about how the translator guesses what to do from context (strong, firm, weak, or soft) and from the type of each subexpression. There is even a wonderful railroad-track diagram, filling over half a page, that endeavors to teach you how to second guess the translator.

Have you spotted the knob on the back yet?

To fully appreciate the effect of this conjecture on the description of Algol 68, you have to repeat the gedanken experiment I suggested above. Take your favorite Pascal or C program and erase all of the indirection operators (^ or *) and all of the empty parentheses. Now explain simply how the translator should put them all back.

My view of Ada goes back about a dozen years. I imagine a committee of university consultants forming, under the benign guidance of the U.S. Department of Defense. On that committee are people who fund their research courtesy of the U.S. government. To this attentive audience, the DOD poses a challenge.

We're going to give you some money to study the state of the art of computer programming languages, says the DOD. We want you to look at what everyone else has done in the way of program design and determine whether:

- *they have already done a better job than you can possibly do in designing a programming language*
- *we should give you lots more money to spend the next several years designing the programming language you've always dreamed of*

You can guess the result.

No, I'm not going to make snide remarks about gold-plated kitchen sinks, or savage Ada in the usual ways. I believe that the people who worked on Strawman, Ironman, Steelman, and the various color-coded candidate languages had good intentions and did the best jobs they could, under the circumstances.

What I'm saying is that the deck was stacked, by those circumstances, in favor of yet another language designed by committee. Even though Jean Ichbiah gets full and proper credit for bringing considerable coherence to the design of Ada, he was in many ways hobbled by an over detailed specification, produced by a committee.

Ada was specified from the start to be a language in which you can write really large programs. It assumes that a typical program will be constructed from multiple modules written by different people. As a consequence, it worries quite a bit about name-space control. Lots of thought was given to controlling just what names are visible at any given point in an Ada program.

Opposing this concern, however, was an important conjecture — that the types and operators of Ada should be extendible. You should be able to introduce, say, the flavor of complex numbers that you like best, and extend the meaning of all the sensible arithmetic operators to cover them. You can, in other words, *overload* the meaning of the operators plus and minus, for instance, to cover complex operands as well.

Overloading operators is certainly a convenience. Nearly every language I can think of lets you write a plus operator in ways that have quite different meanings, depending upon the types of its operands. Algol 68 and other languages let you extend the overloading to cover types that you introduce as well. You can write programs that have a very agreeable notation for performing new forms of arithmetic.

When overloading and extendibility meet up with heavy-duty name-space control problems, however, you can expect complexities. It's no fun to have to qualify every plus operator, for instance, with the name of the module that is providing the appropriate definition. Rather, you want to be able to open up a module, as it were, and dump its contents into the general, unqualified name space. That's fine if you have only one module adding interesting new meanings to the plus operator. But what happens if ten of the 23 modules you are using overload plus in different ways? (Or what if three of these overload it the same way, which is different from the others?)

What you can do with operators, you can also do with function names and other creatures. Ada tutorials devote pages and pages to explaining how the translator can guess which meaning to ascribe to a name that you define multiple ways in the same region of program text. The basic rule seems to be, "If the translator has any chance at resolving the ambiguity, then it must permit the ambiguity and endeavor to resolve it the way it thinks best."

There's the knob on the back once again.

To me, this is like taking the **WITH** statement of Pascal and going wild with it. Or perhaps it can be compared to erasing as many structure specifiers from a C program as you can, changing

```
p->e.o.left->val = x.z;
```

to

```
val = z;
```

until the translator begs for mercy. It might be interesting to start with the minimum number of qualifiers, then add them until the diagnostics go away. But that probably isn't the most productive use of programmer time. Nor is it the most maintainable code.

The point of all of these gripes is the same. A language designer may have a conjecture about how people plan to use a language. Chances are, the designer will fear that a language will not be used if the user has to specify too much. When the designer is a single, gifted person such as Nicklaus Wirth (Pascal) or Dennis Ritchie (C), he or she can often arbitrarily rule in favor of linguistic simplicity. When the designer is part of a committee, however, it is harder to rule arbitrarily against the putative desires of the future user community. Particularly when there are vocal potential users on the committee.

I have characterized the conjectures in each of the three languages in terms of what guesses they require of the translator. It is my belief that high-level language translators have their hands full diagnosing obvious errors and optimizing for less-than-optimal computer architectures. They should not be asked to guess, particularly where a simple word to the wise from a programmer will make their job easier, and the program more readable. You will notice that two of the most successful languages of the past decade, Pascal and C, offer little in the way of shorthand in the areas I have discussed.

I believe that each of the three languages I've taken to task are important languages. I believe that each has many good design features. They have certainly influenced many others, usually to advantage. I have certainly learned many useful principles from studying all three.

Each bears the marks, however, of committee design. Each could be made stronger, I believe, by being asked to do less. And each is hampered by a central folly that causes you to tweak knobs better left hidden. □

Afterword: Rarely does a complex design avoid a central folly. Try your hand at spotting the central folly in UNIX, MS-DOS, C, and C++, just for practice. Learning how to spot such lapses in others can help make you a better designer. The sooner you twig to your own lapses, the better chance you have to mitigate them. At the least, being alert to central follies can make you more tolerant.

5 Safe Math

This essay continues the discussion of computer arithmetic that I began earlier. (See **Essay 2: Computer Arithmetic** and **Essay 3: Floating-Point Arithmetic**.) The last topic I covered was floating-point arithmetic, which I concluded with some general statements about how to write portable programs that perform floating-point operations. I mentioned the function **_prod(x,y)**, and some underlying primitive functions, that I use to avoid having to deal with all the different ways that floating-point overflow and underflow are handled on different computer architectures.

That column stimulated an interesting letter from Paul E. Condon, of San Carlos CA. Here is a summary of his letter:

Mr. Condon begins by observing that you can write a portable version of the **_prod** function in terms of existing library functions. In C terms (although he was speaking FORTRAN), you use the function **fabs** to force each argument positive. You then obtain its logarithm, as in the expression **log(fabs(x))**. Of course, you must first ensure that **x** is nonzero. So to write **_prod(x,y)**:

1. If either **x** or **y** is zero, return zero.
2. Otherwise, compute the logarithm of the (unsigned) product, which cannot overflow if the operands are representable:

   ```
   z = log(fabs(x) + log(fabs(y));
   ```
3. If **z** is less than the logarithm of the smallest representable number (call it **DMIN**), report an underflow.
4. If **z** is greater than the logarithm of the largest representable number (call it **DMAX**), report an overflow.
5. Otherwise, return the product **x*y**, knowing that the result is representable.

Mr. Condon then observes that you can use this code to write code smart enough to run on machines with two different floating-point representations. You can, for example, test on the more forgiving machine whether a calculation would fail if moved to the less forgiving one. Or you can test on the less forgiving machine whether it would help to move a failed calculation to the more forgiving one. Or you could simply select **DMIN** and **DMAX** to satisfy the most stringent range requirements across all machines of interest.

Mr. Condon concludes by presenting a trick. The idea is to look at numbers two different ways by using **EQUIVALENCE** statements in FORTRAN or "type casts in C." He observes that the sign bit of a floating-point number is always in the same position as that of an integer. Moreover, floating-point exponents usually occupy more significant bit positions than the fractions. Hence, a floating-point value treated as an integer is roughly proportional to the logarithm of the proper value. That might save time in the checking procedure that **_prod** uses above.

First, let me say that I applaud Mr. Condon's attitude toward writing portable programs that perform mathematical calculations. The world needs more programmers like him. I have a few critical things to say about his recommendations, and I don't want that important underlying message to get lost.

His implementation of **_prod** certainly does the job. He identifies the primary reservation I have about the function — computing **log** twice takes considerably more time than computing the product alone. This extra time is usually less important than you might think. You probably need to check only a few critical products to make your code safe and portable, and you probably don't know where your program's hot spots are to begin with. Nevertheless, nobody likes to depend upon a staple function that consumes more time than is absolutely necessary.

Mr. Condon characterizes this as a machine-independent function, then points out that you must build into it at least two machine-dependent constants, **DMIN** and **DMAX**. Granted, this is a localized disturbance and the algorithm as a whole is indeed machine independent. And it does permit some pretty sophisticated portability checks, as Mr. Condon points out. Nevertheless, it also compromises the maintainability of the function as portable code.

Complaining about performance and degree of portability is merely carping. It is the last observation in the letter that rang alarm bells for me.

First, a small correction. You can indeed access a floating-point datum in FORTRAN via an **EQUIVALENCE** statement as one or two integers. The comparable trick in C is *not* to use a type cast, however. Casting a value of floating-point type to an integer type would encourage the translator to generate code that converts the representation of the value from floating-point to integer format. What you want to do instead is to place the floating-point value in a union, as in:

```
union {
    float fl;
    int in;
    } x;
```

What you store in **x.fl** as type *float* you can access via **x.in** as type *int*, with no conversion. While there are no official guarantees about accessing the wrong member of a union, this trick works for all of the popular C implementations that I know.

The first alarm bell that rang in my head concerns the relative size of integers and floating-point representations in C. I showed a union containing a *float* and an *int* above. Both are 32-bit quantities on a number of popular architectures, including System/370, VAX, and (sometimes) Motorola 680X0. There are millions of computers, however, for which this trick doesn't work properly. The Intel 80X86 family, used in IBM PCs and compatibles, usually represents type *int* in only 16 bits. Some C compilers for Motorola 680X0 also have a 16-bit representation for type *int*.

FORTRAN promises that types **INTEGER** and **REAL** each occupy a single storage cell, and that type **DOUBLE PRECISION** occupies two cells. C offers an even wider assortment of choices. Floating-point types traditionally occupy four or eight bytes on most popular machines. The new type *long double*, added by ANSI X3J11, may require ten to 16 bytes.

Integers, on the other hand, usually occupy two or four bytes. To get to all parts of a floating-point type, you may have to replace the *int* member in the union with an array of from two to eight *int*s. So in summary, if you want to manipulate floating-point data using integer operations, you are going to have to write a very machine-specific declaration of a union to do so safely and reliably.

There is still another alarm bell ringing. Mr. Condon asserts that the sign bit of a floating-point datum tends to be in the same position as the sign bit in the integer datum you plonk on top of it (via **EQUIVALENCE** or union). Given the discussion above, the first question you must answer is, which integer datum? Hardware designers have been excessively creative, over the years, in deciding how to lay out the bytes of a multi-byte datum in memory. (See **Essay 1: You Must Be Joking**.) The most significant integer is not necessarily the first, or even the last, in the array.

I gather from his letter that Mr. Condon was thinking in terms of comparing the FORTRAN types **REAL** and **INTEGER**, both of which occupy a single cell. (The language doesn't promise that type **INTEGER** uses *all* of a cell, however.) Even in that restricted environment, an important exception springs immediately to mind. On both the DEC PDP-11 family and the DEC VAX family, the sign bit of a 32-bit floating-point datum does not necessarily line up with the sign bit of a 32-bit integer.

If you label the bytes with digits in increasing order of significance, then VAX represents 32-bit floating-point data as **2301** and 32-bit integer data as **0123**. (Some PDP-11 languages represent 32-bit integers as **2301**, some as **0123**.) The sign bits do line up for the 32-bit representations on System/370, Motorola 680X0, and Intel 80X86. For 64-bit floating-point representations, there are all sorts of variations on the same basic theme. (And for 80-bit representations, there are still more.)

So to summarize again, if you want to manipulate floating-point data using integer operations, you need to write a very machine-specific declaration of a union. You also need to know which integer field in the union to look at to inspect the sign bit of the floating-point datum.

I'm still not done with the alarm bells. Mr. Condon is correct in observing that floating-point numbers are often packed with the exponent in a convenient place, and biased by a convenient value as well. All of the popular formats place the exponent in the most-significant bit positions of the representation. All also normalize the fractions. (See **Essay 3: Floating-Point Arithmetic**.) The net result is that the magnitude of a floating-point datum, treated as a binary integer, increases monotonically with the value being represented. Assuming that you can compare integers of the same size as floating-point, and that both values are positive, you can use integer comparisons to compare floating-point values.

You get in trouble with negative values, however. On all of the popular architectures that I have been describing, negative floating-point numbers are represented in signed-magnitude form and negative integers are in twos complement. (See **Essay 2: Computer Arithmetic**.) A comparison that involves two negative values will often yield the wrong answer.

I have written fast floating-point comparison routines on half a dozen architectures, using the basic shortcut that Mr. Condon describes in his letter. In every case, however, I had to add code that converts the operands as signed-magnitude, multi-precision integers to twos-complement, multi-precision integers having the same value. (If the sign bit is set, you ones complement all of the integers, add 1 to the least-significant integer, propagate carries, then toggle the sign bit. This converts –0 to a true zero, by the way.) And in every case, I had to compare the most-significant integers differently (as signed integers) from the remaining integers (which are compared as unsigned integers).

So while Mr. Condon makes an interesting observation about the representation of floating-point values, there are a few practical details you must keep in mind if you want to take advantage of that observation.

One final point, and I will leave the poor letter writer in peace. Given the placement of the floating-point exponent described above, Mr. Condon is quite correct in observing that the integer interpretation closely approximates the logarithm. For all of the popular architectures I have been tracking, the leading bits accurately represent the logarithm, base 2, of the value being represented. If you add two floating-point values as integers (getting the representation of negative numbers right, as for comparisons above), you will indeed get a value that is closely related to the true floating-point product.

This is hardly surprising. If you write two numbers as

`frac1 * 2`$^{\text{exp1 + BIAS}}$

and

`frac2 * 2`$^{\text{exp2 + BIAS}}$

then their true product is

`frac1 * frac2 * 2`$^{\text{exp1 + exp2 + BIAS}}$

If each of the numbers is dominated by its exponent part, then their sum as integers is dominated by the sum of their exponents. Take away the extra **BIAS** and you have a not-unreasonable approximation to the floating-point product.

The only drawback is, you have the worst problems when you're at or near the extremes of the representable range of exponents. If the sum of exponents cannot be properly represented, then it will spill over into the sign bit. Perhaps. Or the resultant exponent will be one of those special values reserved to represent machine infinities and other special codes. Perhaps. Or the resultant exponent might be off by one (or two) because of carries from the fraction part. Perhaps.

In short, there are enough uncertainties that this technique is least satisfying in just those areas where you need **_prod** to help you the most. It is when you are getting close to overflow or underflow that you want to do a safe check before you risk raising a hardware exception when computing the actual product.

I have belabored several aspects of Mr. Condon's presentation, but it is not my goal to beat him up in print. My father told me years ago, "Never argue with a man holding a megaphone." To this day, I am reluctant to write letters to magazines out of fear of that crushing final riposte that begins with, "The author replies..." Once again, I appreciate the letter and the attitude it conveys.

My goal in detailing these problem areas is to demonstrate how perilous it can be to write representation-dependent code. If you want good performance and a high degree of portability (and who doesn't, these days?), then you must isolate representation dependencies in a few well chosen primitives. Use these primitives religiously and you can win with both performance and portability. Let's take a closer look at those primitives I mentioned that are in the Standard C library.

Function **frexp** partitions a floating-point argument into two component results, an integer exponent and a floating-point fraction. If the input number is not zero, then the floating-point fraction is in the interval [1/2, 1). You raise 2 to the integer exponent and multiply the result by the floating-point fraction to get the input value.

On machines with a binary exponent, this simply involves extracting a subfield of the floating-point representation. You add a standard bias to the extracted subfield to get the exponent part. You replace the exponent with a standard exponent value to get the floating-point fraction part. On machines with a hexadecimal exponent, such as System/370, you have to do slightly more work, but not much more. In any case, the **frexp** function is fast, and it involves no floating-point arithmetic.

Function **ldexp** raises 2 to the integer exponent argument and multiplies the result by the floating-point fraction argument to get the function result. As you may have guessed, **ldexp** performs the inverse of **frexp**. If the input number is not zero, you add the integer exponent argument to the appropriate subfield of the floating-point fraction argument and check for overflow or underflow. Once again, there is a bit more work involved on System/370. But once again, this is a fast function.

Function **modf** partitions the floating-point argument into two component results, a floating-point result that is an exact integer and a floating-point result whose magnitude is less than 1.0. Both have the same sign as the argument. You add the two component results to get the input value.

This function is somewhat harder than the two previous ones. If you want to avoid using floating-point instructions, you must do a lot of shifting, masking, and realigning to separate the two components and package them properly. The function is worth calling, however, if you have reason to believe that simply converting a floating-point number to integer form might cause integer overflow.

Function **fmod** effectively subtracts the magnitude of one floating-point argument repeatedly from the magnitude of the other floating-point argument until the residue is less than the value being subtracted. The result is analogous to the remainder you get when performing the integer division **x/y**, for the arguments **x** and **y** to **fmod**. The result is also closely akin to what you would get for a fraction result if you called **modf** with **x/y**, but with a very important difference — **fmod** works hard to preserve all of the bits of precision available in the fraction. Were you to first compute **x/y** and obtain a magnitude larger than one, you would have to sacrifice some bits of precision to represent the integer part that you intend to discard.

This function is very hard to write so that it is both correct and efficient. I used the term "effectively" in describing its operation because that is the easiest way to describe its effect, but no sensible implementor would write the function that way. You have to do some pretty fancy scaling and looping to save time. (The modern floating-point coprocessor chips provide special instructions to do at least part of this job, because it's so important.) Even then, this function can easily take a dozen floating-point comparisons and subtractions. But it's worth it.

Given these primitives, let's take another look at the **_prod** function that started this whole discussion. If you call **frexp** with one of the operands that you wish to multiply together, you extract its exponent and leave a floating-point part that is strictly less than one. You can safely proceed to multiply that part by the other operand, with no fear that the result can overflow. Any overflow will happen when you call **ldexp** to fold the exponent you extracted back into the product. But that is a software operation that steers clear of any hardware exception-handling machinery. So you can write portable code to deal with potential overflows.

If you are also concerned about detecting and handling floating-point underflows with **_prod**, then you need to call **frexp** for both operands. If one operand is near the smallest representable value, multiplying it by 0.5 may cause it to underflow. But if you reduce both operands to the interval $[1/2, 1)$ (or zero), then the product must lie in the interval $[1/4, 1)$ (or zero). You add the extracted exponents and fold them back into the product by calling **ldexp**. If an underflow is going to occur, it will happen then.

This implementation of **_prod** is merely a safe way of profiting from Mr. Condon's final observation. You extract the exponents of two floating-point operands by using integer operations and sum them. You form the product by a safe hardware multiply. You check whether adding the sum back into the exponent of the product will cause overflow or underflow, and handle any exceptions in portable software. The result is a safe floating-point multiply that involves no additional floating-point operations.

Having harped on this subject at length, I would now like to show you a number of concrete examples of how you can (and should) compute real live mathematical functions using code that is simultaneously efficient, precise, portable and safe. You can only truly appreciate the primitives I have been discussing by seeing them in action. That is the topic of the next essay. (See **Essay 6: Do-It-Yourself Math Functions**.) □

Afterword: I really hated to pummel a letter writer, but I couldn't resist the opportunity to discuss so many issues. Writing floating-point software that is at once safe, efficient, and portable is a major challenge. Picking the right primitives makes all the difference. Thanks again to Paul Condon for suffering my diatribe.

6 Do-It-Yourself Math Functions

$\mathfrak{T}$his essay continues the discussion of computer arithmetic that I began several essays back. (See **Essay 2: Computer Arithmetic, Essay 3: Floating-Point Arithmetic** and **Essay 5: Safe Math**.) In the last essay, I described a few low-level primitives from the Standard C library that you can use to write mathematical functions. These functions assist you in constructing functions that are simultaneously efficient, precise, portable, and safe. In this essay, I show examples of how you can practice safe math in the modern world of portable programming.

The examples I have chosen are several of the common math functions. I have written these in many forms over the last quarter century. Each time, I have picked up a bit more technology and (more important) gained a bit more insight into computer arithmetic. The latest versions are decidedly smaller, faster, more accurate, more portable, and more maintainable than the earliest.

It may seem silly to describe in detail how a library function computes, say, a square root. I have preached repeatedly that you should never replicate technology that already exists, particularly technology that requires considerable expertise to master. It is not my intention to inspire applications programmers to run off and belt out several thousand private versions of common math functions. If you can perform the math calculations you need by using the standard library functions that come with your favorite programming language, then by all means do so.

The purpose of this essay is to show you what technology you can bring to bear in those cases where the standard math library does not serve your needs. For instance:

- The Standard C library provides functions only for operands of type *double*. If you need a smaller and faster library for operands of type *float*, you may have to do part or all of the job yourself. Even if you have access to the library source code, you cannot get optimum results merely by changing all the *double* declarations to *float* and recompiling. At best, the resultant code will waste time. At worst, it will give incorrect answers.

- The math functions I describe here exemplify many of the computational difficulties you may encounter when computing more exotic functions. You can learn a lot about computing any periodic function, say, from the way the library computes **sin** and **cos**.

- You may have serious performance problems that are best solved by bootlegging special versions of the standard math functions. A function that computes both **sin** and **cos** for the same argument, for instance, can speed rotations in graphics.

Equally important, knowing what it takes to compute math functions safely may be enough to dissuade you from a marginal enterprise. If the standard library is close enough, you are probably better off just using it. Save your ingenuity for the application-specific part of your program.

Let's begin with one of the easiest math functions, computing the square root. Traditionally, the function is called **sqrt**. It is defined such that, for **y = sqrt(x), x = y * y**.

The first thing to observe is that the square root of **x** is not defined, at least in the world of real numbers, for negative values of **x**. (You can take the square root of any complex number and get a representable complex result, but that is another library.) A mathematician would say that negative values of **x** are outside the *domain* of the function **sqrt**.

Such a *domain error* is not the same thing as an overflow. You get an overflow when the value of the function is well defined for its argument value(s), but is too large to represent with the floating-point format used on this particular machine. Some other machine may have no trouble for the same argument value(s).

You can also get an underflow when the value of the function is well defined, but is too small to represent. (See **Essay 3: Floating-Point Arithmetic**.) A mathematician doesn't believe in overflow and underflow, but a software engineer knows to call these aberrations *range errors*.

You must check for domain errors at the top of each library function that might experience them, and you must report them in some useful way. You must check for range errors wherever they might occur, and you must report them in some useful way. (See **Essay 5: Safe Math**.) It is not acceptable to report a range error for an intermediate overflow if the final result is representable. You must find a way to avoid the intermediate overflow.

Reporting errors from a library function raises all sorts of design issues. At the one extreme, you would like all the help you can get on debugging aberrant behavior. A silly argument to a library function should cause a diagnostic printout, preferably with some trace back to indicate the chain of callers, and probably with automatic program termination.

At the other extreme, you would like your embedded program to keep chugging no matter what. You would like some way for your program to retain control for all possible errors reported by library functions.

There are several solutions to the problem of library error reporting, including:

- Bull ahead with the computation and rely on the hardware to detect and/or report any problems.

- Return some unusual (but incorrect) value when the error occurs.

- Return some in-channel error indicator such as *machine indefinite* or *machine infinity* that the program can check later, even after additional arithmetic has been attempted upon the function result. (Again, see **Essay 5: Safe Math.**)

- Call a standard function to report the error, and return the unusual value or in-channel error indicator only if the error reporter returns control.

As someone who likes both safe and portable code, I always lean toward the last solution. Having the library functions call another function when errors occur gives you the most freedom in responding to the errors. You can provide default error handling that prints a message and terminates program execution. That is what most people want and need, if only in the earliest stages of debugging a program. You can also permit the program to specify alternate behavior when an error is reported:

- If you ask that the error be ignored, the error reporter simply returns to the library function that called it, as I described above.

- If you specify your own handler function, the error reporter calls your function. That function can jerk control back to a higher level of your program, by invoking some sort of exception handler or non-local **GOTO**. (See my essay "Programming on Purpose: Handling Exceptions," *Computer Language*, January 1988.) Or it can take a few notes and return control to the error reporter, which in turn returns control to the library function, which in turn returns control to the caller with its unusual value or in-channel error indicator.

The primitives that I use are two functions called **_domain** and **_range**. Each takes as argument a pointer to an error message that the default error handler will incorporate into its diagnostic printout. Each can return control if the error reporter determines that the library function should return control to its caller.

So, getting back to the square-root function, its overall structure is dictated by the need to detect domain errors:

```
sqrt(x)
    IF (x < 0)
        _domain("square root")
        RETURN (0)
    ELSE
        <compute square root y>
        RETURN (y)
```

For the actual computation of the square root, Isaac Newton developed an algorithm which still cannot be beat. You simply guess some positive value for **y** and average that with **x/y** to get a new **y** that is a better approximation to the square root. You can see that if your initial guess for **y** is too small, then **x/y** will be larger than **sqrt(x)**. Averaging will yield a new **y** that is closer to the square root. And if your initial guess is too large, then **x/y** will be smaller than **sqrt(x)**. The average will once again take you in the right direction.

What is not so obvious is that this algorithm converges really fast. You more than double the number of bits of precision with each iteration. You go from, say, four bits of precision to 79 in just four iterations (9, 19, 39, 79). The only times that the algorithm does not converge, in fact, are:

- when **x** < 0, which is already ruled out as a domain error
- when **x** = 0, which you can handle as a special case
- when you choose a negative value as an initial guess for **y**, a sin which you can easily avoid committing

So your first temptation is to write:

```
y := 1
WHILE (<not close enough>)
    y := (y + x / y) / 2
```

where **<not close enough>** involves checking that the relative difference between **x** and **y** * **y** is sufficiently smaller than **x** to meet your needs.

This works fine. I have even seen amateur square-root functions that do something like this. But it is nowhere near the level of engineering you should demand of an important library function.

Let's get back to those primitive functions I discussed in the previous essay. One of them, **frexp**, unpacks a floating-point number into a fraction (call it **f**) in the interval [1/2, 1) and an integer exponent, base two (call it **n**). If you unpack **x** this way, then:

```
x := f * 2ⁿ
sqrt(x) := sqrt(f) * sqrt(2ⁿ)
```

Computing **sqrt(2^n)** is easy. You just halve the exponent **n** and fold it into the final result by using another primitive, **ldexp**. If **n** is odd, you must also multiply the result by the square root of 2. But that is just a constant factor.

Computing **sqrt(f)** looks no easier than computing **sqrt(x)**, but it does offer two important advantages:

- Because it is in a very narrow interval of values, [1/2, 1), you can easily guess a good starting value. A linear approximation of the form:

```
y := C1*f + C2
```

can start you off with several bits of precision.

```
sqrt(x)
   IF (x < 0)
      _domain("square root")
      RETURN (0)
   ELSE IF (x = 0)
      RETURN (0)
   ELSE
      (x, n) := _frexp(x)
      y := C1*f + C2
      y += x/y
      y := 0.25*y + x/y
      y += x/y
      y := 0.25*y + x/y
      IF (<n is odd>)
         y *= 2^{1/2}
      y := _ldexp(y, n/2)
      RETURN (y)
```

Figure 6.1: *Pseudo code for square-root function.*

■ Because you know how many bits of precision you start off with, you can simply iterate a fixed number of times. There is no need for the time-consuming test for convergence.

Putting all of these shortcuts together gives a first-rate implementation of **sqrt**, as shown in Figure 6.1.

I used the C-style assignment operators (also in Algol 68), **+=** and ***=**, to indicate operations performed in place. They save time if your language supports them. I also unwound the divide-and-average calculations by pairs and regrouped operations to minimize arithmetic. The effect is the same as four divide-and-average iterations, but with a few less operations.

You can determine the coefficients **C1** and **C2** in a variety of ways. My favorite algorithm is to look them up in a book. (But see also **Essay 18: Approximating Functions**.) An excellent source of numerical approximations for all of the common math functions is John F. Hart, et al., *Computer Approximations* (**Har78**). Using coefficients from Hart, this algorithm gives at least 56 bits of precision. That is more than you need for IEEE or IBM System/370 *double* format, and enough for DEC VAX and PDP-11.

You can find $2^{1/2}$ to sufficient precision in many places. A good all-around source of such lore is M. Abramowitz and I. Stegun, *Handbook of Mathematical Functions* (**A&S65**). Whatever you do, don't use your pocket calculator to determine coefficients like this. The result will be good only to about ten decimal places. (I once spent days chasing a small systematic error in a FORTRAN program before I discovered that the author had written π using the junior-high-school approximation 22/7! On the other hand, 355/113 is a satisfactory approximation to π if you are working in single precision.)

You can write a cube-root function, or a function that computes even higher roots, using much the same techniques that I showed here. In fact, Newton's method is good for finding the roots of quite a number of functions. You can also adapt this algorithm to computing square roots to lower or higher precision. Knowing the number of bits of precision you need to develop, you can trade off the complexity of the initial-guess computation against the number of times you need to iterate.

A close relative of the square-root function is the hypotenuse. Often written **hypot (x, y)**, it yields the length of the hypotenuse of a right triangle whose sides are **x** and **y**. It also gives the magnitude of a complex number, or the distance from the origin to a point in the (x, y) plane.

The obvious way to compute the hypotenuse is:

```
hypot(x, y) := sqrt(x*x + y*y)
```

By now, you are alert enough to recognize the potential pitfalls:

- Either **x*x** or **y*y** may overflow, even when the result is representable.
- The sum may overflow, even when the result is representable.
- The result may not be representable.

What to do? If $|x| < |y|$, then you can recast the formula above into the safer form:

```
r := |x|/|y|
hypot(x, y) := |y|*sqrt(1 + r*r)
```

You may get an underflow when doing the divide, but it is safe to accept the usual zero fixup when that occurs. If the result is unrepresentable, then you will get an overflow on the final multiply by $|y|$. For this operation, you can use the safe function **_prod** that I described at length in the previous essay.

If $|y| < |x|$, then you can do the same as above by reversing the roles of **x** and **y**. The only other possibility is **x = y = 0**, which is easy enough to handle as a special case. (You treat special cases separately only to protect an algorithm from blowing up. If you have good reason to believe that you will get a speedup because the special case occurs so often, then handle it separately, but by all means label the code as an optimization. Otherwise you will drive maintainers crazy.)

Putting all these considerations together, you get:

```
hypot(x, y)
    IF (x < 0)
        x := -x
    IF (y < 0)
        y := -y
    IF (x < y)
        r := x/y
```

```
ELSE IF (x = 0)
   RETURN (0)
ELSE
   r := y/x
   y := x
RETURN (_prod(y, sqrt(1 + r*r)))
```

As you can see, the difference between a mathematically correct function and a computationally safe one can be considerable, at least in terms of apparent complexity.

Now let's look at another widely used function, for computing the sine of **x**, usually written **sin(x)**. It is, of course, closely related to still another widely used function, the cosine of **x**, or **cos(x)**. So intimately related are the two that both are typically computed in the same library module, using much the same code for both functions.

At first blush, in fact, you might observe that:

$$sin(x) = cos(x - \pi/2)$$

If you write **sin(x)** this way, by subtracting $\pi/2$ from its argument and calling **cos**, you are asking for trouble. Tiny values of **x** will lose all significance when combined with $\pi/2$. The value of the function will suffer along with **x**. Even larger values can easily lose at least one or more bits of significance. You do slightly better by writing **cos** in terms of **sin**, but you still risk measurable loss of significance. And either way, you are performing an additional floating-point addition or subtraction, which costs extra time.

This typifies an important principal in writing safe math functions. Never subtract (algebraically) two floating-point numbers that might be comparable in magnitude. The result invariably has a large relative error, which often results in avoidable loss of precision in the final result. A corollary is that you should never add two numbers if there is any chance that you later will wish to subtract out one of them. A larger number will swamp the precision carried by a smaller one.

So what do you do? Well, **sin** and **cos** are periodic functions. You can add 2π to the argument (mathematically at least) and get the same value for the function. It makes sense to use this identity to reduce an argument to the interval $[-\pi, \pi]$. There are enough additional symmetries that it makes even more sense to reduce an argument to the interval $[-\pi/4, \pi/4]$, by repeatedly adding or subtracting $\pi/2$ and counting the number of times you do so. All you need to keep track of besides the reduced argument are the low two bits of the count. These bits tell you what quadrant the argument is in. If you reduce the argument this way, then the difference between **sin** and **cos** is whether you start counting from quadrant 0 or 1.

You do not want to divide **x** by $\pi/2$. The integer part of the quotient may overflow your largest available representation, and the fraction part will lose significance. You probably do not want to actually add or subtract $\pi/2$ repeatedly. For a large argument, that can take a long time. (Never mind how meaningful the result is.) This is an ideal application for the **fmod** primitive I described in the previous essay. It forms the residue carefully, as if by repeated subtractions, but much more quickly. The version of **fmod** that I favor also safely delivers up the low order bits of the add/subtract count, no matter how large the count might be.

Once you have reduced the argument, all you have to do is compute **sin(x)** (if the quadrant count is even) or **cos(x)** (if odd) for $|\mathbf{x}| <$ $\pi/4$. Both **sin** and **cos** are sufficiently well behaved that you can approximate each by a polynomial in **x**. What is the polynomial? A natural candidate is a truncated version of the Taylor series:

```
sin(x) = x - x³/3! + x⁵/5! - ...
cos(x) = 1 - x²/2! + x⁴/4! - ...
```

You need to retain about seven or eight terms for a *double* result.

You can reduce the number of terms you need to compute, however, by "telescoping" the truncated Taylor series. What you observe is that a linear combination of powers of **x** will have its worst error at the extremes of the range, where $|\mathbf{x}|$ approaches $\pi/4$. A truncated series that is barely acceptable at the extremes has far more precision than you need for smaller values of **x**. Wouldn't it be nice if there were some way to adjust the coefficients of the truncated polynomial to sort of smear the error over the whole range? An approximation that wiggles back and forth around the exact result has to be better than one that steadily diverges for larger magnitudes of **x**.

There is a set of functions, called the Chebychev polynomials, that wiggle just this way over a unit interval. The trick is to fit a linear combination of Chebychev polynomials to your truncated series, then discard the highest-order polynomial. The resultant polynomial has one lower power of **x** than the original, and has an error that wiggles nicely about the exact result. What you see as a result of this process is a set of coefficients that are tweaked up and down slightly to do a better job over the finite interval in question. For a more detailed description of telescoping polynomials, see F. Acton, *Numerical Methods that Work* (**Act70**).(See also **Essay 19: Economizing Polynomials**.)

An even better way to improve upon a truncated Taylor series is to browse through Hart, et al. (See above.) You are sure to find just the coefficients you need for whatever precision you are striving for. To develop a *double* result on most popular machines, you need polynomials of order 6 for both **sin** and **cos**.

The final result is show in Figure 6.2.

```
sin(x)
   RETURN (_sin(x, 0))

cos(x)
   RETURN (_sin(x, 1))

_sin(x, quad)
   (x, n) := _fmod(x, π / 2)
   quad += n
   y := x*x
   IF (quad & 1)
       y := _poly(y, cos_tab, 6)
   ELSE
       y := x * _poly(y, sin_tab, 6)
   IF (quad & 2)
       RETURN (-y)
   ELSE
       RETURN (+y)
```

Figure 6.2: *Pseudo code for sine and cosine functions.*

Here, I also make use of the primitive **_poly**, which computes a polynomial given the value of its independent variable, a table of coefficients, and the order of the polynomial. It is a tight loop that computes the polynomial very efficiently using Horner's method, a succession of multiplies and adds. (On the DEC VAX, **_poly** is a single instruction.) You can see how a well chosen set of primitives distills out all but the unique aspects of computing **sin** and **cos**.

Many other periodic functions also fit this mold. Once you reduce the interval over which you must approximate a function, you have a broad assortment of techniques for picking the most economical form. Acton gives some useful guidelines in his book that I cited above. A few of them are:

- If it wiggles like a polynomial, approximate it with a polynomial.
- If it approaches an asymptote, use a truncated continued fraction or a ratio of two polynomials.
- If you are near a singularity mathematically, you are *at* a singularity computationally. Factor it out or perish.

Armed with this sage but general advice, and the handful of primitive functions I have discussed these last two essays, I have tackled many a nasty problem in approximating mathematical functions. With a proper respect for the limitations of floating-point arithmetic, you can too. □

𝕬fterword: Computing math functions well has been a preoccupation of mine for most of my career. I risk boring others in my zeal to explain the technology involved. Still, I know of few sources that cover everything you need to know in one place. When you have to compute a function with accuracy, robustness, and efficiency, you'd better know what you're doing.

I revisit this theme in two later essays.(See **Essay 18: Approximating Functions***and* **Essay 19: Economizing Polynomials.***)*

7 Locking the Barn Door

Information has value. Many of you who read this collection earn the money to pay for it by creating information. And you depend upon a vast infrastructure to protect the value of that information and ensure that the proper owners benefit from it. You also have a personal responsibility to ensure that the information you work with is protected.

People who manufacture, say, lawn chairs understand value and protection. You don't spend all day turning out chairs, only to leave them unattended on the sidewalk in front of the store overnight. It is a matter of time before someone takes advantage of your laxity and walks off with a chair or three. Never mind that it is illegal, never mind that the city employs a police force and courts to protect your property rights. You still have an obligation to do your part in protecting your goods from theft. You take the chairs inside the store at night and lock the door.

People who manufacture jewelry understand value and protection even more. Their stuff is much more highly valued than lawn chairs. It is also much more portable. If you manufacture jewelry, you don't display it out on the sidewalk. Many thieves would risk a snatch and run in broad daylight for the chance of nabbing a $5,000 bracelet. You don't depend on just locking up the store at night. There are enough thieves who would risk breaking and entering to haul off $100,000 worth of assorted jewelry. Jewelers must invest far more than furniture stores in private methods of protection, such as armed guards, burglar alarms, and safes.

When it comes to tangible goods, we have several millennia of experience in how to behave. We understand that gray area where we must provide our own protection, even though society nominally provides it for us. We understand that the investment in protection must be proportional to the value that is at risk. We understand that nothing is ultimately safe from theft, but that everything can be made safe enough if we make life tough enough for prospective thieves.

When it comes to information, however, we encounter greater difficulties. Information can be copied, often quite cheaply, so that thieves can benefit from it without having to pay the cost of generation. There is a thriving black market for pirated software, audio cassettes, video cassettes, and inside information on mergers and acquisitions. Information can be corrupted or blocked, often without a trace, so that enemies can deceive you into believing untrue data. Whether you make a bad marketing decision, an unwise stock transaction, or an unsafe military maneuver, corrupted information can be disastrous.

Worst of all, we tend not to think about the value of our private information, so we forget to guard it. There are still communities in the United States, mostly rural, where people leave their homes unlocked at night or when left unattended. Sadly, those communities have become the rare exception. A typical multi-user UNIX installation, on the other hand, is like a rural farmhouse in Central Park. Its neglected defenses leave it at the mercy of the first aggressive assailant. And those assailants are more numerous than you might think.

As you may have guessed by now, this essay is about protecting information. There is some really neat technology to help you keep information private and uncorrupted, as I indicated in an earlier essay. (See my essay, "Programming on Purpose: You Can't Do That," *Computer Language*, September 1988.) You should know what is possible these days in both single-key and public-key cryptography, so you can avoid the more obvious oversights in this twisty business. At least as important, however, is to be aware of what *protocols* you must follow to ensure that your efforts at protection are not misplaced. The vast majority of successful security attacks are akin to finding the door key under the welcome mat. And most responses to invasion amount to no more than locking the barn door after the horse has been stolen.

To protect information properly:

- you must first notice that you have information that is worth protecting
- you must avoid subverting whatever protocols you have for protections that are already in place
- you must be sure that the protections you use raise the cost of assault to a sufficiently high level

If you fail to notice that you have information that is worth protecting, then the game is over before it is begun. What you tend to overlook is that information has no special value to you if you cannot control access to it. A wise general knows that a wanton killer makes a bad soldier, and a mob is no substitute for an army. It is the ability to turn an armed force on and off at will that makes for military might. Similarly, a mining engineer has no interest in a powerful explosive if it is also unstable. The engineer favors dynamite over nitroglycerin because the former is easier to control.

You can control information by limiting access to it. Do you have a software product? Then show the source code only to customers who pay good money and sign a well crafted license for the privilege. Don't let your employees take it home on diskettes. Put copyright notices on it, in case it does go astray. You might even ask yourself whether a neighbor might enjoy browsing through your dumpster.

Do you have a customer list? Then treat it like the gold that it is. Don't disclose it to other customers, and certainly not to competitors. Don't tell anybody what your gross sales are, or your market share. Public corporations must disclose a lot, but even they are permitted a few secrets.

If you find an atmosphere of secrecy repulsive, you need to readjust your thinking. Many of us enjoyed the open and liberal atmosphere of college. We learned to associate secrecy with acts that are illicit or unethical. But I am not talking about coverups or clandestine operations. I am talking about privacy. What you do in the bathroom is no secret, but it is private. The same should be true of your checkbook and your company's customer list.

I am continually amazed at the inconsistent way most companies protect their information. One company that I have had recent dealings with is very closed about its other business relationships. But it maintains a visitors' log in the lobby that I read with interest every time I sign in. Knowing who my competitors are, and when they visit, has helped immeasurably in my negotiations.

I have two guidelines for determining when to protect information:

- How much would I enjoy learning similar data from a competitor?
- How much did it cost me to acquire the information?

If either of these questions rings a bell, then I start locking the barn door before it is too late.

To understand the importance of observing protocols, you should read Clifford Stoll's "Stalking the Wily Hacker" (**Sto88**). It describes the antics of an assailant, evidently somewhere in West Germany, who successfully invaded dozens of computer systems over a one-year period. Some unusually alert and responsible people at Lawrence Berkeley Labs caught him in the act, then set about monitoring his actions while various law-enforcement agencies cooperated in tracking him down. The intruder was patently on the lookout for military information.

What is sobering about Stoll's account is the ease with which the assailant found his way around a network of several hundred machines, and his success rate in invading many of them. This was no *War Games* whiz kid, nor any sort of computer genius. The assailant succeeded with a little knowledge of common security gaffes in UNIX systems, and a lot of persistence. Fully 13 per cent of all systems available to the assailant gave at least some information about their operations. Five per cent let him log in, and two per cent granted him system-manager privileges!

You should understand that UNIX is capable of being a reasonably secure system. When you specify your password for subsequent logins, the system does not save a copy of it in a file, as many earlier systems have done. The best protected file can always be read by someone. Rather, it encrypts your password using a scheme that is known to be very expense to invert, even if you know the algorithm. The encrypted password is stored in a file that need not be protected from arbitrary readers. Whenever the system requests your password, it encrypts what you type and compares the result with the encrypted password. Plaintext versions of passwords have a very limited lifetime.

Each program runs in protected mode, so that it can perform certain operations (such as file I/O) only via system calls that check access permissions. The access permissions on each file can be set to prohibit your altering any programs which have permissions beyond your own. Dennis Ritchie was even granted a patent on the "set-user-ID" access protection, which lies at the heart of the ingenious but simple UNIX protection mechanism.

There is no reason, in principle, why a UNIX system cannot be made arbitrarily safe. In practice, however, users subvert the protections in a number of ways. Stoll reports that 20 per cent of the passwords at LBL fell to a simple guessing attack. I have found about the same ratio over many years of working under multi-user systems. If I have to guess login IDs, I begin with **root, bin,** and **guest.** I proceed with known users' surnames, first names, and initials. For passwords, I try **password, foo,** and **bar.** I proceed with login IDs, followed by names of children, spouses, and pets, then license-plate numbers. I can usually score enough hits to acquire a useful assortment of permissions.

I often find that just logging on to a UNIX system gives me all the access permissions I need, because system managers are lax about limiting access to critical files. If I can read the raw devices on which file systems are written, I can read any file regardless of its protection. If I can write on a file with set-user-ID permissions, I can replace it (temporarily) with my own shell. If all else fails, there is usually a version of mail or emacs lying about that I can subvert into corrupting a system file on my behalf. And by judicious juggling of the login history file and the date command, I can erase any tracks I make in my wanderings.

To the best of my knowledge, I am no more adept at cracking UNIX systems than the wily hacker described by Stoll.

One of the most adept assailants, naturally enough, is the guy who developed UNIX. Read Ken Thompson's Turing Award Lecture, "Reflections on Trusting Trust," (**Tho84**). He describes a marvelous double Trojan horse that he insinuated into an early version of UNIX. Thompson devised a simple change to the **login** utility that would let him bypass the normal password check when logging on in a special way. He then replaced that change in login with a special pattern of code, and altered the C compiler to replace the special pattern with the desired change. Now you could inspect the code of login and not see the Trojan horse.

To protect the C compiler, Thompson repeated the process. He replaced the Trojan horse with another special pattern of code, and altered the C compiler in a different way to replace the second special pattern with the double Trojan horse. After one recompile, he discarded the intermediate version of the C compiler. The final product was innocent-looking source code for both login and the C compiler, and a perverted binary for the C compiler.

As icing on the cake, the new C compiler source made use of one or two small extensions over the previous version. I remember getting the source of the new compiler and being annoyed that the old compiler balked at it. A quick phone call to Murray Hill saved the day, however. Thompson cheerfully agreed to send me the new binary (complete with double Trojan horse) to help me convert to the new dialect of C. What a guy.

I have also been guilty of installing a Trojan horse in the UNIX login command. Not being as subtle as Thompson, I used the purloined-letter approach. You could stare straight at the new code in login and not see its malicious purpose. Forgive me if I don't tell you what use I made of the modified command. I also had occasion to augment a file-encryption utility, so that it wrote to a secret file all passwords it used. That ploy gave me legitimate access to some very useful information. And it taught me that it is easier to steal keys than to pick locks.

Now for the technology. You can often get adequate protection just by limiting access to your valuable information. No technology needed, it's all protocol. If you must transmit information via public channels, however, then you need to use some form of encryption.

The simplest scheme is called *single-key encryption*. Sender and receiver agree on a method for mapping plaintext to a cryptogram. The encryption must, of course, be reversible, so that the plaintext can be recovered by a corresponding decryption mapping. Many methods take the form of a generic mapping algorithm plus a variable key. Sender and receiver share the key in secret.

The simplest of these simple schemes is also the best. It is the only one I know that serious cryptographers agree cannot be cracked. The key shared between sender and receiver is a thick pad of text. For each transmission, the sender tears the top sheet off the pad and uses its text as the encryption key. Each character of the cryptogram is a function of the corresponding characters in the message and the key. If you represent characters by numeric codes, such as ASCII for example, you can simply exclusive-OR the key and message characters to produce the cryptogram character. You can then decrypt the cryptogram by performing the same operation with the same key. Because there is no redundancy in this "one-time pad" approach, assailants have little to analyze.

For shipping megabytes of information, however, this scheme presents problems. You need some way to distribute megabytes of keys by some safe channel, so why not use that channel to send the information in the first place? It is clearly desirable to be able to use short keys, and to be able to reuse keys. Much of the science of cryptography concerns itself with finding safe ways to use short keys. (The rest concerns itself with subverting these efforts.)

Julius Caesar used a simple encryption scheme which is still popular today. The key consists of a permutation of the letters of the alphabet. You encipher plaintext by replacing each letter with its corresponding letter in the permutation. It is a simple scheme with just one principal drawback — it is practically worthless.

Today this encryption scheme is used as an idle amusement. Most collections of crossword puzzles come with a dozen or so cryptograms encoded by simple letter substitution. Millions of people crack messages as short as one sentence, using only a basic knowledge of English word patterns and letter frequencies. If we amateurs can be so successful, you have to wonder what the professionals can do when the stakes get high.

You can do a few things to help simple substitution codes. Since the letter **e** occurs frequently, you can replace each **e** by randomly choosing from a group of replacement sequences. You can drop in occasional noise letters, such as the letter **x** in places where it obviously does not belong. You can run the words together. All of these changes are fairly easy to unravel when you decrypt the message, and interfere nicely with the normal fun of cracking substitution ciphers.

If you want state of the art encryption, however, don't waste your time with incremental improvements on a basically unsafe approach. The best known technology for single-key encryption is the Data Encryption Standard published by the National Bureau of Standards (**NBS77**). First published in 1977, the DES algorithm has been the subject of intense scrutiny by the best in the trade. To date, nobody has reported a successful method of attack that does not involve an exhaustive search over nearly all possible keys.

DES uses only a 56-bit key, which puts exhaustive search within the realm of possibility for today's ever more powerful computers. But there are various techniques for performing a sort of "lapstrake" encryption, where encrypted text is fed back to confound the encryption process even more. And you can always double encrypt with two keys to up the ante.

There are some who fear that NSA, or some other perennially suspect government agency, knows how to crack the DES. These people are certain that the government is encouraging the use of DES because it eases the task of spying on the private communications of private enterprise. Personally, I have an aversion to paranoid thinking. My anodyne to paranoia is: If everybody's behavior can be explained by simple stupidity and greed, there's no point in assuming a conspiracy. Besides, what are you doing to attract the attention of NSA? If you're not, then you have nothing to worry about. If you are, you have more to worry about than having your mail steamed open.

DES is used widely to secure and authenticate electronic funds transfers. You can buy chips that will encode a data stream using DES at a respectable bit rate. You can buy library functions that will let your PC or your mainframe speak DES as well. If you have private data that you must send over public channels, my advice to you is to get on the DES bandwagon now, before you lose any (more) horses.

The next step up in sophistication is to use two-key, or public-key, cryptography. It is the topic of the essay that follows. (See **Essay 8: Half a Secret.**) □

Afterword: People are becoming more aware of the need for confidentiality, but only slowly. Programmers are becoming more aware of encryption technologies, but not much faster. I focus on the simplest technology in this essay, because it is often sufficient. No point in putting a fancy lock on the barn door until you get in the habit of closing the door behind you.

8 Half a Secret

One of my favorite Sunday comic strips, as a child, was "Uncle Remus." This was a Walt Disney product, based on the delightful fables by Joel Chandler Harris. I suspect much of the strip was contrived by the folks at Disney Studios, not derived from Harris's tales, but the spirit of the original was well preserved.

A particular favorite of mine among these strips concerned the on-going rivalry between Br'er Rabbit and Br'er Fox. Br'er Rabbit was growing tired of Br'er Fox stealing watermelons from his watermelon patch. One day, he got a bright idea. He put up a sign in the middle of his watermelon patch. It said, "Br'er Fox, you'd better not eat any of these watermelons, because one of 'em is pizened." He reckoned that Br'er Fox wouldn't dare steal any of the watermelons, for fear of eating the poisoned one.

Next day, he returned to his watermelon patch to find that no watermelons had been taken during the night. That was the good news. But scribbled across the bottom of the sign was the addendum, "Now *two* of these watermelons is pizened!"

I remember delighting, even as a child, in the elegance of the stalemate. Each of these perennial connivers knew half a secret, which watermelon he himself has poisoned. (Of course, either or both may have poisoned no watermelons at all, or several of them. That scarcely altered the value of the information each of them held.) Safe consumption of watermelons was possible only if the two pooled their information. That gave Br'er Fox a strong bargaining position with the luckless owner of the watermelon patch.

In another essay, I described several clever techniques for solving problems that seem impossible, at least at first glance. (See my essay, "Programming on Purpose: You Can't Do That," *Computer Language*, September 1988.) I ended that essay by alluding to a companion problem to Br'er Rabbit's dilemma — how do you prove conclusively to somebody that you know a secret, without revealing just what that secret is? In other words, how do you tell half a secret? The fascinating technology of public-key cryptography lets you do just that. By the sheerest of coincidence, that same issue of *Computer Language* contains an overview of encryption systems, by T.A. Elkins (**Elk88**). I recommend that you read it.

In the previous essay, I discussed at some length the ways in which information has value. (See **Essay 7: Locking the Barn Door.**) I also described some of the ways you can protect your valuable information:

- by keeping it secret
- by encrypting it with state-of-the-art techniques
- by honoring the necessary protocols to ensure that neither secrecy nor encryption are compromised

I continue that topic in this essay by discussing public-key encryption.

The people who thought up public-key encryption are W. Diffie and M.E. Hellman. They wrote a landmark paper called "New Directions in Cryptography," (**D&H76**). In that paper, they explored what you could do if you could, indeed, split a secret in half. Half the secret is how to encrypt a message. The other half is how to decrypt it. If you could devise a scheme, the authors argued, whereby the encryptor could not decrypt messages and the decryptor could not encrypt messages, all sorts of interesting problems in authentication and secure communication could be solved.

Diffie and Hellman offered some suggestions for how to pull off such a trick, as did others. Over the years, however, many of the methods proposed for partitioning secrets have succumbed to the intense analysis of code breakers. One of the best survivors, to date, is called the RSA cryptosystem, in honor of its authors, R.L. Rivest, A. Shamir, and L. Adleman (**RSA76**). Before we get into the various uses for public-key cryptosystems, let's look at how the RSA approach works.

One good way to curdle numerically encoded information, so that it is hard to read, is to exclusive-OR it with an encryption key, as I discussed in the previous essay. You get the information back by repeating the exclusive-OR operation with the same key. Still another way is to raise each code value, **X**, to some power, **E**, then reduce the computed value modulo some base, **N**. The effect is much like flicking the spinning arrow on one of those children's board games. Even if the arrow head sweeps through an arc of predictable length, where it ends up pointing around the circle is hard to correlate with where it started out. You can take a numerical sequence of codes and end up with a sequence of encoded values that are distributed with a satisfying pseudo-randomness.

You get particularly satisfying results if the code value and the base **N** are relatively prime. That is, they have no common factors other than 1. Or to put it in terms of the greatest-common-denominator function (**GCD**):

```
GCD(X, N) = 1
```

Whether you add **X** repeatedly to a running sum, or multiply **X** repeatedly into a running product, you tend to get sequences that repeat no values until you have iterated **N** times. Such behavior is not always essential to good encryption schemes, but it helps to confuse matters.

℣o decrypt information encoded this way, you have to spin the arrow again in such a way that it ends up where it started. For a code value raised to the **E**th power, you can find the **E**th root (modulo **N**, of course). Or you can compute the logarithm and scale it appropriately (again modulo **N**). It would be nice, however, if you could raise the code value to still another value, **D**, reduce it modulo **N**, and obtain the original code value. That has the advantage of using the same machinery for decryption as for encryption. It also means that either exponent can be used as the encryptor and the other used as its corresponding decryptor, since any value raised to the **D*E** power equals the same value raised to the **E*D** power.

It may sound expensive to take on an encryption scheme that involves all of this exponentiation. Certainly it is more time consuming to perform multiplies than to perform exclusive-OR operations. But the cost need not be outrageous. The standard way that library functions raise **X** to an integer power **E** takes time proportional to the logarithm of **E**. In other words, the number of multiplies you have to perform is proportional to the number of bits needed to express the value of **E**. In pseudo-code:

```
pow(X, E)
    ans := 1
    FOREVER
        IF (E & 1)
            ans *= X
        E /= 2
        IF (E = 0)
            RETURN (ans)
        X *= X
```

The trick is to build just those binary powers of **X** that might contribute to the final result. Along the way, you fold into the result, `ans`, just those binary powers of **X** for which there are corresponding 1 bits in the exponent **E**. Note that the two in-place multiplies above, signaled by the operator ***=**, should be performed modulo **N** for this particular application.

𝕬 more important matter is, do such pairs **D** and **E** exist, for a given **N**? Certainly they do if you choose **N** to be the product **D*E**. Pierre de Fermat showed over three centuries ago that any positive prime number you can write (modulo **N**) when raised to the **N**th power (modulo **N**) equals itself. So, for instance, you could represent a 64-character alphabet with the code values 1 through 64. If you pick **D=5** and **E=13**, you get **N=65**, which can represent all of the code values. You encipher each character by raising its code value to the 13-th power (modulo 65). You decipher each character by raising the cipher value to the 5-th power (modulo 65).

Of course, this yields just another one-for-one substitution code. We dispatched those as incredibly weak in the previous essay. You can salvage the approach, however, by picking **D** and **E** much larger. Then you encrypt large blocks of text all at once and smear many adjacent characters into the same ciphertext. The numeric value you encode is the large number you get by treating the individual characters as digits, base 64. You might use the leftover zero code as a padding character, both for filling out short blocks and for insinuating occasional nonsense in the message stream. This is comparable to the old practice of peppering extra **X**s in a message to disrupt the expected patterns of English text. The padding characters are easily filtered out when you decrypt the message.

So we know that it is possible to find triples (**N**, **D**, **E**) that can provide separate encryption and decryption keys. Unfortunately, the particular scheme I just outlined does not chop the secret in half. You have to know **N** and **E** to encrypt a message. Knowing those two values, it is an easy matter to determine **D**. It is simply **N/E**. We need a sneakier way of picking the triple so that:

- you can't easily deduce **D** given only **N** and **E**
- you can't easily deduce **E** given only **N** and **D**
- you can nevertheless easily contrive the triple

The first two requirements are met by what are called *one-way functions*. These are functions that are reasonable to compute, but very unreasonable to invert. The Data Encryption Standard I described in the previous essay (**NBS77**), like any good enciphering algorithm, is a one-way function. There is no easy way to look at the ciphertext, in the absence of the encryption key, and determine either the plaintext message or the key.

The third requirement is met by what is called a *trap-door one-way function*. This is a function that you can easily invert, but only if given some extra bit of information. Naturally, you keep this extra information secret. The nice thing about the use of the trap-door here is that the secret need not be shared between encryptor and decryptor for the two to cooperate in exchanging secret messages.

The RSA approach takes advantage of several properties of prime numbers and modulus arithmetic. I won't go into all of them, because I don't intend to prove that the cryptosystem is correct. I just want to describe how it works. See the May 1988 issue of the *Proceedings of the IEEE* for a number of excellent articles on cryptology. There you will find all the mathematical backup you could possibly want. I leaned heavily on that issue in writing this essay, particularly James L. Massey's, "An Introduction to Contemporary Cryptography," p. 533 (**Mas88**). See also Martin E. Hellman's, "The Mathematics of Public-Key Cryptography," in the August 1979 issue of *Scientific American* (**Hel79**).

In the RSA cryptosystem, you determine two large primes, called **p** and **q**. You keep these primes secret. What you use for the base **N** is their product, **p*q**. You then pick a candidate value for **D**, which must be relatively prime

```
rsa_pair(D, p, q)
    bp := 0
    b  := 1
    c  := (p-1)*(q-1)
    d  := D
    FOREVER
        q := c/d
        r := c % d
        IF (r = 0)
            IF (d <> 1)
                <error>
            ELSE IF (b < 0)
                RETURN (p*q - b)
            ELSE
                RETURN (b)
        t  := bp
        bp := b
        b  := t - q*b
        d  := r
        r  := q
```

Figure 8.1: *Pseudo-code to determine an RSA key pair.*

to **(p-1)*(q-1)**. The corresponding value for **E** is then the unique value
for which **D*E** has the value 1, modulo **(p-1)*(q-1)**. Given **p**, **q**, and **D**,
you can determine **E** by an extension of the standard algorithm for computing GCD. I adapted the pseudo-code in Figure 8.1 from Don Knuth's
The Art of Computer Programming, Volume 1, p. 14 (**Knu68**).

This code reports an error if **D** is not relatively prime to **N**. Otherwise it
returns the value of **E** that corresponds to **D**. For the example above, with
p=5 and **q=13**, you can use this algorithm to determine the four (**D, E**) pairs
(5, 29), (11, 35), (13, 37) and (19, 43). There are also seven other candidate
values: 7, 17, 23, 25, 31, 41, and 47. These form pairs with themselves, such
as (7, 7), which may not be a wise choice.

The "trap door" here is knowing **p** and **q**. You need them to determine
the critical modulus **(p-1)*(q-1)** that relates **D** to **E**. You can in principle
determine **p** and **q** from the published value of **N**, which is **p*q**. But to do
so requires you to factor a very large number.

𝒜 modern supercomputer takes about a day to factor a 250-bit number.
For every 50 bits you add, the time required goes up about tenfold.
Considerable attention has been lavished on the problem of factoring
numbers (inspired, in part by RSA). And the price of computer power has
dropped impressively over the past decade. Nevertheless, there is no
serious hint that we will need values of **p** and **q** with more than a few
hundred bits to make codes that are safe for the foreseeable future.

One technical problem remains. How do you determine the large primes **p** and **q**, if it is so expensive to factor very large numbers? The answer is that you only have to be reasonably certain that **p** and **q** are primes, and you can determine that certainty to whatever degree you wish. In the range of numbers we are talking about, approximately one per cent of all odd numbers are prime. So what you do is guess an odd number, **X**, at random. Then guess about a hundred or so numbers less than **X** and see if each of them obeys the theorem of Fermat's that I mentioned earlier. If all hundred-odd guesses pan out, you are virtually certain to have guessed an **X** that is prime. Otherwise, go back and guess again. Within about a hundred guesses for **X**, you should strike a prime. So you see that it is much easier to determine that a number is quite likely to be a prime than it is to prove that the number is definitely not a prime by factoring it.

So what can you do with this elegant machinery? First of all, you can forget about replacing your DES applications with RSA. It is *much* slower. Instead, you should consider distributing the secret keys you need for DES via a channel protected by RSA. That takes best advantage of the respective strengths of both methods.

The nice thing about RSA, in fact, is that you can freely publish the pair (**N**, **E**) for both friends and enemies alike to peruse. Your friends can encrypt messages that only you can decrypt. You still have the problem, in the presence of thine enemies, to authenticate any messages sent your way. Remember that information forged, corrupted, or lost can be just as damaging to you as valid information that falls into the wrong hands. Public-key encryption doesn't make this problem any worse, only more apparent.

Every message that might be forged needs some form of signature (discussed below). Every message that might be corrupted needs enough redundant structure (also discussed below) so that any corruption is likely to be detected. Every message that might be lost needs a deadline, sent in an earlier message.

Your friends also have an obligation to compose messages that don't leak information in subtle ways. Say, for instance, you are expecting a simple yes or no answer. Your enemy can use (**N**, **E**) to encrypt the messages **yes** and **no** to see what they look like. When he sees your friend send a cryptogram that matches one of these simple patterns, he knows the answer without having to decrypt anything. Remember that even the mere *presence* of a message can convey information. There's much to be said for padding a communication channel with baseball scores and idle chit chat.

You can publish instead the pair (**N**, **D**). Any cryptogram you send out can then be decoded by the world at large. But only you can contrive a cryptogram that decodes properly for a given (**N**, **D**). That's one way of proving, electronically and from afar, that you are who you say you are.

No, you don't simply encrypt a static message such as, "Hello world. My name is Joe." Once you send that, anybody can copy it and present it as your forged signature. Instead, you encrypt part of the accompanying message, or the current date and time, as proof that you can repeat your magic trick on demand.

Say you have a file of information that you wish many people to peruse. But you want to protect your friends from an enemy corrupting the contents of the file. A checksum over the file can determine whether its contents have been altered, but an enemy can change the checksum to match. So you encrypt the checksum by your secret pair (**N, E**) and advertise the pair (**N, D**). Your public can decrypt the checksum to validate the file. But your enemy cannot forge a valid cryptogram with a new checksum.

Someone has even worked out a way to use the RSA cryptosystem to help verify treaty compliance (**Sim88**). Imagine a seismograph provided by the U.S. to monitor nuclear testing within the Soviet Union. The U.S. wants to receive telemetry with some assurance that the Soviets are not altering it in any way. The Soviets want to be sure that only seismic telemetry is being sent out. Both sides have a stake in being able to demonstrate noncompliance to a disinterested third party. The solution involves stuffing a computer down the bore hole, along with the seismograph, so that the instrument can concoct its own triples (**N, D, E**). Beyond saying that, I won't even begin to describe how all the protocols hang together. But it's neat.

I believe we have only begun to think of ways that public-key cryptography can be used in our everyday affairs. Already there are credit cards with logic and memory sandwiched inside. I have no idea how far we are from having cards that can use RSA to prove they are not forgeries, but I'll bet it's closer than you imagine. That should either elate you or frighten you, depending on whether you're an optimist or a pessimist. Either way, it's exciting.

As an occasional writer of speculative fiction, I can't resist a creepy addendum. It is clear to me that the current methods of personal authentication are becoming strained. Too many people are adept at cribbing credit-card numbers, forging signatures, impersonating voices, or imitating appearances. The technological choices on the horizon for safer authentication involve matching fingerprints, matching retinal patterns, or public-key cryptography.

Imagine a near future where these technologies compete for dominance of the growing commercial authentication market. Imagine trying to explain such a future in terms understandable to a person living before the age of high tech. Now consider the description of the "beast" that conquers the world for a time in Revelations 13:16-17:

And he causeth all, both small and great, rich and poor, free and bond, to receive a mark in their right hand, or in their foreheads.

And that no man might buy or sell, save that he had the mark, or the name of the beast, or the number of his name.

Before you send me any tracts, please understand. I am neither preaching the coming of the Anti-Christ nor making fun of St. John the Divine. Having been raised in the hills of West Virginia, then later trained as a nuclear physicist, I try to keep an open mind on these matters. If any of this makes you feel queasy, however, you can take some comfort in the verse that follows:

Here is wisdom. Let him that hath understanding count the number of the beast: for it is the number of a man; and his number is Six hundred threescore and six.

At least we know how to charge things to his Visa account. □

Afterword: Public-key cryptography is one of the more sophisticated topics I've tried to cover in these essays. I introduced an error or two in the original version (corrected in this presentation). I ruffled a few feathers with my biblical excursion at the end. And I dated the essay more than I ever expected by discussing Cold War applications. But all in all, I'm happy that I handled a difficult topic without compromising the facts.

9 It's (Almost) Alive

When I was about ten years old, I sat down one day and made a list of all the things I wanted to learn about. It was a long list. Three topics stood out at the top of the list, however:

- **Cybernetics** — I wanted to understand the mechanics of how people think, and the discipline that would help us replicate thought and think more clearly ourselves.
- **Computers** — I wanted to understand the mechanics of how computers work, and the discipline that would help us use them more effectively.
- **Natural philosophy** — I wanted to understand the mechanics of how the real world operates, and the discipline that would help us more quickly discover and understand natural laws.

These three topics are mushed together in my brain in ways that I cannot yet articulate well. Somehow, I see them as different manifestations of the same fascinating topic.

In my freshman year at college, I realized I would have to trim my list, at least for the time being. Princeton only let me take five courses per semester. So I struck from my long list all those topics that I felt I could satisfactorily address later in life merely by spending a few thousand hours pawing through library card catalogs and reading into the night. That took care of history, literature, philosophy, and a few branches of mathematics.

My top three items remained on the list, however. I trimmed the short list with a cold-bloodedness that I find, with hindsight, almost terrifying in a seventeen-year-old:

- **Cybernetics** was still in its infancy. I would defer serious study of it until others had laid more groundwork. I am still waiting.
- **Computers** were just becoming available on campus, but there were no computer science courses in those days. I could learn enough simply by working as a programmer a hundred hours a week during the summer and thirty hours a week during the school year.
- **Natural philosophy** required me to exercise skills at which I am not very strong. I got mostly Bs, with an occasional A or C, in math and physics courses. So the obvious thing to do was to major in physics and have the stuff forced down my throat. I earned a Bachelor of Arts in physics at Princeton and a Doctor of Philosophy in nuclear physics at Michigan State. (And I haven't done a lick of physics since the day I took my orals.)

I recite this history not to brag, but to show how you can turn an undisciplined ne'er-do-well (like me) into a yuppie over achiever. There's nothing like the joy of playing with expensive toys (computers) and the terror of final examinations (in physics) to keep your attention focused.

I also recite this history by way of introduction to an essay whose focus I cannot well articulate. Recent progress in these three separate fields has created a growing number of bridges between them. I feel a growing excitement that we are close to achieving a new level of understanding about how people think and how we can reflect those thought processes in software and hardware.

I freely confess to general ignorance about the current state of the art in artificial intelligence. (What I am maundering about isn't exactly artificial intelligence, but that's the closest discipline to it that has been actively pursued, at least until recently.) What I know I have learned from reading the trade press and popular literature, not from writing Lisp and Prolog programs.

Nevertheless, like any other Philistine, I know what I like. It seems to me that the recent progress in AI has resulted primarily from the astounding drop in the cost of raw computer power. The same paradigms that investigators pursued twenty years ago still dominate the field today. If there have been significant breakthroughs in the algorithms used to model human intelligence, I have yet to see the payoff in their application. My focus is a little outside the AI spotlight (as I understand it).

To clarify this focus, I would like to again go back in time to my days as a graduate student. I encountered then three computer programs, each of which offered tantalizing hints about the peculiar nature of living things. Bear with me while I recount these anecdotes.

Interestingly enough, all three programs were written by one person. John Kopf was (and remains) a close friend and fellow programmer who masqueraded for a time as a physicist. He is currently a senior staff scientist at a company in Cupertino CA. In those days before structured programming, John was a remarkably disciplined assembly-language programmer. He also had a peculiar gift for making programs come alive.

On one occasion, the MSU Cyclotron Lab played host to some visiting biologists. The laboratory director asked John to provide a demonstration of our little on-line computer (one of the first in physics research) that a biologist could relate to. John responded by making a DNA molecule out of a yard of paper tape. If you stuffed the strip of paper tape in the reader and hit the bootstrap switch, the computer would read in the head of the tape and transfer control to it. The head consisted of a small program which copied itself to the paper tape punch, then copied the tail from the reader to the punch. *Voila,* reproduction.

John demonstrated his little DNA program and let the visitors turn out half a dozen replicas. It was cute, but rather trivial. They got the point very quickly. But the real fun began when John handed a visitor a hole punch and asked him to "mutate" a DNA molecule. The results were fascinating.

Chances were that a random hole would end up in the tail, since it was much longer than the head. If the hole was in a data track, the bad parity light would come on during the read, but the change took effect. It appeared in the daughter molecule, with the parity corrected. The daughter molecule produced future generations with the same mutation (and no parity gripes). If the hole was in the parity track, the bad parity light would again come on, but the change disappeared. The genetic damage was repaired during reproduction!

If the visitor punched a hole in the head of the molecule, it could almost never reproduce. A parity hole was corrected, as with the data tail, but any other change would alter the program. And the program was so tightly written that any change at all would alter its behavior unacceptably.

People who work around radiation know how silly are most of those sci-fi films that center around mutated monsters. Sterility is the most likely result of random damage to the reproductive machinery. And it is an axiom of genetics that sterility is not hereditary. John's program did a marvelous job of illustrating the behavior of life at its lowest levels. We used up several hundred feet of paper tape getting educated that afternoon.

The second program was almost as simple as the DNA molecule. John read an article (in *Scientific American*, as I recall) about a random sentence constructor. You fed it short lists of nouns, verbs, and adjectives and it followed the basic rules of English to construct well formed but silly sentences.

The program John wrote was a sort of automated Mad Lib generator. Depending upon the vocabulary you fed it, it was as insulting, profound, or licentious as you wanted to make it. Unless you have a preadolescent fondness for Mad Libs, such games get old after a short time.

What made the program interesting to me was a combination of two factors. First, it was capable of generating recursive structures, such as "The book that you ate is humble." And second, John put a fairly shallow stack in the program. On stack overflow, the program simply emitted a despairing "... fooey!"

As a result, about one sentence in 50 would degenerate into Teutonic convolutions, then terminate the whole exercise with admirable impatience. It was heart warming to see such utterances as, "The computer that the byte that a diode that ... fooey!"

Many years later, I learned from Larry Constantine why I found the program's behavior so endearing. Larry showed me a sentence that proves that we carry only a limited push down stack around in our heads. It reads, "The girl the boy the dog bit hit cried." I believe this sentence is discussed in Yourdon and Constantine's *Structured Design* (**Y&C79**), but I can't locate it now.

If I tell you about a boy the dog bit, you can understand me. If I tell you about a girl the boy hit, you can understand me. But if I pack both appositions into one sentence, you suffer stack overflow and get lost. Even Germans, who exercise their push-down stacks heavily in everyday speech, seem to let the leftover *gewesen*s and *worden*s sort of trail off in idle conversation. They reserve their pride in recursive exactitude for written essays.

I found it humbling to learn that I was just as limited in some ways as a program that could be represented in a few kilobytes. I also found it pleasantly surprising to see a very human trait — impatience — modeled so simply.

The third program of the Kopf suite was by far the most complex. John read yet another article (again in *Scientific American*, as I recall) on a program that could play checkers. By today's standards, the strategy was pretty naive. It had a simple board evaluator and a move generator that could look ahead only a few moves. There was no tree pruning. John coded it up quickly to demonstrate our newly acquired display scopes.

Had he done it right, he would have produced a program that played mediocre checkers and dragged out its inevitable loss with tedious insistence. Instead, John inadvertently wrote a program with two significant bugs.

The first bug lay in the min/max algorithm for deciding which move to make. It was supposed to pick the move that would give the computer the best future position assuming that the human opponent was doing his or her level best to defeat it. Instead, the program essentially assumed that the human opponent would make a colossally stupid move at every opportunity. As a result, the program itself made colossally stupid moves, one after the other. Young children took particular delight in playing a much vaunted computing machine and beating the pants off it.

And that exposed the second bug. John forgot to program for the eventuality that the program might lose. When defeat became inevitable the program misbehaved in an utterly charming fashion. It would cheat. Frequently, it would jump its remaining checker to some random position of temporary safety. I once saw it flood the board with its own kings. If you think kids liked beating a computer fair and square, you should have seen their delight when they drove it to cheat.

I don't recall whether John ever fixed the bugs in his checker program. There was a strong lobby against any such interference. I do recall that the buggy version was a mainstay among demo programs for some time.

I also recall being once again struck by how an irrational program appeared so much more human than the various sophisticated attempts at modeling the best of human reasoning. And even though it was more complex than the sentence generator, John's checker playing program was still astonishingly simple to simulate human behavior so well.

I suspect that what made me remember this trio of computer programs was a recent presidential election campaign. Nothing underlines the basic irrationality of human thought half so much as watching reasoned arguments repeatedly fall before a well orchestrated emotional appeal. We are repeatedly assured that rational thought is of paramount importance in picking our nation's leaders, but the campaign managers charged with getting candidates elected know better than to count on (or worry about) that.

Before you assume that I have something against your favorite candidate, let me assure you that I am talking about the whole process, not specific individuals. If some were more successful than others at subverting reason in the selection process, it was not because the others weren't trying much the same tactics.

The next thought that probably springs into your head is that I am indulging in the usual elitist bleatings about the incompetence of average folk to determine their own government. Far from it. I firmly believe that democracy is our best shot at good (or adequate) government, and that people usually choose the government that is right for them, whether vociferous individuals concur or not.

I believe we are wrong to lament a lack of reason where we have no reason (!) to expect it in the first place. Who says that being logical is a survival trait? All that nature requires of a species is that it survive. No brownie points are handed out for doing it a certain way. Whatever it is that human beings have been doing with their much vaunted intelligence for the past million years has demonstrably worked. For whatever reason.

Certainly being intelligent in our society has only limited benefits. "If you're so smart, why ain't you rich?" is a common challenge, and a legitimate one. If anything, there is considerable evidence that people skilled in rational thought don't land the most desirable mates or the best paying jobs. That other set of skills we call *common sense* or *street smarts* is at best loosely correlated with logic.

On the other hand, what has kept us ahead of other life forms (by some metrics, at least) for the past million years may not be adequate to see us through the challenges of our successes. If we quadruple the current human biomass, overheat the planet, or detonate but a fraction of our nuclear arsenal, you may not like what passes for human survival in the years that follow. If triumphs of reason gave us the technology to get into this narrow strait, many argue that only a more consistent exercise of reason will get us out of it.

So to summarize:

- We shouldn't confuse thinking with logical reasoning.
- Whatever we do that passes for thinking has kept us going this far.
- Rather than fret that we are either too logical or too emotional, we need to learn how to balance the two and to be better at both.

What Kopf's trio of programs suggest to me is that the calculus of thought is probably not as complex as we have tended to view it. I feel that there is such a calculus, that it is knowable, and that it is reproducible. Looking for the roots of that calculus in logic is probably not fruitful.

I see lots of evidence that the outcome of our thought processes has almost as much to do with the current chemistry of our blood as the neural networks so carefully laid down by nature and trained by nurture. Thinking that is slow and error prone when we are tired comes easily the next morning. A donut or a cup of coffee does more than satisfy hunger pangs. Some of us get buzzed sufficiently by carbohydrates and chocolate that we can just say no to stronger ways to edit our moods.

The exciting thing to me is that researchers are forming links between physics and life at all levels of abstraction, from the workings of DNA to the beating of a heart to the development of artistic creativity. Almost every issue of *Physics Today* now contains some mention of the order to be found in the chaos of life, or the living chaos available in the most ordered of systems. And a colleague just showed me *Artificial Life: The Proceedings of an Interdisciplinary Workshop on the Synthesis and Simulation of Living Systems Held September, 1987 in Los Alamos, New Mexico,* edited by Christopher G. Langdon (**Lan89**).

You can see the ferment in the popular press as well. A recent issue of the *Boston Globe* (January 16, 1989) contained the following articles:

- "Scientists link attitude to course of AIDS," by Richard Saltus, on p. 3 (**Sal89**)
- "A paradox of the body: Order may be unhealthy," by David L. Chandler, on p. 4 (**Cha89a**)
- "Fractals: Out of the studio, into the lab," by David L. Chandler, on p. 45 (**Cha89b**)
- "A glimpse of how mind produces art," by Tom Valeo, on p. 45 (**Val89**)

Each of these articles deals with a different aspect of the confluence between cybernetics, computability, and physics.

$\mathfrak{J}$f we can better understand how we really think, then we are in a better position to program (or wire) computers to think as well. It will probably still require gigabytes and kilo-MIPS just to sort garbage. And I fully expect thinking machines will make mistakes and get moody, but what the heck. That has to be better than balancing parentheses in a gigantic Lisp program.

If we can better understand how we really think, then we will almost certainly begin to do a better job of it. If you dig your well downhill from your latrine, you are likely to get sick more often than if you separate the two properly. That is now obvious to us, but it became common knowledge in Europe only about a thousand years ago. We need the same improvement in collective mental hygiene now that we saw in physical hygiene back then.

It just might trigger another renaissance. □

$\mathfrak{A}$fterword: I didn't know where I was going with this essay until I got there. Finally, I realized I was making a plea for a broader, and simpler, view of artificial intelligence. Artificial rationality has its uses, to be sure, but I somehow suspect that reason and survivability are distinct skills.

10 The (Almost) Right Stuff

We all strive for perfection. It is the elegant algorithm that wins our hearts, the super performer who wins our admiration. In our culture, it sometimes seems like there is no credit to be earned for near perfection, no glory in being second best.

Yet much of the world must be less that perfect, almost by definition. We muddle through with approximate theories. We win many a ball game with the second string. It's nice to have "the right stuff," like Tom Wolfe's characterization of the original seven Mercury astronauts. But most of the time we get the job done with the almost right stuff.

By long-standing tradition (this is the third year in a row), I have celebrated the month of April by criticizing the shortcomings of other people's designs. What better way to honor April Fool's Day, said I, than to shine a harsh light on the follies that haunt the most successful designers of computer software and hardware?

In the process of gathering also-rans for this year's essay, however, I found myself drawn to more abstract themes. There are no names to be named this time. I also found myself being more tolerant of ideas that have proved to be less than perfect. Perhaps I am mellowing in my old age.

For whatever reason, I'd like to share with you several approximations to perfection that have demonstrated redeeming social value over the years. You can look on it as my contribution to a kinder and gentler April Fool's Day.

Let's start with a few numbers that are almost right. The one you're doubtless the most familiar with is the number hiding behind that upper case "K" you see in all those ads for computer memory. When computer types talk about 640K of memory, you know and I know that they really mean 640 x 1,024 bytes, or 655,360 bytes of memory. The K is cribbed from the table of standard prefixes of the International System of Units (SI). It indicates a multiplier of 10^3, or 1,000. That's not exactly 1,024, but it seems to be close enough to satisfy most of us. We must consider it an amusing accident of nature that 2^{10} is so close to 10^3.

It doesn't hurt that you get an extra 24 bytes with every K you buy — I'll bet if the actual number were less than 1,000 all of those ads would have to carry tiny footnotes warning us unsuspecting consumers of the shortfall. (How about something like, "Memory is sold by weight. Contents may settle after packing.") I have no idea who first commandeered the K. As far back as I can remember, it has been in common usage among computer types.

What I find interesting is that the error builds as you piggy back on ever higher SI prefixes. A 2.4 per cent error around a thousand grows to 4.9 per cent around a million. Yes, we cribbed the "M" for mega from the same source as K for kilo. We are all happy to get a five per cent bonus in disk space, or even memory space with today's megabyte desktops. We are even happier to get a 7.4 per cent bonus on a gigabyte of storage, cribbing the "G" for giga to represent 2^{30} as almost the same value as 10^9.

I wonder at what level will the purveyors of huge storage devices feel compelled to emphasize the bonus. Here is the current table of SI prefixes and the associated errors in approximating powers of two:

Prefix	Symbol	Value	Error
kilo	K	10^3	2.4%
mega	M	10^6	4.8
giga	G	10^9	7.4
tera	T	10^{12}	11.0
peta	P	10^{15}	12.6
exa	E	10^{18}	15.3

Perhaps it will be a nonproblem. By the time you see exabyte add-on drives advertised in the back pages of *Computer Language* for a mere $new 5,000, none of us will be in a mood to sweat an extra sixth of a billion billion bytes. It's close enough.

I can't help drift away from computers a bit while on the subject of almost right numbers. One of my favorites is the remarkable coincidence that $2^{7/12}$ is very close to 3/2. That coincidence is why there are twelve different notes in every octave on a piano keyboard.

Here's why. The simplest harmony you can make with a musical note is to double it. That harmony is so basic that we assign the same letter name to all notes obtained by doubling a given frequency. Middle C is 256 Hz (cycles per second), the next C up is 512, and so on. The next simplest harmony is the frequency that is 3/2 that of your starting note. (It is called a *fifth* for ancient reasons.) In the scale starting at C, G meets this requirement. You will find that many of the simple, happy melodies of Western music are rooted deeply in C/G-type harmonies.

But what if you want to start with G and make a simple harmony? Then you need a note at 3/2 the frequency of G, which happens to be D. Start at D and you need to add an A. In principle, you would need an infinite number of notes to complete this sequence. In practice, however, you can do an adequate job with a very finite set.

If instead of making G 1.5 times the frequency of C you set it at $2^{7/12}$, you introduce just a tiny error. The error is about one part in a thousand, which is hard for even a trained ear to detect. It certainly does not jar. Continue adding notes at this ratio (halving frequencies from time to time to stay in the same octave) and the series closes on itself. Since 7 and 12 are relatively prime, the series closes after you have produced 12 distinct notes.

Each of the notes lies at a frequency $2^{1/12}$ above its lower neighbor, about 5.95 per cent higher. Among the twelve notes you will find reasonable approximations to the seven notes of the traditional Western harmonic scale — CDEFGAB. (Now can you guess why the interval from C to G is called a fifth?) None are perfect, but all are close enough not to jar the ear.

This scheme of tuning an instrument is known as *well tempering*. It lets you play music written in any key without having to retune the instrument when you shift keys. It has been known since the time of Bach, who wrote *The Well Tempered Klavier* as a sort of promotional for the scheme. (There are twelve preludes and fugues, each pair written in a different key.) Perhaps this explanation of well tempering will help you see why music has such an appeal to the mathematically inclined, including many good computer types I know.

$\mathcal{S}$till one more diversion, this time from the world of astronomy. It is well known that there is a North Star, a.k.a. Polaris, but there is no South Star. It is less well known that Polaris is not exactly at due north. My copy of Norton's Star Atlas puts it at declination 89 degrees, 2 minutes, almost a full degree off due north. Nevertheless, it is close enough to true north that we are happy to call it the North Star, even though it moves in a circle about the pole whose diameter is about four times the width of the full moon.

The interesting exercise is to use this data to estimate the number of visible stars in the sky. We have as samples two circles each about a degree in radius. Each of the circles covers about one ten-thousandth of the area of the sky. Within these two circles lies a grand total of one star. Ergo, we would expect to see about 5,000 visible stars spread over the entire sky. And indeed, that is approximately the generally stated figure. (It's not easy to be exact, what with the tremendous variation in viewing conditions.)

So once again we have a number (the number of pole stars) that tells us as much about the people who use it as it does about the universe being observed. Human's can't feel a 2.4 per cent counting error well enough to sweat the difference. They can't hear frequency errors well enough to complain about the compromises made by piano tuners. And they can't see a one degree error well enough to dethrone Polaris. All three numbers are arguably close enough.

$\mathcal{N}$ow let's get closer to home. A pet peeve of mine in language design is the length of identifiers (names) that a language should support. Implementors have been known to pick rather small upper bounds, ranging from an obscene low of one character (BASIC), to a miserly six-ish (FORTRAN, early C), to a fairly generous 30-ish (COBOL, PL/I). Purists repeatedly insist that there should be no limit whatsoever on the length of identifiers. The question is, how do you pick a reasonable number as a compromise when one of the values you must weigh is infinite?

When X3J11 was standardizing C, I argued repeatedly (and successfully) for picking a finite limit for name length. Implementors are, of course, free to support names longer than the limit, but users are cautioned that some implementations may support names no longer than the limit. (This is another one of those treaty points that make up much of a language standard. It is the meeting place between producers and consumers.)

The limit X3J11 agreed upon was 31 characters for internal names. (We reluctantly retained the long-standing caveat that existing assemblers and linkers may impose a 6-character, 1-case limit on external identifiers, but that is another story.) We felt that 31 characters was long enough to encompass nearly all sensible names created by human beings in the course of writing computer programs. The idea was to pick a limit which was essentially infinite, yet still finite enough to protect implementors from the trouble makers.

Trouble makers come in two guises, in the world of programming languages at least. There are the amateurs, who literally stay up nights looking for gotchas so that they can write arrogant letters to standards committees. This tribe delights in keeping responsible adults busy sifting through trivia. (They also keep us honest, and make sure we dot the "i"s and cross the "t"s, so what the hell.) There are also the professionals.

The professionals write verification and validation suites for languages. Serious customers buy these suites and insist that vendors pass all their tests before they will shell out good money for the language implementations. It doesn't matter how beautiful a job you do as implementor, if you happen to fail three esoteric tests in a validation suite. You will be stigmatized for those three failures, your successes forgotten. Professional implementors quickly learn to tune their products for the extant validation suites at whatever cost, just to stay in the ball game.

So what happens when a language imposes no limit on the length of identifiers? The answer is simple. The author of the validation suite picks a comfortably large length (or uncomfortably large length, from the implementor's viewpoint) and writes a test to see if identifiers of that length are accepted. Where the standard is silent, the only voice heard is that of the validator. The net effect is that the most popular validation suite becomes the de facto standard in this area. All customers look for the tested name length and all smart vendors work to that specification.

The Pascal and Ada standards took the route of requiring arbitrary length names. Their respective validation suites defined the finite enforced limit. I have seen repeated references in the literature to those finite limits as being the defined limits for identifiers in these languages. Nobody bothers to point out that either of these limits is literally just one person's opinion as to how long is long enough.

So while it seems like the right idea to insist on arbitrary-length identifiers in designing a language, in practice the ideal doesn't hold up. The standards-forming body may as well take responsibility for determining a finite limit. If they don't, someone will finish the job for them. Arbitrary length identifiers are almost a good idea.

Another one of those almost-good ideas is block-structured languages. I have read numerous paeans, particularly in introductory computer texts, to the virtues of using block structure to control access to identifiers on an as-needed basis. If you write your programs top-down (as all right thinking programmers are supposed to do all the time), then you will naturally form a hierarchy of functions and working data. Block structure gives you just the scope and visibility you need for functions and data shared in a hierarchy.

The ointment contains one or two flies, however. The first is that a pure hierarchy almost never proves to be adequate for non-trivial programs. You are probably going to make use of a library of functions. The same workhorse function will likely be called from several places in the hierarchy. You are faced with an uncomfortable choice. Either you replicate the function at each point in the hierarchy where you use it, or you push the function up the hierarchy until it is high enough to be visible from all points that need it. The first solution forces you to replicate the code in the interest of doctrinal purity. The second weakens the information-hiding properties of your hierarchy.

Even if you don't make use of an existing library (a rare and dubious feat among large programs), you will probably end up inventing your own. The process of abstraction and information hiding pushes you inexorably in the direction of making common access functions that are callable from many places within a hierarchy. And if you have to share static data among functions, the problem is even worse. I have seen many a Pascal program with pages of data declarations at the outermost block, yielding all the maintenance problems of a 1960s COBOL program. All that beautiful hierarchical scoping goes out the window when performance is on the line.

Even if you stubbornly hold onto a pure hierarchy, you can't avoid the forward-referencing problem. Sooner or later, you are going to want to declare two functions that call each other. Worse, you are going to want to declare two data objects that refer to each other.

Every block-structured language I know must face the forward-referencing problem in at least one guise. And every block-structured language I know indulges in its worst design kludges in this area. The Pascal rules for declaring pointers to other types, for instance, contain some real eyebrow raisers. They impose scoping limitations on the type names that are designed to give you a fighting chance at writing mutually referencing data types. But the cost is considerable head scratching in situations where mutual referencing is far from your central focus.

The X3J11 committee indulged in one lulu of a kludge in this area. They chose to address the problem of two structures that refer to each other, as in:

```
struct x {
    struct y *py;
    . . . . . };
struct y {
    struct x *px;
    . . . . . };
```

This is mostly straightforward stuff, except when you wish to drop such a pair of declarations blindly into the middle of a nested block of code. (The declarations may be part of a generic macro that is expanded, for instance.) Now you have a potential problem.

Should the containing environment happen to have a declaration for **struct y**, then the first structure will point to an instance of the existing structure definition, not forward to the (as yet undefined) following declaration. If you knew that was a possibility, you could reverse the declarations. But then, what if the containing environment happens to have a declaration for **struct x**? You're screwed again. And if both structures might be defined at the start of the block, you have no way to write the mutual reference safely.

So X3J11 introduced an artifice. When you write the declarations:

```
struct y;
struct x {
    struct y *py;
    . . . . . };
struct y {
    struct x *px;
    . . . . . };
```

you are guaranteed the behavior you want, because the first declaration unconditionally introduces a new instance of **struct y** within the current block. It cauterizes any references to the containing environment. It's a kludge, pure and simple, but it does rescue an almost-right idea from a nasty little black hole.

The fact remains that hierarchical decomposition is a good way to construct many programs. And block structuring is a good way to control most of the name scoping in those and other programs. Because block structuring is almost the right stuff, we should not be quick to ignore it just because it has a few annoying shortcomings.

𝕴 can make a similar harangue about object-oriented programming. It looks like a great organizing principle to first identify all of the data types you're going to need, then define all of the operations you're going to perform on them. You end up with a program that is at least as tightly structured as one built by pure hierarchical decomposition. And you avoid a number of the design and maintenance issues I touched on briefly above.

You also acquire a fresh set of headaches. I have been reading with amusement the new breed of publications that have picked up the torch of Better Program Design. There's the *Journal of Object Oriented Programming*, the *Journal of C, Ada, and Modula-2*, and the newly arrived *C++ Report*. All are worth reading, but all indulge in the same excuses that every other revolutionary design method tried on for size:

- You don't really want to do that anyway. That's the old-fashioned approach.

- Existing programmers have trouble understanding this stuff, but newcomers take to it naturally.

- The first few projects have a high learning cost, but then your productivity goes up fivefold.

Yup. (See my essay, "Programming on Purpose: The Seven Warning Signs," *Computer Language*, October 1989.) The simple fact is that object-oriented programming has something to offer, but it also gets in the way sometimes. Just like every other method for organizing programs. Since I'm one of those unreconstructed oldsters (and a C expert at that), I'll sidestep any detailed criticism of OOPs. (What a lovely acronym!) When I get a little more experience under my belt, and when the religious fervor dies down a bit, I'll be back. □

𝕬fterword: This, obviously, is the third in my series of April Fool's essays. I used it as an opportunity to trot out a number of numerical almost coincidences that have fascinated me for years. (I left out 355/113 as a remarkably good approximation to π, however.) It also offers a semi-humorous way to introduce the creative art of approximation. John Archibald Wheeler taught me to appreciate this art in honors freshman physics at Princeton. Ever since then, I've been trying different ways to teach similar skills. I still can't come close to Wheeler's effectiveness. But I'll keep trying.

11 Instant Lies

Well, it's that time of year again. Regular readers should know by now that I celebrate only one holiday religiously in these essays. No predictions for the year to come from me. No silly-season nonsense to make it through the summer doldrums. No annual year-end wrap-up.

Instead, I save my special efforts for that one time of year that keeps us all humble. I like to think of it as a kind of secular Day of Atonement, open to Jew and gentile alike. It's the day upon which we can reflect upon our past follies. And take a few salutary potshots at the follies of others.

I refer, of course, to April Fool's Day.

For my fourth annual April effort, I thought I'd examine a few of those words and phrases in our field that have come to annoy. It's a semi-serious gripe session about terms that never mean exactly what they say. I think of them as *instant lies*.

An instant lie is not exactly the same as oxymoron. We've all laughed at those phrases that appear to be self-contradictory. I suspect that "limited nuclear war" is one of the best examples of oxymoron. (Some would say "military intelligence," but I am more charitable than that.)

An instant lie goes beyond mere self-contradiction. Consider the statement, "I'll be with you in a moment." It is most often spoken by an airline representative, waitperson, or bureaucrat. Whoever utters the phrase, you can be sure of one thing. The speaker will most definitely *not* be with you in a moment. Otherwise, said person would simply be with you. No need to utter the temporizing lie.

A subtler instant lie is the Hollywood connective "starring." You see it following the title of a movie or TV show. It alerts you that the name following is supposed to be that of the star of the show. Only problem is, that's not what star billing is all about. You get star billing when your name comes *before* the name of the show. If it follows the word starring, you don't have star billing. You are a participant in an instant lie.

Are you starting to get the drift? Then you understand why I dislike the adjective "adult." It's almost invariably applied to fiction, movies, and emotional positions that are demonstrably adolescent. Anyone who is truly adult never says, "Look, let's be adult about this."

You might also understand why I blanche when a hospital reports that a guy hit by a truck (or bullet) is in "good condition." *Nobody* admitted to a hospital is likely to be in good condition. Otherwise, he would be out walking around. Right? Instant lie.

I could go on in this vein for some time, but I will stop with one final non-computer example. Beware of the scientist who says that a result is "correct within an order of magnitude." Since an order of magnitude is a factor of ten, that can be pretty far from my notion of correct. Pay me an eighth of what you owe me and the sum is correct within an order of magnitude. I call it simply incorrect.

Now that you understand my bias, let's look at a few of those phrases I warned you about earlier.

A good one to start off with is "reduced-instruction-set computer." We all know that RISC machines are the wave of the present and our hope for the future. (Yes, I know that "RISC machine" is redundant, since a computer is a machine. But that's what everyone else says.) Any number of people assure us that they are much better than the old-fashioned variety. I refer, naturally, to CISC, or "complex-instruction-set computers."

The whole thing started at U.C. Berkeley several years ago. VLSI chip design was just coming within reach of organizations that lacked highly skilled designers and the odd million dollars to spare. It looked like it might be possible to get an advanced class to design and fabricate a working CPU chip in an academic year, more or less.

Of course, nobody expected to produce a commercially viable product. Like those innumerable Pascal and Modula-2 compilers that come out of universities, a few pieces had to be left out. A CPU can be said to work if it can load, store, add, jump conditionally, and reset. Just getting a class to do that with a real VLSI chip would be a major accomplishment. And indeed it was.

All would have been fine had the result not been *strongly hyped* (to commandeer Andy Koenig's choice phrase). Making a virtue of necessity, the designers praised the simplicity of the chip. They argued that a stupid computer can go faster than a smart one. This is believable. They argued further that the speed advantage can more than offset the stupidity. This is conceivable but by no means automatic.

Next thing you knew, every new computer architecture that came along billed itself as a RISC design. Puns and pundits abounded. Of course, none of these were nearly as RISCy as the original Berkeley offering. Some, in fact, were downright CISCy. But the RISC aspects were what was touted.

I believe this happened for two reasons. One is that any new architecture can and should be extensively simulated before it is finalized. (By contrast, I am told that System/360 enjoyed at most a few thousand lines of trial code before it was frozen.) Oodles of studies have shown that programs spend most of their time doing simple things like moves, adds, and conditional branches. It is only natural that a well designed modern architecture should do a handful of simple operations very quickly.

The other reason for emphasizing the RISC aspect is political. Customers have developed considerable resistance to shifting to new architectures. (Again, it was the move from the IBM 709X and 14XX class machines to System/360 that first gave customers second-degree burns.) The advent of retargetable C compilers has lowered this resistance, but it is still there.

You don't sell people on a new architecture just because it is nice. As the saying goes, "Ya gotta have a gimmick." You need something to sell management on why it's worth paying the steep, and open-ended, conversion costs. The hook these days is RISC.

I brand RISC an instant lie because no commercial computer is truly a RISC design. Nor are RISC computers necessarily faster than CISC for comparable VLSI technology. But it sure sounds nice.

Now let's talk about "object oriented." It's a topic I have written about a great deal, lately. (See "Programming on Purpose: Abstract It," *Computer Language,* November 1989, "Programming on Purpose: Encapsulate It," *Computer Language,* December 1989, and "Programming on Purpose: Inherit It," *Computer Language,* January 1990.) I feel that I have to talk about it, since everyone else seems to be. I also believe that the object-oriented approach has something real to offer. But then I believe that adult is a legitimate adjective. Both terms just get misapplied a lot.

Object-oriented programming goes back many years. Two obvious early progenitors are the languages Simula and Smalltalk. Both lean hard on the notion that objects are the central players in an executable program.

You don't call functions with copies of stored or computed values as arguments. Instead, you "send a message to an object." The object decides for itself how to carry out the action requested in the message. The same message can have quite different effect on different objects.

What this gets you is systems that are incredibly extendible. Each object has so much autonomy that you can defer all sorts of bindings to runtime. That permits incremental construction of complex systems. It also encourages reuse of general-purpose objects. And it helps you erect debugging scaffolding as you go.

In short, you have a tinkerer's paradise. Anything within the ken of a single person (or a small, cooperative group) goes together with relative ease. It is only when the number of objects begin to balloon that you begin to see the limits. With enough tinker toys and enough authors, shared conventions begin to break down. It is one thing to tailor the message `display_yourself` to the peculiarities of a given object. It is quite another when different objects choose different display devices.

$\mathcal{B}$ ut that's not what kept Smalltalk from taking over the world. The problem with this approach is that performance suffers badly. When you defer binding, you pay more in runtime lookups. Do that once per function call and you have serious problems. And that is indeed the case.

Nevertheless, the object-oriented approach has its merits. It is particularly good at limiting name-space clutter in some cases. One of those cases is when you have a bunch of related data types and a bunch of functions that work on them.

Graphics is a prime example. Window interfaces come close behind. When modern bit-mapped displays got cheap enough, there was a sudden upsurge of interest in both topics. Start writing a C or Pascal interface for either and you quickly go into overload. You soon have several hundred functions with silly names like **WinFlapMagentaShutter**. You soon begin to scream for help.

Some of those screams woke up the older programmers down the hall. They saw the problem, smiled, and said, "Have *we* got the language for *you!*" The screamers listened a bit, smiled tentatively, and said, "That's nice, but can it mix with C code?"

The object-oriented hands winced and explained about paradigmatic purity, or something equally pompous. The screamers tried to talk about performance. (That's why the old hands were down the hall and not in the main room, remember?) The alliance that formed was equal parts enthusiastic and tense.

The result has been languages like C++ and its brethren. All are much more procedural than their purer antecedents. They tend to mix in enough object orientation to make a difference. But none buy the whole package of beliefs.

So that's why I say that object-oriented programming is an instant lie. What has caught on these days is not exactly object oriented. It is more "object preoccupied." Or perhaps "object tolerant." But you can't say that, can you?

$\mathcal{N}$ ow let's consider that older standby, "What you see is what you get." Even marketing types wince at that chestnut now. The roots of the term are honest enough. Back in the distant past there was a big difference between the seeing and the getting. Brian Kernighan developed one of the first document-formatting programs in the era of punched cards. He worked out some neat conventions for specifying which letters to capitalize. (Few keypunches made it easy to punch lower case letters.)

Thus was born one of the first runoff programs, if not the first. Punching those card decks was not easy, but it produced nice results in the end. People skilled in the art could earn extra money preparing input. Then along came interactive time sharing and things got a little easier. More people could type directly into the computer. More terminals had lower-case characters. Still, the terminal was a bottleneck.

When you can print only ten characters per second, you cut corners. The first interactive text editors favored terse commands and a minimum of feedback. Dennis Ritchie's **ed**, the first editor on UNIX, is probably the most representative example of this class of editors. And you certainly didn't want the computer to try to format as you typed. CPU cycles were too scarce and paper was too permanent for the flexibility we now take for granted.

When document formatting moved onto the interactive systems, terseness prevailed. You prepared a text file with a minimum of *markup*. A separate program used your markup hints and some preprogrammed common sense to format pages to a printer. The turnaround took a bit of time.

The famous WYSIWYG phrase evolved to describe the first programs that would format as you typed in text. A dedicated personal computer has the CPU cycles. A glass TTY can rewrite a line of text in reasonable time. A printer is just another device for laying out a fixed set of characters on a regular grid. You could at least see on the screen a chunk of the page you would later get on the printed page.

It is a rare combination of display and screen that really look alike, however. At the best of times, WYSIWIG involves a bit of hyperbole. I won't even discuss the software that generates hard copy with different logic than for the display. Too often, WYSI not quite WYG.

I have cheerfully moved into the era of PC typesetting and bit-mapped displays. It's fun to see an approximation to the final copy take shape before ones very eyes. I was dismayed, however, to find that the approximation can be pretty shoddy at times.

It seems that screen fonts occasionally bear only a loose family resemblance to what the PostScript printer gens up. And screen aspect ratio, size, and dot resolution often matches the final output only in the loosest sense of the word. Color has an even shoddier track record to date.

In short, very few systems today are honestly WYSIWYG. They're certainly easier to use than a keypunch. And they certainly try. But they don't do what they say.

Then you have phrases like "user friendly." Any software that is truly user friendly doesn't have to say so. It just is. Only when there is some doubt do the manufacturers dust off this fib.

I am still grappling with the problem of classifying UNIX. It's a system that I took to almost instantly back when it was first developed. It was very clear to me, and a number of my colleagues, that this was one friendly environment.

I could get all sorts of things done under UNIX that I literally only dreamed of with other systems. Kernighan and I endeavored to explain part of the UNIX phenomenon when we wrote *Software Tools* (**K&P76**). We succeeded in part, but we left out a large part of the story.

Then people started telling each other that UNIX wasn't friendly at all. Its commands were too terse. It was so powerful as to be dangerous to mere civilians. It was a system that only a programmer could love.

Well, maybe. But as I have remarked in the past, saying that UNIX is not user friendly implies that some operating system out there *is*. MS-DOS certainly doesn't fit the bill. It's a cheap imitation of UNIX at best. Some of you might hasten to mention the Macintosh. I personally get tired of pointing and clicking so much. I miss my shell scripts. User friendly is not synonymous with simplistic, nor with condescending. Not in my book.

So maybe I don't know what is truly user friendly. But I certainly know when something is not. And the one sure way to know a thing is not is when its proponents insist that it is.

I have a few other terms on my list that I feel less strongly about. Take "well documented," for instance. That is simply a synonym for "over described and under explained." Anytime someone develops a five-foot shelf of manuals for a product, this instant lie pops up. Government contracts have a way of specifying documentation so elaborate that it is worthless. Even worse, it soon gets out of phase with the code so that it actively misleads.

My idea of good documentation begins with one paragraph of installation instructions. It is followed by a three-page overview that describes the product in general terms. Any reference material that follows has an index that is almost as big as the text itself. And the three terms I want to look up are in the index.

In a similar vein, "real-time" is usually a misnomer. It means, "preoccupied with performance." Or, "pushing the state of the art in a way that should impress you."

"Strongly typed" refers to languages that get in your way. The term is a clue that you'll have to write something truly unreadable to get good performance. What is weakly typed by comparison is a language like C. C is a blue-collar language suitable only for writing programs. It is clearly inferior to any language that endeavors to protect you from writing bad programs.

Last on my list is the adjective "structured." I won't even bother to lambaste it, however. Criticizing that term is like shooting at life rafts. Everyone knows it's a lie. □

Afterword: This essay started out as a gripe session of sorts. I quickly recast it, however, as a techie's version of "The Emperor's New Clothes." So many simple concepts get hyped to the point where otherwise sensible adults start soberly debating their merits. Sometimes we need to reclaim a bit of ground lost to the marketing types.

12 What Meets the Eye

I recently described my evolution from physicist to programmer. (See "Programming on Purpose: The Physicist as Programmer," *Computer Language*, June 1990.) I now take the opposite perspective. I want to talk about the times when a programmer should think like a physicist.

Most of the time, of course, you don't have to bother. Your assignments are sufficiently clear cut, or your latitude is sufficiently constrained, that you just do what you must. But every once in awhile, you should take a look at the world outside. It just might affect how you write your next program.

For example, I have long been concerned with the production of images by computer. Interactive displays deal with one class of imaging problems. Printers deal with another. It would be nice if the two classes were not so disjoint, but right now they are. I am happy to see so many people working on making displays and printed output look more alike.

It was not so long ago that character-oriented images were considered acceptable for most applications. Certainly they are simple enough to deal with. You only have one or two hundred distinct little pictures to generate. (They're called *glyphs* in the trade.) You only have to display them at a couple of thousand distinct places within a page image.

That makes it much easier to ensure that what you see on an interactive display resembles what you get on the printed page. It also makes for much less traffic along serial communication lines to transmit page images. And it greatly simplifies the processing of text with multiple filter programs, as in a UNIX-style pipeline. Or clipping and pasting text between windows.

But the world did not stand still at that level of technology. Too many people demand multiple fonts or colors instead of just one. Too many programs benefit from being able to display arbitrary graphics along with text. Too many new applications need gray scale or color images as well.

We are well into the era of the graphical user interface (GUI) and the bit-mapped image. Both have introduced a complexity into programming that often dominates the writing of new applications. A typical GUI has an interface defined by upwards of a thousand functions. A serious commercial application may have to produce bit-mapped images for dozens of different devices. This does not make for elegant programming.

One of the least-appreciated successes of the UNIX operating system was the way it tamed character streams. In the late 1960s and early 1970s, when UNIX was invented, displaying text was not so simple. Your program had to be privy to various properties of the display device.

Is the first character of each line a FORTRAN-style carriage-control character, or does it print? Do you provide a character count for each line, or an explicit terminator? If so, do you terminate a line with a carriage return, a line feed, or with both? And can the device handle horizontal tabs, vertical tabs, and/or form feeds? Write a program with one device in mind and expect it to work horribly with another. Or be prepared to stuff the output through some multipurpose reformatting program.

What UNIX did was standardize on an internal representation for a stream of characters. It defined a mini-language for placing characters within a succession of page images. The peculiarities of individual devices were isolated at the edges of the system. A UNIX device driver translates to and from this internal character-stream language as need be for each device. The need for reformatting programs is largely eliminated.

Most programmers take that sort of device independence for granted nowadays. They would scoff at the arguments used against the UNIX approach in the early 1970s:

- We can't afford the overhead of another layer of mapping software between the program and the device.

- Our mini-language is superior and contains features that many applications will need.

- You should know what device you're driving anyway, so you can take maximum advantage of it.

Nevertheless, we are now struggling through a similar process with GUIs. The need for device independence is more widely accepted, but the preoccupation with performance necessarily remains. Several candidates are contending for the leading role as device-independent GUI. All trade off performance for some semblance of portability. And all still involve far more complexity than I am comfortable with. We have yet to see the breakthrough we need in the linguistics of graphical displays.

We cannot sit around and wait for the problem to be solved, however. The need is too great for solutions *now*. Probably, we need more experience with existing GUIs before we learn how to isolate the complexity. So we live with Windows, and PostScript, and Motif, and all the other bold attempts at solving parts of a very difficult problem.

None of this current technology should blind us to what we *really* want in the way of displayed images. That is a function of the human eye and the brain behind it. It is not a question of whether Windows or Presentation Manager makes better use of an Intel 386 with four megabytes of memory and a VGA display. We should look on character-oriented devices and current graphical displays as just steps in the right direction. We want to draw prettier pictures, and we want to draw them more elegantly.

That's where the physics comes in. Pretty may be in the eye of the beholder, but pretty enough is determined primarily by the physics (or physiology) of human vision. I assume, for now, that the images we generate by computer are for human consumption. If our goal is to record more detail than the eye can see, naturally different criteria apply. I also assume, for now, that developing an elegant GUI language is a separable problem. Certainly the solution will be shaped by the needs of the final imaging devices.

Let's begin by looking at spatial resolution. That's a common enough preoccupation these days. Usually, people talk in terms of dots per inch (dpi), but that tells only part of the story. What counts to the human eye is angular resolution.

For example, it is widely accepted in the printer industry that 300 dpi produces (barely) adequate fine detail for mimicking the typesetters' art. That assumes that you regard the output from a normal reading distance. Call that distance 18 inches and you're talking about an angular resolution of 200 microradians, or 1/100 of a degree.

Press your nose against the image and the angular resolution gets ten times worse. You also lose if you project the image on a large screen and stand too close. So whether you're generating slides, dart boards, or billboards, you know what you need. If you want to get the same effective resolution as a 300 dpi laser printer on letterhead, you must provide at least 100 dots per angular degree of vision. Now you know why the typical terminal screen looks crummy at 30 dots per degree.

That value of 300 dpi is slightly misleading. Printers have known for years that you can get away with much less spatial resolution when printing illustrations. Newspaper photographs are typically printed with a *halftone screen* of 60 to 80 lines per inch. The screening process breaks up the image into a grid of dots much like the pixels on a computer-generated display. The major difference is that the dots on a halftone screen can vary in size. Hence, the dots can represent a number of different shades of gray. A laser-printer pixel is usually just a black dot or a white space, period (at least until recently).

I will not pretend that newspaper quality is acceptable for reproducing images in arbitrary applications. On the contrary, I find it to be about the minimum tolerable. But even the glossiest of magazines needs nowhere near 300 lines per inch. In fact, high-grade paper stock can't support that much resolution. Ink from adjacent dots begins to run together and smear once they get close enough. Printers say that the paper *can't hold the ink*. The finest screens top out around 150 lines per inch. And they do a fine job of reproducing the detail that the eye demands.

Those shades of gray really make a difference in the number of dots you need. They are also very necessary if you want to display an image containing grays. Once you get beyond type and line drawings, the world is seldom black and white.

You can make shades of gray even if your display produces only black dots. Halve the spatial resolution of a 300 dpi printer and you have four dots at each printing position. Print differing numbers of dots in a given position and you generate three shades of gray between black and white. That's not many shades, so try halving the resolution again. Now you have newspaper resolution at 75 dpi and 16 dots to play with at each position. You now have 15 intermediate shades of gray.

There are 16 different ways of displaying only a single dot at a given printing position. There are even more ways of producing other intermediate shades. (Hint: Think about Pascal's triangle and its role in combinatorics.) It would be nice to do something useful with those 65,536 different ways to represent 17 shades.

It turns out there is. If you always use the same pattern for each shade of gray, the human eye quickly detects your laziness. The repetition stands out, particularly in a region of uniform shading. It can distract. Unless your goal is to add a touch of surrealism, you want to avoid this sort of thing.

The answer is to choose bit patterns at random for each shade of gray. The eye sees only noise and filters it out without fuss. This technique is known in the trade as *dithering*.

I haven't commented yet on whether our trusty 300 dpi printer can do a decent job of reproducing photographs. Certainly, newspaper resolution is the best you can hope for. The question is, do 17 distinct shades suffice to simulate a halftone screen? Some people might think so, but I don't. The eye can detect far more than 16-odd shades of gray. Worse, it is not particularly pleased by the set of shades you get this way.

You have to remember that the eye is tremendously adaptable to variations in light. Those of us who were photographers before cameras became so automatic had to learn about shutter speeds and lens apertures. On a sunny day, you might have to set your camera at 1/1000 sec. at f16. In a dimly lit room, you might try for a shot at 1/8 sec. at f1.4 to deliver the same amount of light to the film. Those two exposures differ by a factor of 16,000. Yet your eye can tolerate brighter sunlight and function in much darker situations. In fact, the human eye can respond to individual photons, detecting one in ten that hit the eye.

We are far from being able to produce computer images that span much of this tremendous range. Fortunately, we don't have to. Through several mechanisms, the eye adjusts its sensitivity in response to ambient light. At any given adaptation, it can distinguish only a limited range of intensities.

Any light that is too dark looks black. Any light that is too bright looks white. The ratio of light intensities between barely black and barely white is about 1 to 1,000.

That's still a pretty broad range. The eye deals with it by another trick used widely in the sense organs of animals. Its response to variations in intensity is logarithmic. That means that the eye detects *ratios* of intensity, not differences. Say light B produces twice the energy of light A. Your eye sees it as a lighter shade of gray. Now adjust light C so that it is brighter than light B by the same shade. Light C must have twice the intensity of light B, or four times that of light A, to look one shade brighter.

Your eye can distinguish about ten such shades, or doublings of intensity, between barely black and barely white. We old photographers used to call a factor of two change in light intensity one *f-stop*. Disciples of Ansel Adams learned to use a related but different terminology in the darkroom. He called each doubling one *zone*. His Zone System helped print makers make accurate exposure decisions without the confusion of logarithms or f-stops.

A slide in a projector can reproduce the full ten zones our eye is prepared to distinguish. A photographic print on glossy white paper can reproduce about eight. (That's one reason why slide presentations have more punch than posters — provided they do not record your Uncle Louie's vacation). These are the criteria by which we must judge computer displays and printed output. Not enough dynamic range of intensities and an image looks flat and lifeless.

Another important parameter is the number of different shades the eye can detect. Ansel Adams taught us to split a zone into much smaller pieces than was customary in the past. His richly detailed prints were proof of the pudding. My experience with printing color negatives was that I could barely discern 1/30 of a zone. That fits well with the growing popularity of scanners that distinguish 256 shades of gray. (Thirty steps times eight to ten zones yields 240 to 300 discernible shades.)

Let's get back to those 17 shades of dithered gray from the laser printer. First, it's clear that we need many more shades to please the eye. Even newspaper halftones do better than that. Second, it's now apparent that the eye sees even fewer shades than 17. There's only one step between a density of one dot and two dots. There are eight steps between eight dots and 16 dots, even though it looks like the same total change in shade. Dithering does not come off as a good way to trade angular resolution for gray shading.

So a good display will cover ten zones of intensity, or a thousand-fold change. It will display 256 different shades along the way. And it will distribute those shades along a logarithmic scale of intensity. It might also give you some control over the exact shape of the gray scale.

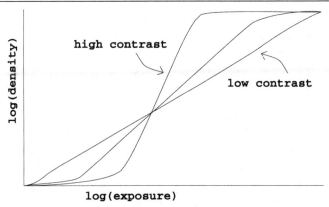

Figure 12.1: *Density/exposure curves with three different values of γ.*

Photographic films and papers are characterized by how they respond to various degrees of exposure. Plot the logarithm of exposure intensity along the X-axis. That's the shade of gray you want to capture. Plot the logarithm of the density of the image produced along the Y-axis. That's the shade of gray you get. A good film or paper will have a response curve that lies close to a straight line over a wide range of exposures. Photometricians traditionally refer to the slope of this line by the Greek letter gamma (γ). See Figure 12.1.

A gamma greater than one indicates high contrast, or an overreaction of the film to changes in shading. X-ray film is often designed this way to emphasize detail. A gamma near one characterizes a film that accurately reproduces the range of grays it sees. Slide film perforce aims for accurate reproduction.

A gamma less than one indicates low contrast, or a compression of shades. Most of the negative film you buy in a drugstore has a gamma of about 0.6. That lets it capture additional information in case you overexpose or underexpose the subject of interest. You can rescue an improperly exposed negative where you can't save a slide. The printing paper you use with such film has a gamma of about 1.6 to compensate. You can even get black-and-white papers with gammas above and below this value, to alter the effective contrast of the scene.

𝕴 recite all this technology as an existence proof. We know we want to fiddle with contrast because people have been doing so for the century and a half since photography was born. The software that runs the newer scanners often lets you alter the effective gamma of the scanner. Good gray-scale editing software even lets you work over the shape of the response curve. It is not unreasonable to want similar control over the images produced by a computer.

I am pleased to see that scanners are, in fact, starting to capture publication-quality images at home-office prices. All you need is the megabytes of memory and disk to hold all those bits. Printers aren't quite there yet. You can get production-quality gray-scale images, but they don't come cheap. What is in reach for many of us can be good for black and white, but inadequate for gray-scale. Interactive displays have a long way to go.

One reason for this recitation is to show that there is real room for improvement. I weary of the perennial articles that question why computers need to keep getting faster. If you can't see beyond running a simple word processor on an EGA screen, don't deny the rest of us our ambitions. *We* can think of uses for *lots* more power.

Another reason is to show that there is such a thing as enough. At least for awhile. At least in a given direction. Once you deliver all the quality in an image that the eye can appreciate, it's time to put your energies into some other part of the system. Like dirt-cheap memories, or lots more specialized processors.

For all the numbers I have bandied about, I still have only touched the surface. Image quality is important, but so is image size. Have you though about how big a display you'd *really* like to work with? And what would you do if your workstation had lots more horsepower for producing images? You might think more seriously about color, and high-fidelity sound. And perhaps even 3-D pictures, and stereo, and animation. Then you could start thinking about how to address your other three senses. But more on all that later. □

*fterword: This essay turned out to be the first of a four-part series. (See **Essay 13: Technicolor and Cinemascope**, **Essay 14: What Meets the Ear**, and **Essay 15: Warm Fuzzies**.) Each explores a different aspect of the human senses from the standpoint of computer input and output. I've never seen all this information put in one place before. As my commentary reveals, I acquired it from a variety of sources over many years. We need to gather this much information just to answer such simple questions as, "How good a display is good enough?" With computers growing ever more ubiquitous and powerful, such questions are becoming paramount.*

13 Technicolor and Cinemascope

$\mathfrak{J}$ talked at length in the previous essay about computer displays and printouts. (See **Essay 12: What Meets the Eye**.) Starting from the physiology of human vision, I discussed what we need to reproduce adequate resolution over an adequate range of shades of gray. I ended that essay with a brief list of other considerations when interfacing computers to people. I continue that discussion by addressing some of the items on the list.

Let's begin with color. Human vision can distinguish many thousands, perhaps millions, of different colors. We know that color is an important signal. Flashing red lights warn us of danger. Subtle hues add an important sense of realism. Lots of us want good color for lots of good reasons.

The human eye is sensitive to light with wavelengths between about 400 and 700 nanometers. (A nanometer is one billionth of a meter, or ten Ångstroms. It has also been called a millimicron.) We see the shorter wavelengths as blue and the longer ones as red. In between lie all the colors of the rainbow. Different mixtures of light at different wavelengths yield oodles of additional hues.

You probably know by now that the eye constructs the sensation of color from three kinds of sensors. One kind is most sensitive to red light, another to green, and a third to blue. (Discrimination between red and green is a recent evolutionary invention. A small genetic hiccup leads to the commonest form of color blindness, a failure to distinguish red and green.) For a person with normal color vision, all mixtures of wavelengths that stimulate the three sensors appear to be the same color.

That means that you can reproduce nearly all colors by mixing three light sources that address the eye's sensors independently. (Life is never quite that simple, but I don't want to get any more detailed right now.) Press your nose against a color TV screen while it's on. You will see the red, green, and blue dots that make up the image. Even better, watch the stage lights the next time you're in a theater. I'm continually amazed to see red and green lights combine to produce yellow, with no sensation of either primary color.

Red, green, and blue are the colors you use when mixing lights. They are called the *additive primaries*. When you mix pigments to produce colored inks, however, you need a different set of primaries. Press your nose against the Sunday comics and you will see the three colors. Your kindergarten teacher probably taught you that these *subtractive primaries* are red, yellow, and blue. Your kindergarten teacher was wrong.

That alleged red is really magenta, a mixture of red and blue. You can also think of it as the absence of green. The alleged blue is really cyan, a mixture of green and blue. You can also think of it as the absence of red. Yellow is correct, a mixture of red and green. It is also the absence of blue.

In principle, you can mix varying quantities of cyan, yellow, and magenta pigments to make an arbitrary color. In practice, it's hard to produce the full range of grays that's possible with black ink and gray-scale reproduction. (Last month I observed that glossy paper can capture eight zones, or density doublings.) The blacks just aren't as black as you'd like. Printers solve this problem by adding black ink to the soup. Equal quantities of cyan, yellow, and magenta are effectively replaced with the proper measure of black, to good effect. That's why printers talk about four-color reproduction, even though our eyes work on only three primaries.

Color displays have been with us for some time. We have the technology of television to thank for that. They generally lack the snap and sharpness of gray-scale displays, however. And they cost considerably more. That's because of the need to stuff three color dots into each pixel. But resolution and cost are improving rapidly.

Also important is the number of distinct hues that a display can represent. The more hues, the more bits you need for each pixel. At 300,000 pixels for conventional VGA, eight bits per pixel takes nearly a third of a million bytes. And that gives you just 256 distinct colors. Cost and writing time both go up as you increase the number of distinct hues.

One popular trick lets you dramatically increase the number of distinct colors you can display without increasing bits per pixel. Each display is accompanied by a *palette* that maps the code stored in each pixel to the color you wish to display. At eight bits per pixel, you need a 256-entry palette. At 16-bits per pixel, you can display 65,536 distinct colors. You just can't display all those colors at once. Instead, you choose which subset of 256 does the job well enough for each picture. That's what you store in the palette.

But let's say you're not in the mood to compromise. How many bits do you have to store in each pixel to represent all the colors your eye can distinguish? In the previous essay, I concluded that 256 shades of gray are probably sufficient if you don't care about color. It helps if you can also map code values to shades of gray by some nonlinear scale. (The human eye responds logarithmically to light intensity.)

It makes sense, then, that 256 shades of each primary should do a good job of covering all the colors the eye can distinguish. And indeed, that seems to be the case. It is probably more than enough. The eye is noticeably less sensitive to changes in blue shades than to changes in red and green. (Blue vision seems to have evolved earlier and is more primitive in several ways.) You might cut corners here. You might also cut corners in the almost-black or almost-white regions. The eye is fussiest about color near the middle grays.

People have tried a variety of encodings with these thoughts in mind. Some 16-bit encodings give good coverage, in part by short changing the blues. The simplest brute force approach is simply to allocate eight bits to each of the three primaries. That yields the 24-bit color you hear more about every day. Adding to the confusion, some people set aside 32 bits per pixel. The additional eight bits don't participate in the color information. They just help round the storage size up to four bytes, a size beloved of much computer hardware.

Today you can buy scanners and displays that support 24-bit (or 32-bit) color. That's wonderful, except that displays still need better spatial resolution. Color printers have the spatial resolution, but typically lack the color resolution. I will be happy only when the norm for scanners, displays, and printers uniformly meets the demands of human vision. That means 100 dots per degree and 24-bits of color information per dot.

Now let's talk a bit about image size. The conventional output device these days is the page printer. In the U.S., the de facto standard page size for letterhead is 8.5 by 11 inches. All the rest of the nominally civilized world uses the metric standard A4. It is a little skinnier and a little longer than the American page. The differences are just enough to drive you up the wall if you have to reproduce a mixed bag of correspondence from around the world. (Sorry, I promised not to gripe about my problems with standards activities for awhile.)

Naturally, there are other widely used paper sizes as well. U.S. lawyers insist on a slightly longer legal-size page. Some applications need the larger 11-by-14-inch page. The metric world has its A5, B4, etc. At least these tend to be even multiples or divisions of each other. For now, however, I confine my attention to standard letterhead pages.

When I discussed resolution in the previous essay, I was careful to distinguish spatial and angular resolution. Spatial resolution is about how many dots per inch you use to construct an image. Angular resolution is about how many dots per angular degree you see, regardless of viewing distance. The same spatial resolution can yield quite different angular resolutions under different viewing conditions. It is angular resolution that your eye cares about.

The same is true of image size. Words typed in ten-point Courier on a sheet of letterhead are easily read at arms length. Post the same sheet near the top of a bulletin board and you'd better write larger. The larger print size regains the angular resolution you need to make the words legible. But now you can write fewer words per page. Nail that same sheet to a telephone pole across the street and you can convey even less information.

Anything more detailed than a single peace sign or smiley face will go unrecognized.

What's changing here along with angular resolution is called *solid angle*. It is a measure of field of view that is independent of viewing distance. Imagine yourself suspended inside a sphere one mile in radius. By looking in all directions, you can see the entire inner surface of that sphere. The area of the sphere is 4π square miles. Saw the sphere in half and each part has an area of 2π square miles. In fact, any field of view you can delimit can be projected onto the spherical surface. The projected area in square miles is a measure of the solid angle of the field of view.

The sphere on which you project the field of view can of course be any size. Just divide the projected area on the sphere by the square of the radius of the sphere. You will obtain a dimensionless number between zero and 4π. People nevertheless ascribe a unit of measure to this dimensionless number — the *steradian*. I will present all solid angles in units $1/1000$ as large, or millisteradians.

Now let's get back to our sheet of letterhead. Held at arm's length, it subtends a solid angle of about 300 millisteradians (msr). Double the viewing distance and it subtends only a quarter as much, or about 75 msr. Ten times the viewing distance yields one per cent of the original solid angle, or 3 msr. As you can see, you lose a lot of viewing angle if you have to step back.

The problem with current interactive displays is just the opposite. They're not big enough. The VGA display on my Compaq SLT/286 is rather nice, and it's pretty much state of the art. At normal viewing distance, it subtends about 15 msr, or about half a sheet of letterhead. That's fine for many uses, but it's maddening when I compose page images with Ventura Publisher or Corel Draw. I feel like I'm looking at the world through the porthole of a ship.

Then I see ads for various windowing environments. Invariably, they show a standard terminal screen decorated with half a dozen or more images overlapped in various ways. We are supposed to feel reassured by this clutter because it follows the infamous "desktop metaphor." Just as we push bits of paper about on our work desks, we can manage our computer-hosted work the same way. No need to learn any scary new ways of doing business.

The multiple images are supposed to convince us that we can share information between any number of applications that are active simultaneously. They give me a headache. I already have eyestrain from peering through the porthole. Why should I obscure the limited view with an assortment of sticky yellow notes?

ℱred Brooks, of *The Mythical Man-Month* fame (**Bro75**), puts it even better. He says that the desktop metaphor is misleading. It should be called an *airplane-seat* metaphor. You are sitting in one of those horrid middle seats in coach class. Hefty people are seated on either side of you. You are trying to organize your work on that tiny little tray table in front of you. You have no elbow room and no place to put extra papers, except possibly your shirt pocket. I have indeed worked that way more often than I care to count. But it is not my favorite environment.

My idea of a desktop environment is far more ambitious. I have tried full-page displays and I find them little better than conventional ones. A typical desktop has room for a dozen sheets of letterhead, without overlap. You can tolerate even more clutter, with overlapping piles, for short periods while you are organizing papers. If you want to sell me on the desktop metaphor, give me a display as big as a desktop. That means a viewing angle of of at least 2,000 msr. And give me 100 dots per degree resolution over the entire view, with 256 shades of gray at every pixel. (Even better, give me 24-bit color.) Oh yes, and keep it cheap, please.

Actually, I am even more ambitious than that. I attended an engineering-preparatory high school in Baltimore. There I learned to love drafting tables. I like to really sprawl when I work. My study desk through college was a drafting table, and I still have one or two kicking around the house. My idea of a CAD/CAM station is a drafting table with an active surface. Now we're talking around 4,500 msr.

Some people are beginning to experiment with artificial realities. A (very hot) computer generates everything you eyes see and everything your ears hear. You manipulate this world through gloves that sense your hand motions and offer believable resistance to those motions. Artificial realities make many demands on the human interface. Some I will eventually discuss further. For now, I simply observe that each eye must be presented with an image that subtends over 6,000 msr.

If it's any consolation to hardware designers, there is a limit to my ambition. A solid angle of 12,500 msr is an acceptable upper bound. That controls everything you see in all directions, except for a small hole for the projector lens. I'll settle for that.

𝕆ne of the special demands of artificial realities is to produce realistic 3-D images. The challenge is to produce two distinct images and to present them independently to different eyes. Where the eyes must focus provides depth information out to about twenty feet. Small differences in the perspective of the two images provide additional depth cues, particularly for distant objects.

If you can slap goggles on the observer, you have the easiest solution. A small imaging device can subtend a large solid angle. Clever optics can produce images at a variety of perceived distances. And it is easy to keep the signals for the two eyes separate. The problem is that even the wispiest of goggles can annoy. I assure you that current technology requires goggles that are a long way from wispy.

One way to keep the goggles wispy is to separate the imaging function. Do the hard work out front on a screen or some other active device. Leave the goggles the lesser job of keeping the images separate. The earliest 3-D movies achieved this noble goal with red and green cellophane filters in cardboard frames. They sorted out red and green monochrome images projected onto the same screen. Photographs of audiences from that era are often more entertaining than the movies they watched.

A later improvement supported color. The filters are neutral gray polarizers aligned at right angles to each other. They separate the two images projected with appropriately polarized light sources. As far as I know, that remains the most inexpensive approach that can be considered at all adequate. Holograms and "xenon mists" are still just the stuff of science fiction. As for me, I am willing to wait a bit longer for three-dimensional displays to become commonplace.

I am less willing to wait for animation. By that term, I mean moving displays in general. My living desktop should be able to display a few TV-quality pictures of various sizes. Some can be from broadcasts, some from a large online data store. (I won't bother restricting the store to being a VCR or optical disk.)

It should also be able to compute and display graphs evolving in real time. I want to unleash subatomic particles in various potential fields and watch the probability waves slosh back and forth. And it should let me storyboard a presentation and interpolate the intermediate frames of action. (Cartoonists call this *tweening*, a process often still performed by platoons of human *in-betweeners*.)

If the display goes dark after it shows each frame of animation, it had better show the next one soon after. Otherwise, you get perceptible and annoying flicker. Countries that favor 50 Hz power also tend to favor television sets with 50 Hz refresh rates. To me, they constitute just one more source of headaches in a headache-infested world. I feel that 60 Hz is a better minimum refresh rate. Some folks consider 100 Hz a more tolerable minimum.

One trick for lowering flicker is to increase the persistence of each image. With phosphors painted by flying electron beams, you must strike a delicate balance. Persistence that is too long blurs motion and smears scene changes. Of course, a display that doesn't fade between frames has fewer problems in this area.

A remaining problem is simulating smooth motion. (This is not the same as eliminating flicker.) The 60 Hz scan of American TV actually offers only

30 new frames of information per second. If the broadcast source is a movie, the rate drops to 24 distinct frames per second. (Some get shown twice.) That seems to be enough to do the job.

I suspect that by now I have lost most of the pragmatists among you. Asking for an active display with 300 dpi is pretty ambitious. Insisting that each of those dots display any of 16 million different sends the cost way up. Demanding an active area a yard on a side makes the cost outrageous. Then requesting that the display be refreshed 60 times per second simply puts the icing on a very expensive cake.

For memory, I'm talking a hundred million pixels, each with three bytes of color information. That's 300 megabytes just for the active screen memory. Refresh it at 60 Hz and you need to process 1.8 gigabytes per second. Some people would consider that a serious data-processing load.

I can only observe that display demands have been soaring all along. Twenty years ago, ten bytes per second was all you could stuff into a Model 33 Teletype. Ten years ago, you were happy to get 1,000 bytes per second. Today, 100,000 bytes per second is a not-uncommon display load. I'll bet that those 1.8 gigabytes have lots of redundancy. Specialized processors will handle most of them as a matter of course. We can probably get away with a traffic of a mere 10 megabytes per second. That keeps us closer to the exponential growth curve.

The main point is that we really do need displays like this. Many of you won't believe that until you see them, but I am absolutely convinced they're vital. Human vision is such an important communication channel, we need to make full use of it when we interact with computers.

Of course, the other four senses are also important. And I still haven't talked about them. □

Afterword: I knew I'd have to build up to the conclusion I reached in this essay. By today's standards, the numbers are staggering. Still, I'm convinced that my "desktop computer" will one day have a display as big as a desktop — and it will be an active one. I can hardly wait.

My happiest artifice here was to express all solid angles in millisteradians. I confess that I got the idea from reading any number of essays by Isaac Asimov. Immortality takes many forms.

14 What Meets the Ear

$\mathfrak{I}$ have spent the last two essays discussing the physiology of human vision. (See **Essay 12: What Meets the Eye** and **Essay 13: Technicolor and Cinemascope**.) A computer display or printer must, in the end, meet the needs of that very demanding consumer, the typical person. Until we consistently hit the limits of visual perception, we can expect steady pressure to improve displays. And we have a long way to go.

On the other hand, we at least know when we get there. There is no point in providing significantly more resolution, for example, than the eye can discern. (I continue to ignore for now the problem of storing large quantities of information for future machine processing. That is a subject for a different set of essays.) We have a good idea when enough is enough.

As important as vision is to people, we do have four other senses. At the very least, they supplement what we see with additional cues that add realism. At the most, they convey information or sensation that cannot be communicated by pictures alone. We should consider all possible ways that computers can present data to people.

Hearing is second only to vision as a sensory channel. It is only fitting that we consider it next. That is the topic for this essay.

$\mathfrak{L}$ong before there was commercial television, radio was painting verbal pictures in the minds of listeners. I am old enough to have cut my teeth on Sky King and Fibber McGee. I can attest that it can rival TV in dramatic impact. Today, we rely on radio primarily for music, news, and the modern equivalent of back-fence gossip with the neighbors. The emphasis has changed, but the importance of radio remains.

The booming business in audio recordings attests to the powerful grip that sound has on our aesthetic sensibilities. (I refuse to haggle over the relative merits of the Boston Symphony and Madonna.) And the telephone dominates many of our lives. Just try to ignore yours the next time it rings.

Despite all this, computers have been slow to exploit sound. The earliest interactive terminals were equipped with a simple bell. Send an ASCII BEL code (decimal 7 or control-G) and the bell would ring. Send a sequence of BEL codes and many terminals would jam for the duration. The best ones would ring the bell two or three times per second until the codes ran out. It is hard to achieve elegant communication with this sort of machinery.

When CRTs began displacing mechanical terminals, they simply mimicked existing functions. Dings turned into beeps or boops. A series of dings usually ended up as a protracted boop. Big deal.

The first computer I encountered with a programmable speaker was the SDS (later Xerox) Sigma 7, built in the late 1960s. You could toggle a flip-flop to make square waves. Timing was a matter of delay loops and watching the real-time clock tick away. Nevertheless, my friend John Kopf contrived several video-gameish fweeps with it. (See **Essay 9: It's (Almost) Alive**.) He even generated a passable rendition of Bach's "Jesu, Joy of Man's Desiring."

When IBM planted a speaker in its first PC, it was not significantly smarter. You can make a few tinny sounds, if you work at it. No dog would mistake it for his master's voice, however. Later computers have invested steadily more in sound generation hardware and firmware. But only a handful can honestly claim acceptable fidelity or flexibility in programming.

So how good is good enough? My bet is that more of you know the parameters of human hearing than know vision. Home and car sound systems have been a technical sell for several decades now. Still, it's interesting to put all the numbers in one place.

The analog of brightness in light is loudness in sound. Human vision can encompass a tremendous range of light intensities, as I discussed two essays back. (See **Essay 12: What Meets the Eye**.) Human hearing has an even more astonishing dynamic range for loudness. In both cases, our senses respond logarithmically to the powers they detect.

I talked about the stop and the zone in photography. Both are ways of describing a doubling in the intensity of light from a subject or a reproduction. Each doubling looks to the eye like a uniform step along the gray scale. That's the effect of the logarithmic response.

Naturally, it is too much to expect sound measurement to share any technology with light. The power of a sound signal we call *loudness*. The unit of loudness (or power amplification) is the bel, after Alexander Graham Bell. Never heard of it? Then perhaps you know its little brother, the decibel. Increase sound power by a factor of ten and you increase loudness by one bel. Or more commonly, by ten decibels. That makes a decibel equivalent to a power ratio of the tenth root of ten, or about 1.26.

It turns out that the smallest detectable change in loudness is about one decibel. That means you have to increase sound power by 26 per cent, roughly, to make a noticeable difference to a human listener. If you interpret that to mean that the human ear is not very sensitive, you've missed the point. The tradeoff for this relatively coarse incremental sensitivity is a broad dynamic range.

A person with normal hearing can hear sounds of just a few decibels. That same person can probably tolerate sounds as loud as 120 decibels, at least for short periods. Sound becomes pain if it's loud enough, and prolonged loud sound is literally deafening.

computer need not produce such a broad range of sounds to make credible noises. I pointed out that the human eye, for all its dynamic range, distinguishes at most ten zones in any given scene. Similarly, the human ear is content with about 80 decibels variation in loudness in a given program. That seems to do justice to either the Boston Symphony or Madonna.

Paltry as it sounds, 80 decibels still represents a change in sound power of one hundred million to one. Compare that to the thousand-to-one ratio of powers that the eye can distinguish in a given scene. Little wonder that it has taken decades of aggressive research and development to perfect high-quality sound recording and playback.

The current state of the art in sound recording, in fact, is the compact disk, or CD. To do its magic, it represents sound amplitude as a regular sequence of digital samples. Each digital sample is a 16-bit unsigned integer. That provides for 65,536 different amplitudes.

During playback, a CD player has to do some pretty fast arithmetic on those samples. It basically turns the sequence of samples into a voltage signal whose amplitude is directly proportional to the sample values at each instant. If a speaker is a purely resistive load (and engineers keep trying to better approximate that ideal), the resultant sound power is easy to compute. It is proportional the square of the voltage amplitude at each instant.

For each bit you add to the digital sample, you double the range of voltage amplitudes you can represent. Double the range of amplitudes and you quadruple the range of sound powers. A factor of four in sound power is very close to six decibels. (That's another consequence of the interesting numerical accident that 2^{10} is very close to 10^3, which I discussed awhile back. (See **Essay 10: The (Almost) Right Stuff.**) Thus, 16-bit samples can represent a dynamic range of 96 decibels. That's more than enough.

It's not as much overkill as it seems, however. When I talked about gray scales, I observed that a linear increase in density has its drawbacks. The eye sees the darker shades as coarser steps than the lighter ones. Logarithmic response strikes again.

Those linear steps in sound amplitude cause similar problems. Some distortion occurs because the amplitude can assume only a finite number of distinct values. The smallest representable change, naturally, occurs when you add one to a sample value. Add one to a small sample value and you get a bigger apparent change in loudness than if you add one to a large sample value. Go 80 decibels down from the loudest sounds in a recording and the sampling distortion gets significantly worse.

An earlier digital recording technique used 14-bit samples. It had enough dynamic range, but not enough resolution at low sound levels. We should all be happy that the industry decided to indulge in the apparent overkill of 16-bit samples. It turns out that you need much of that headroom in dynamic range to keep the ear happy about distortion.

So we have a good notion about how good is good enough when it comes to representing sound amplitudes within a computer. Whether the program plays back captured sounds or generates them internally doesn't matter. We want 16-bit sample values.

The next question is, how frequently must the samples occur? That is a function of the range of frequencies that the ear can detect. Human hearing varies considerably, but we know some acceptable outer limits.

If your goal is to reproduce human speech adequately, you should study the telephone. A century of experience tells us that you can get away with a remarkably narrow band of frequencies. The band corresponds roughly to the middle seven octaves of the piano keyboard, topping out at about 3 KHz. (That's 3 KiloHertz, named in honor of Heinrich Hertz. In earlier times, people would say 3,000 cycles per second.)

Our more ambitious goal is to present the ear with all the sound information it can handle. That is generally taken to be a frequency range of 20 Hz to 20 KHz. Of course, the ear is less sensitive at the extremes of this range. It is also less sensitive to variations in sound power at the extremes. Errors as large as 3 decibels (a factor of two in power!) can be hard to discern at the lowest and highest frequencies.

To reproduce a pure tone at 20 KHz, you have to provide samples at more than twice that frequency. That means you have to provide more than 40,000 samples per second. You can cut corners some, but only by introducing a rather nasty form of distortion at higher frequencies. This particular form of distortion is called *aliasing*.

Think back to those Western movies with the Conestoga wagons crossing the plains. Perhaps you've noticed that rolling wagon wheels almost invariably look funny. Either they appear to be moving too slowly forward or they appear to be moving crazily backward. Occasionally, they even appear to be stationary. Only slowly moving wagons have wheels that look sensible.

The illusion is an artifact. A movie camera samples the view 24 times per second. Our eye and brain stitch samples together and endeavor to make sense out of the changes between samples. (Persistence of vision eliminates the flicker.) We expect to see each spoke of a wagon wheel progress in small steps around a circle, in the direction that the wheel is rolling.

At low speeds, each spoke makes a very small step. We stitch the pictures together just the way we expect to. But when a spoke rotates more than halfway around to where the next spoke was, we get confused. It is easy to confuse those identical spokes. We mistake "this spoke moving a bit forward" with "that spoke moving a smaller bit backward." The eye and brain conclude that the wheel is rolling backwards, against all common sense.

When a spoke rotates exactly to the position of the next spoke between samples, the wheel appears stationary. When a spoke goes just a bit farther, the wheel appears to be moving more slowly than it really is.

In all cases, the captured sequence of frames has at least two distinct interpretations. (Actually, there are an infinite number of interpretations, depending upon how fast you are willing to believe that the wheel is truly spinning.) You could say that the faster motion appears under an alias. Any noun can be verbed, and eventually will be by some American bureaucrat or engineer. So what people usually say is that the faster motion is *aliased*, or distorted by aliasing.

The same thing happens when you sample audio signals. A pure tone is a simple sine wave. Sample it at more than twice its frequency and you can reconstruct it adequately. Sample it less often and it looks just like a lower frequency sine wave. That is its alias. A high pitched tone comes through as a low pitched tone. This does not sound good.

The net effect of all this is that you have to be careful when digitizing sound. You must pick a sampling frequency more than twice as high as the highest frequency you wish to reproduce. You must filter out any frequencies higher than this before sampling, lest they alias back in band. And you must filter out those frequencies yet again when you reconstruct the signal. Fortunately, none of these steps is particularly onerous. But they do add up to a nontrivial package of operations.

So now you should know how many samples a computer must generate to make good sound. We want at least 40,000 per second to match human hearing. As a matter of fact, CDs are a bit more meticulous than that. They capture 44,100 samples per second. And they sound pretty good to my (fairly sensitive) ear.

But we're still not done, because we have two ears. Those ears have evolved to determine the direction of a sound as well as its loudness and mix of frequencies. They determine direction by comparing the signals that reach the different ears. Small differences in arrival time and loudness serve as cues. For many sound sources, you can close your eyes and point toward them with an accuracy of perhaps thirty degrees.

That's not very many bits of information, at least for a single sound source. For a roomful of sources, however, it starts to add up. Echoes and reverberations add to the sense of realism or *presence*. By the time you capture them as well, you need a lot more bits. The easiest thing to do is to capture separate signals for each ear. That's called stereophonic sound, or stereo for short.

So now we can add up the information required to please our ears. We want two signals. Each signal should be sampled at 44.1 KHz. Each sample should occupy 16 bits, or two bytes. That's a total data rate of over 175,000 bytes per second. Good sound doesn't come cheap.

Compared to the demands of an active visual display, however, this is small potatoes. In the last essay, I estimated the data demands of a *real* desktop metaphor. I postulated a fully animated display the size of a real desktop, a meter square with full spatial and color resolution. That gobbles up 1.8 gigabytes per second, or *ten thousand* times as much information as our ideal sound machine.

Would you like your workstation to play the "Pastoral Symphony" (or "Like a Virgin") in the background while you work? Would you like an icon to whistle for your attention when you get mail? Would you like an active computation to mumble reassuringly while it runs? I know that I would. At the very least, I want to know the cost incurred when I ask for it.

Let me conclude this essay with two observations. The first is one I also made in conjunction with generating pictures. Most sound contains lots of redundancy. Generated music probably has the most. The number of bytes you have to present to a MIDI interface can be substantially less than a CD delivers, if you are content to synthesize the voices of various instruments. Human speech is a lightweight load, if you synthesize it as you go.

Even when you record arbitrary material, you can save a lot of bandwidth. Speech compression techniques go way back. Better coding techniques are appearing with exciting regularity. As digital signal processors increase in power, we can afford to trade even more computational complexity for information bandwidth.

In short, we should not let that figure of 175,000 bytes per second loom too large. Such data rates may appear only in dank corners of future sound systems. Data compression techniques are also fascinating, but I will save their discussion for another time.

My final point goes the other way. It increases the demands made on future workstations. So far, I have discussed primarily the production of pictures and sounds. We also want computers to see and to hear, however. And we already know that those operations are not easy.

It's hard enough to scan pictures and record sounds. Those activities have only recently moved from the research lab to the personal workstation. They still have not reached the limits of human perception, as I have been talking about here. At least not at civilian prices.

It's much harder for a computer to interpret what it sees and hears. Optical character recognition was once neither cheap nor reliable. Now, at least, you get to choose between cheap and reliable. It will be nice when you can have both. Speech recognition is even further up the pipeline, but it's coming.

I won't even talk about the problems of having a computer *understand* what it sees and hears. At least not in the human sense. At least not right now. □

Afterword: Compact-disk technology made this essay easier to write than the previous one. People had already worked out the technical parameters of good digital sound. (I'm only glad they didn't compromise at almost good enough.) All I had to supply was a bit of physiology. And some perspective. That makes this essay another of my Asimov-inspired treatises.

15 Warm Fuzzies

This is the fourth in a series of essays on interfacing computers to people. (See **Essay 12: What Meets the Eye, Essay 13: Technicolor and Cinemascope,** and **Essay 14: What Meets the Ear.**) So far I have talked about vision and hearing. In both cases, I have explored the limits of what each sense can detect.

I don't care (for now) about what is minimally acceptable. I want to know how much information, in what form, is required to give each sense all the data it can process. Only when we reach such limits will we be able to simulate reality believably. Only then will we be able to refine the human/computer interface to the utmost.

Vision and hearing are the two best sensory channels for conveying detailed information. We know quite a bit about the energy sensitivity, frequency response, and discrimination of our eyes and ears. We are sophisticated at making effective sounds and pictures. A generation of television addicts might even tell you that sound and light are all you need to reach out and touch someone.

But then why use that word "touch?" Sure, it's a figure of speech. But all figures of speech are deeply rooted in our experience of the world. It's one thing to *hear someone out*. It's better to *get the picture*. But only rarely are you also *touched* by what you experience.

Touch, smell, and taste are three powerful senses. They certainly convey much less information than vision and hearing. Perhaps for that very reason, their impact is all the more profound.

Smell is an ancient sense. Its roots go deep into our animal brains. And taste is a close cousin to smell. A peculiar aroma or flavor can invoke crystal memories long lost to other associations. More than once, I've been yanked back to childhood by an impudent clover blossom or apple pie. I suspect you have had similar experiences.

Touch has to be at least as ancient. The earliest organisms had to care as much about what was poking at them as what chemistry experiments they stumbled into. Whatever its etymology, touch is a heavy-duty channel to the human psyche. Babies know this, with the nearest thing to instinct that our species has. If you've lost touch with your sense of touch (as it were), try to spend an afternoon making mudpies with a two-year-old. You will be grounded in practically every sense of the word.

I see a real growth industry in computer peripherals that address these three primitive senses. Frankly, I'm not prepared to discuss how to exploit taste and smell. At least not yet. But I can see many ways that touch is under utilized, even with today's technology.

So my topic in this essay is the sense of touch. How is it used to interface people to computers? How can it be used? What are the limits of information processing with this sense? I don't pretend to be very knowledgeable about this area of physiology. That has never deterred me, however, from having opinions on a subject.

Before computers became interactive, you couldn't touch them at all. You clutched your deck or cards, or box of cards for a large program, until the operator snatched it away. You fondled the listing you got back while you worked at squeezing the maximum information from it. Two or three submissions a day was felt to be good turnaround.

Then one day the keyboard went on-line. That became your point of physical contact with the abstract world of data processing. Your fingers push the keys, your eyes (and occasionally your ears) get the feedback.

Feedback through the fingertips is largely passive with most keyboards. Good ones have little bumps on the **F** and **J** keys. Or maybe **ASDF** and **JKL;** are dished a little deeper. (Go take a look at yours.) Many people learn to find these *home* keys by touch without ever becoming consciously aware of their education.

Good keyboards also reward a keystroke with a satisfying thunk. You feel slight resistance as you push against the key. Once it passes the point of no return, its resistance suddenly drops. The key hits ground decisively. You don't know how nice that behavior is until you have to live for a bit with one of those toy affairs designed by a non-typing Philistine.

Really good keyboards tell you when you strike two or more keys at once. Depressing one key mechanically locks all the others. My all-time favorite keyboard in this regard is the one on the old electromechanical IBM Selectric typewriters. Push a key and a metal tab elbows its way into a raceway full of ball bearings, displacing one bearing. The raceway contains only $N-1$ bearings to accompany the N keys. Try to push another key and the bearings firmly resist. Elegant.

The trend today is to resolve roll-overs electronically. One key wins the race and has its code latched. No new keystrokes are recognized until all are released. That approach neatly avoids curdling codes, but it doesn't tell your fingers which one won.

I should tell you that I learned how to type as a college freshman reporter. On an old Royal portable. Sitting on bleachers typing summaries of lacrosse and soccer games. In the rain. My audience was my fellow members of the Princeton University Press Club, and the Western Union operator. We put a premium on speed and semantic accuracy. Aesthetics got murdered in a hail of Xes.

As a result of this upbringing, typing is a particularly sensuous experience to me, I want my keyboard to communicate with me by touch. I don't want to have to look at the screen or the paper to see the result. I don't want to have to look down to see where the backslash key is on this particular keyboard. So I welcome almost any form of tactile feedback, even if it is only a local conversation between me and the keys.

I have encountered one form of feedback from computer to human via the keyboard. Unfortunately, it is not my idea of user-friendly interaction. Some systems can mechanically lock all the keys when the computer doesn't want to be distracted. You try to type and the keyboard tries to break your thumbs. A kindly system may warn you with a loud snick, and/or a "Kbd Lock" indicator, before it rebuffs you. I prefer to have my typing ignored to having my fingers bruised.

So much for keyboards. Fortunately for all of us, hardware designers have been willing to experiment with other ways for us to use our fingers. One of the earliest alternatives I got to play with was the light pen.

A light pen is a device that you hold up against a CRT display screen. It is designed to be an absolute pointing device. The computer determines exactly where you are holding the pen on the screen. The software relates this position to whatever it is currently displaying. A typical light pen also has a trigger button so you can input the one-bit message (in time and space), "Now."

I liked using a light pen. I liked the natural motion of reaching out to touch the thing I wanted to select. True, the thing was just an abstract picture. It had no tactile feedback to reassure me that it was more than a shadow. But it was right there at my fingertips. I didn't even mind the tired arm I got from holding up a light pen to a vertical screen for several hours.

Light pens are largely passé, of course. I think that's because they are such a nuisance to program. The pen has to see an illuminated dot on the screen for the computer to know where it's pointing. That calls for extra logic intimately associated with the display to sensitize the pen at just the right instances. It also calls for messy software to hunt for the pen if you're drawing freehand or pointing at a dark area.

A modern incarnation of the light pen is the so-called touch-sensitive screen. A halo of infrared emitters and detectors frames the screen. Your pointing finger interrupts horizontal and vertical beams. That gives both X and Y coordinates and the "Now" signal.

Such gadgets are useful for displaying multiple-choice menus without too many options. Resolution tends to be too coarse for drawing — the devices I've played with seem to have about 30 to 60 lines in each dimension. And you can't simulate a proper keyboard — they detect the presence of your finger, now how hard you push. I find touch screens cute, but no substitute for other pointing devices.

*V*ideo games taught me to like joy-sticks. Good ones have resistance that increases the further you deflect the wand from dead center. Really good ones send a signal to the computer that accurately reflects how far you deflect the wand. Once again, the tactile feedback is local. What the computer is thinking or doing has no effect on it. Still, I find it helps.

I have saved for last the most popular hand-operated pointing device. The mouse has largely displaced light pens and joy-sticks. It has held at bay such workalikes as track balls and sketch pads. It is as cheap to make and interface as any of these alternatives. It is arguably as easy to use as any for pointing, selecting, and coarse free-hand sketching.

Sadly, it also ranks near the bottom in terms of tactile feedback. All a mouse tells you is where it is on the work surface. The proprioceptors in your hand and arm supply that information when they tell your brain how muscles and bones are deployed. You have to look at the screen to relate that to where the computer thinks you're pointing.

The newest mice have variable ballistics. The faster you move your hand, the coarser the motion specified by the mouse. That's a real help in moving around a large screen. But it means that the cursor doesn't return to the same spot when you return the mouse to the same spot. Once again, you need loosely coupled hand/eye coordination where a direct touch is more natural.

I have reviewed this technology in detail to emphasize a simple point. We currently make very limited use of our sense of touch. It is confined to the hand, often just to the fingertips. It is used more to help generate input than to interpret output from the computer. Even for those limited goals, it often fails to make the best use of our sophisticated hand/eye coordination.

*L*et's look at the various ways that touch can be used to convey information. You can probably find an instance where each way has been used as part of a computer interface. Some are common enough, but limited. Some are used only in exotic devices. None have come close to being fully exploited.

I should say up front that I'm not looking for high channel capacity here. Braille writing is proof that you can read with your fingertips. It is not a skill easily learned, however. If you are blind, you have a strong motivation to learn that skill. I understand that most sighted people read Braille with their eyes, rather than educate their sense of touch. We should not expect civilians to embrace a difficult discipline.

We can estimate the spatial resolution of human skin. It is measured in small numbers of millimeters, or fractions of an inch. It is doubtless finest on our fingertips, somewhat coarser on palms and face. It is probably coarsest where you sit down. The actual limits don't matter too much, for the reasons I indicated above. Few people educate their skins to distinguish distances smaller than the width of a Band Aid.

There are still a variety of signals we can exploit, however coarse their dimensions. The first one that springs to mind is simple resistance to motion. You push against something, it pushes back. How hard it pushes back can be a measure of its mass, if it continues in motion. Or it can measure its springiness, if it bounces back. Or it can measure its viscosity, if it remains deformed. All are useful cues for animals evolved to manipulate their environment.

Imagine a joy-stick, mouse, or trackball that fights back. Its contribution to a flight simulator is obvious, but there are others. Drag a big document toward the printer icon and the pointing device resists more than for a small document. Or mass up an icon by its execution priority, or the number of edits since the last backup. My ideal desktop display would create a similar sense of gumminess (don't ask me how) when you press your hand against a page image and push it to one side.

A device that can vary its resistance is but a step away from one that can move on its own. Here you have to be careful. The goal is not to move things about. Robots do that and are best given a wide berth. I'm talking about gadgets that can nudge, twitch, or tickle.

The problem with most computer-controlled motion is the lack of pressure-sensitive feedback. You don't want to be poked by something that doesn't know its own strength. Or that can't distinguish a poke in the ribs from a poke in the eye. A flight simulator is more realistic if it can make a joy-stick dance like a Cessna in a down draft. But it shouldn't be allowed to break your kneecap.

Vibration is a subtler form of motion more easily controlled. It also comes in many distinguishable flavors. An icon can hum reassuringly while it computes or buzz a nasty warning for errors. You can take in half a dozen such summaries where you rest your arms. No need to look away from the business at hand.

In the early days of UNIX on minicomputers, I used to tune systems by feel. I found it most useful to sit astride two disk drives and stare at the console lights. The lights told me which part of the system was active, the shaking told me what each drive was doing. Even if that part of my anatomy had only coarse spatial resolution for touch, it was more than enough. I could literally work by the seat of my pants.

Your skin is also sensitive to changes in temperature. Heat a spot ten degrees above ambient temperature and just about anybody will get a strong signal that something is out of the ordinary. Chilling a spot is generally harder and not quite so loud, but that too is effective. The neat thing is that hot and cold are cues with many cross cultural meanings. Red says, "Watch it" to cultures with traffic lights, but hot says it louder to everyone.

Yes, I know that heating and cooling take lots of energy. I understand that thermal inertia severely limits how fast the signal can vary. I have no idea how to make a practical display, or even a pointing device, that has hot spots. Still, I can dream.

While I'm dreaming, I can also hope for a device that can change its texture. That's even harder than generating vibrations or temperature changes. Still, it would be nice to commandeer the warm fuzzies and cold pricklies of pop psychology. They are freighted with useful overtones. And they are just part of an open-ended set of sensations that can help computers communicate with people.

When you look at this list of stimuli, you develop a fresh respect for your skin. It's amazing what a variety of sensations you can get from something counted as a single sense. It's a pity we haven't devised more ways to exploit touch as a form of computer output.

I confined most of my usage examples to things you can do with your hands. Certainly, they are a principal portal for tactile sensations. And certainly, we all feel most comfortable keeping many contacts at arms length, as it were. You can almost always wash your hands.

Still, there are applications where people would gladly accept a wider range of tactile stimuli. (You can supply your own leers and sniggers at this point.) We are heading steadily in the direction of full reality simulation by computer. Sight is very important for that, and hearing is close behind. But until you introduce touch, you're well short of the mark. And whatever sensation comes next is a distant fourth. □

Afterword: I couldn't be nearly as quantitative in this essay as in the previous three. That tells you, more than anything else, how little we have exploited our sense of touch. I believe we will see great strides in this area in the near future. We may also see progress in the use of smell and taste, but I am less sanguine about that prospect. That's partly why I chose to limit this study of the human senses to three out of five. Anything I could say would be too speculative even for my catholic taste.

16 Font Follies

It's that time of year again. Regular readers of these essays know that April is the cruelest month. I set aside my usual saint-like compassion and focus more intently on the foolishness that pervades the software business. Pagans used to celebrate the summer and winter solstices. I feel it more fitting that programmers paint themselves blue and dance about naked on April Fool's Day.

My topic this time around is font software. If you've ever dug into the stuff, you already know what a rich vein of complexity awaits the strike of a pickax. I long suspected as much, but managed to put off any serious delving until about half a year ago. Then, fool that I was, I jumped in feet first. I am still waiting to hit bottom.

My descent into this particular mine shaft began many years ago. Upon reflection, I realize that it probably began with two recurring daydreams that I indulged in as a child. At the time, I saw no connection between the two dreams. I now know better.

The first was part of my dream of becoming a writer. Who knows what makes a particular vocation look appealing — what turns some of us into computer programmers and others into accountants or publicans. Maybe, in my case, it was my early introduction to science fiction. I somehow got the notion that science fiction writers were godlike creatures with profound insights who, incidentally, attracted hordes of admiring women. (I have since learned better, on all counts.)

So I wanted to write, for whatever misguided reasons. But that wasn't the end of it. From early on, I dreamed of having strict control over what I wrote, from inception to black marks on paper. Twenty years before the first commercial word-processing software hit the dealers' shelves, I was determined to do my own document formatting.

It's not that I'm above having my work edited. I recognize the need for someone to tone down my hyperbole and catch grammatical lapses. Some of my best work has been with co-authors who fill in my perceptual lacunae. I just want to be responsible for the final product. If it contains any typos, they had better be my fault.

Fortunately, I was at Bell Labs when some of the earliest document-formatting software came into being. Neglecting an abstruse paper or two in nuclear physics, I can report that all my published work went through a computer. Every textbook that I've written or helped write came out of a phototypesetter under my control or that of my co-author. I am grateful that the technology fell into place in time, if only barely, to satisfy my early dream of control.

The second childhood dream was to make the perfect character set. On rainy days, I used to take a sheet of graph paper and divide it up into dozens of equal-size boxes. The challenge was to make easily distinguishable, and pretty, letters and digits with an economy of dots or lines. I spent a significant chunk of the 1950s pushing the limitations of seven-bar digit displays and bit-mapped character sets.

In time, all sorts of vendors were repeating my childhood studies in pursuit of serious profits. I could buy terminals and printers that exhibited the best and worst of economical character sets. That's probably why my interest has drifted, over the years, away from the minimalist toward the more aesthetic. I no longer care much what a designer can do with a 16x16-dot matrix. I want to see Goudy Old Style rendered well enough to compete with hand-set type on vellum.

My two daydreams began to merge a few years ago when I bought the first release of Ventura Publisher. This is a typesetting package for the IBM PC family that rivals the early successes of the Apple Macintosh family. It lets you format documents containing mixed type faces, line drawings, and bit-mapped graphics. A document can be as simple as a single-page flier or as complex as a book divided into numerous chapters. Ventura Publisher is a complex program that is hard to learn, but for my needs it is well worth the effort.

Before Ventura came along, I did all my serious document formatting with the nroff/troff package that comes with UNIX. To back up to the beginning, *roff* stands for "run off," as when you *run off* a good draft. Brian Kernighan developed the first program of that ilk (at least that I know of) as a graduate student at Princeton. You had to submit the paper on punched cards, but you got pretty output on the high-speed IBM chain printer. Brian solved the problem of specifying mixed-case printout using single-case input and a minimum of *markup,* or meta-information, interspersed in the printable text.

Joe Osanna wrote a "new runoff" program at Bell Labs, based loosely on prior experience with several versions of roff. His nroff became the vehicle of choice for formatting papers to computer printers. It had gazillions of commands, which you can bundle into macros that defined your own nifty markup language. Model 37 Teletypes eliminated the fuss about single-case input. They also opened the door to Greek letters and half-line vertical spacing. With nroff, you could work minor miracles of formatting. Provided, that is, you were content with a couple hundred printable characters all of the same width.

Along came the first of the (relatively) inexpensive phototypesetters that could be driven by minicomputers. Joe mucked over nroff extensively to produce troff, for "typesetting runoff." It had gazillions more commands and still more macro capabilities. You could contrive macro sets that nroffed a document onto a printer with one version or troffed it onto the photo-typesetter with another. Suddenly, we had oodles more characters to display, in a myriad of sizes. The world is now awash with laser printers. It is hard to imagine today the thrill we got back then producing papers, letters, even mock ransom notes without involving professional printers.

Input was still a problem. Sure, you had lower-case letters by then, but it was all computerese. And the markup didn't help readability. It's hard to see **\fIwow\fP** as italicized *wow*, or **\ (em** as an em-dash (—). It's even harder to debug page layout if you have to run a separate formatting program every time you want to see the effect of a change.

That's where Ventura Publisher really makes a difference. You can still type those files with markup if you want to. The markup is still hard to read — **<MI>wow<D>** and **<197>** are no better than their precursors. But you can load a file into Ventura and watch it format before your very eyes. Make a change and the effect percolates through instantly. Ventura even saves the changes as a file with markup codes. That lets you muck it over with a more powerful text editor, between Ventura sessions.

To make all this magic happen, you need a new flavor of software. A common barbarism for it is *fontware*. It is the stuff that specifies the shapes of all those pretty letters on the screen and on the printed page. Fontware goes far beyond the 95 ASCII graphics built into most character-mode terminals and letter-quality printers. It includes hundreds of glyphs (the proper term for the visible form of a character), possibly in hundreds of different fonts (the proper term for a type face at a given point size).

The printer needs fonts. A typical PostScript printer these days has 35 different type faces stored in an internal ROM. Essentially all have at least 13, including variations on Times, Helvetica, and Courier. (Helvetica, Helvetica Italic, Helvetica Bold, and Helvetica Bold Italic count as four faces.) Each face is scalable almost continuously from ridiculously tiny to ridiculously huge. You can specify a seeming infinity of fonts.

For some of us, however, an infinite number is not enough. We want access to even more faces. The very fact that these 35 faces are in so many printers has made them shopworn. I weary of books and papers set in Times Roman with Helvetica Bold heads and computer text in Courier. Perhaps that is variety for its own sake, but so be it. We want more choices than you can possibly count.

A number of companies are happy to address this growing hunger. Some printers take plug-in cartridges with additional fonts in ROM. You can buy them from lots of sources. Others, such as the PostScript jobs, will let you download *soft fonts* from the computer. That can be slower, but it's a lot more flexible. Just know that if your printer doesn't have the fonts you want on board, you will have to pay extra to get them there.

𝔜our display screen also needs fonts. At 80 dots per inch, or thereabouts, the screen can't make characters look nearly as pretty as the printer should. A *letter quality* printer needs at least four times that much linear resolution, or 16 times as many dots per hectare. But what you see on the screen should be a reasonable facsimile of what you get on the printer. Otherwise, much of the power of a package like Ventura Publisher is wasted. Worse, bad screen fonts can drive you up the wall. Place the cursor here, do an edit, and watch some characters over there twitch. That's worse than reading markup language.

The first version of Ventura Publisher I bought ran under GEM, a windowing environment from Digital Research. GEM needs screen fonts in fixed point sizes. That doesn't sit well with an application that traffics in a continuum of sizes. Even if you set a document all in ten-point Times Roman, you need three different screen fonts. Ventura has three levels of magnification for displaying typeset pages.

So you compromise. You give GEM an assortment of fonts for each face. Try to display one that isn't there and GEM has to guess. Should it choose one that's close enough, by some metric? Or should it scale an existing font? Too often, GEM goes for close enough. The result is the misaligned cursor madness I described above (hereinafter MCM).

Another kind of substitution also occurs. Try to display a face that has no fonts at all and GEM really has to guess. It maps every face onto one of the three standbys from the early days of PostScript. Some faces have serifs, those little nubbins on the corners of letters. (Roman stonemasons carved serifs two millennia ago to minimize cracking. Talk about form outliving function.) All such faces display as Times.

Some faces are sans-serif, literally "without serifs." They display as Helvetica. A monospaced font has fixed-width letters, just like a typewriter or a standard computer printer. They display as Courier. The result works, but it can often be nowhere near what you get on the printer. Particularly for the more ornamental faces that are sometimes fun to use. MCM again.

𝕴 lived with this clunky machinery for over a year. Then, one day, I took the first step toward the bottomless pit. I saw an ad that promised GEM screen fonts for all 35 common PostScript faces, in a rich assortment of point sizes. The cost was a pittance. I got them, managed to install them, and was amazed at the transformation. Zapf Chancery appeared in all its scrawly elegance. Dingbats looked dingbatty. All it cost me was another chunk of disk real estate and an extra fifteen seconds startup time for Ventura. I was hooked.

Then I got an excuse to expand my horizons. I edit a computer magazine that displays its computerese in Letter Gothic 12. That's not one of the 35 infamous faces in my PostScript printer. So it's not among my GEM screen fonts either. The magazine uses Ventura Publisher, lucky for me. But without Letter Gothic 12 screen fonts, I was back at MCM.

So I finally broke down and bought some soft fonts from Bitstream. They had a decent rendering of Letter Gothic 12. While I was at it, I bought a bunch of other faces I had always admired. Bitstream cleverly gives away a sampler with each copy of Ventura Publisher. (I think they learned marketing from a drug dealer.) I already had a copy of Fontware, the program that generates the various font files from the diskettes that Bitstream ships.

Only Fontware didn't work right. After a day of fussing, I started making phone calls. Seems I had failed to upgrade to the absolute latest version of Fontware. Ventura, or GEM, was gagging over some subtle change in file format. Fine. I got the new version, installed it, and made my fonts. I now had a reasonable assortment of screen fonts plus downloadable soft fonts for my NEC PostScript printer. For almost two weeks, I was in pig heaven.

Then I heard that Ventura Publisher was moving to Microsoft Windows. I didn't hesitate. After all, Windows 3.0 works pretty hard to look like a Macintosh. (No copyright infringement implied.) And the Mac has done more than most gadgets to make *font* a household word. I got Windows 3.0 and learned how to use it. When Ventura for Windows came along, I got that too.

Only then did I learn that all my beautiful fonts were dead meat. After all, they were in GEM format. Windows demands its own format. Reasonable, I suppose. It's a bit early for ANSI to belt out a common font-interchange format for low-to-medium resolution screens. Maybe I could rescue the Bitstream stuff with another day of work, but I still needed facsimiles of the 35 standard fonts. I had to do something.

That was when I tripped across a copy of Bitstream Facelift. This is a wondrous product that works with Microsoft Windows. Forget all those tough decisions about what point sizes to install. Facelift lets you install a single outline file for each type face. Then it scales them on the fly. Evidently, Windows has a hook in its screen driver that gives packages like this a chance to intercede. If a character owned by Bitstream goes by, Facelift steps in and contrives the appropriate-size glyph while-u-wait. Naturally, it takes a bit of caching to make all this stuff go fast enough.

On top of everything else, Facelift came with a fistful of type faces that I didn't yet own. They're the sort of thing you use for wedding invitations and fliers that sell used cars, but what the heck. More fonts.

o I bought Facelift and hurried home to install it. It came right up, with all its fancy type faces working with Windows Write and Ventura. Mazeltov. Then I tried to reinstall my existing Bitstream fonts. No go.

After two days of frustration and reading the manual from cover to cover five times, I broke down and called Bitstream. They live 15 miles from my home in Concord, Mass. The nice folk there explained that they had changed file formats with the release of Facelift. Diskettes with a diamond logo were digestible by Facelift, older ones were not. On the other hand, they were willing to ship me my old wine in new bottles if I could show proof of recent purchase. So I did and they did.

I got the scalable screen fonts working and set about making download-able printer fonts. No go. Seems I now owned three flavors of fonts. The old ones could be stuffed through Fontware to make downloadable printer fonts. The diamond-logo jobbers could not. The ones I got with Facelift proper also came with downloadable versions, but in a different flavor. (I won't bore you with the differences among PostScript-compatible font file formats.)

I camped on Bitstream until they sent me files in enough different formats to do the trick. In the end, I had to obtain a still later version of Fontware to get around some bugs. But all the fonts are now installed, both as screen fonts and as downloadable. It bugs me that the same information has to appear in two different forms on the disk. At 50 kilobytes per type face, two dozen faces eat over a megabyte. I hate to pay that tariff twice. At least it's all in and working. Mostly.

Then I ran across Adobe Type Manager. This is a package that does for Adobe fonts what Facelift does for fonts from Bitstream. Remember those 35 faces I kept babbling about earlier? Well, they come from Adobe along with PostScript. I still needed good screen fonts for my original set. Why not get them straight from the horse's mouth? I figured that Adobe Type Manager would have to give me accurate replicas of the printer fonts on the screen.

art of me knew I was insane. Windows 3.0 is a new and complex piece of software. I have already reported a fistful of bugs in it. The same is true of Facelift and Type Manager. What are the odds that two (count 'em, two) complex packages can share a complex hook into Windows and not try to kill each other? I've been writing software for nearly thirty years. I should know better than to put my writing and editing productivity at the mercy of such a combination.

Well, guess what. They work together. I'm sure that Type Manager occasionally savages Windows. Type Manager goes nutty from time to time, but stumbles on. Windows screws Facelift all too often. But then, Facelift more often screws itself. I have never caught Type Manager and

Facelift harming each other. The whole mess hangs together often enough for me to get serious work done.

Adobe Type Manager comes with the Original Stale Thirteen faces. You can buy a supplemental pack to flesh out the standard 35. So I did that. Naturally, I had to give up yet another chunk of memory for Adobe to cache expanded characters. You could hardly expect it to share a cache with Bitstream. I discovered that Type Manager could, however, manage some of the Bitstream faces. But not all. In the end, I decided to keep each in its own ghetto as much as possible. I was getting headaches from chasing installation bugs.

It took me a full two weeks of full-time work to get Facelift and Type Manager working. Ventura didn't start working right until Adobe told me about a patch I needed. (Xerox gave me the same news under my maintenance agreement, two months later.) I downloaded the patch from CompuServe and got it going.

My story is not over. I also use Corel Draw, a wonderful drawing package for the PC. I use it to make textbook illustrations that are beyond the capabilities of Ventura Publisher. (In fairness, Ventura is great at letting you import stuff from fancier word processors, drawing programs, and image manipulators.) Corel can also bend, stretch, and twist type in marvelous ways.

Corel comes with a rich set of faces for you to mangle. Only problem is, none of these exactly match the Adobe 35, much less any of my Bitstream acquisitions. When I make textbook illustrations, I want the type faces to agree.

Corel nicely provides a font-file reformatter called WFNBOSS. I unleashed it on my miscellaneous assortment of font files. No go. Some files seemed to translate okay, but Corel crashed when I tried to use them. Others substituted funny characters. Still others came out with funny spacing.

After another day of struggling, I called Corel. Guess what. I needed a later version of WFNBOSS. They let me download it and most of my problems disappeared. The rest I worked around. Two more days gone.

At this point, I had a wobbly mass of software that mostly worked. Every once in awhile, Facelift shut down without warning. I learned the incantations that brought it back to life. Type Manager developed a funny interaction with Windows. Even with the Windows flavors of Courier and Times disabled, some part of Windows still seemed to be second guessing Type Manager. Both Microsoft and Adobe agree that bugs remain. To date, nobody has called me with a fix or work around.

I was left with one fundamental problem. My Compaq SLT/286 was now too slow. After two years of noble service, it finally found itself outclassed. I conferred with my wife, studied my checkbook, and ordered a Compaq

SLT/386-s20. It arrived in due course and I shifted my software over. I was back in pig heaven.

𝕴 am now in Australia for a year, fonts and all. For the price of a small car, I have Ventura Publisher running under Windows with two flavors of scalable screen fonts. Six megabytes of disk real estate and half a megabyte of RAM are devoted to helping my 20 MHz 386 paint screens fast. Some fonts exist in three different forms. The software kicks up from time to time, but it mostly works. When it works, it is great. When it doesn't, I spend time making expensive phone calls. Or I do without.

For example, I installed Facelift with my NEC PostScript printer connected to LPT1. I am now using an Apple LaserWriter II connected to COM2. Facelift flatly refuses to download fonts to the new printer. Or to a file. Or to anything except a PostScript printer connected to LPT1. I can get Facelift to scale fonts on the fly for the printer as well. That takes five minutes per page instead of five pages per minute.

The Australian rep for Bitstream has yet to answer the phone. But then it's summer here. If you've ever seen a Sydney beach in summer, you know why nobody answers phones.

Where does the folly lie? Decide for yourself. □

𝕬fterword: The fun never stops. Since I wrote this rambling diatribe, I have discontinued use of Bitstream Facelift. Many of the troubles I blamed on Adobe Type Manager turned out to be insidious Facelift bugs. One by one, I eliminated the bugs described here, acquiring new ones at a mercifully slower rate. Over time, I have been able to get Adobe Type 1 versions of all my fonts. That lets me depend on Type Manager alone for screen fonts.

Then along came Windows 3.1 with the new TrueType format. After a bit of experimenting, I turned off most of TrueType and stuck with Type Manager. Better the devil you know. But the font business is far from settled down.

The real reason for this essay, of course, in not just to talk about fontware. Rather, it illustrated how ever more complex software can dominate our lives. For more on that subject, see "Programming on Purpose: The Cycle of Complexity," Computer Language, June 1992, and "Programming on Purpose: Piled Higher and Deeper," Computer Language, September 1992. It's a recurring theme because it's a recurring problem.

17 Text Editors

No topic stirs the passions of your average programmer half so much as the relative merits of different text editors. Folks who are otherwise (mostly) sane and agreeable wax poetic about their editor of choice. They heap scorn upon those who find other editors in any way preferable. They marshal all sorts of intellectual arguments to support the conviction they feel in their guts.

Arguments about text editors are usually branded as "religious." I think that term is right on the money. The wellspring of religion is a deep and abiding faith that transcends reason and logic. That's a pretty accurate description of the mind set of your typical editor devotee as well. Both demand respect. You get in trouble only when you insist on dragging conviction into the realm of the rational. The issues are simply orthogonal.

I have long stood in awe of this phenomenon with text editors. What is it about them that fires people up? Sure, you have your compiler devotees and your spreadsheet loyalists. Brand loyalty is no stranger to the world of computer software. Still, text editors seem to stand apart. They bring out the zealots in all of us like no other tools we use.

One conjecture is that programmers use editors quite a lot. Your average computer user may deal with a handful of applications. Many applications generate files, to be sure. But they handle the formatting details for you. The user speaks only a restricted language to the application.

A programmer, on the other hand, performs a broader spectrum of tasks. Keying in and editing program source is just one job. Preparing test input is another. Generating initial versions of configuration and database files is yet another. As a programmer, you work daily with text files in a broad assortment of formats. For that, you need a general-purpose text editor.

You don't want a text editor that is too presumptuous. Any structure it imposes on a file may be fine in some cases but is sure to cause trouble in others. About the only structure you can abide is the partitioning of the character stream into lines. Each line should be terminated in accordance with local custom — carriage return plus line feed, line feed alone, or whatever. Files generated by the text editor must be digestible by the local assembler, compiler, display driver, and printer. Beyond that, the less said the better.

Herein lies a fundamental dichotomy. What a programmer often wants to control is the pattern of bytes stored in a file. What a text editor offers as feedback is a pattern of marks on screen or paper. You type at the editor, or point and click with a mouse, and the display changes. Presumably, those changes reflect changes in the pattern of bytes stored in a file.

The design of a text editor defines the mapping between displayed marks, typed commands, and stored bytes. You as user of the editor form some mental model of this mapping. If your mental model is reasonably accurate, you use the editor with assurance. You build a history of successes in defining the patterns of bytes you need in files of varied formats.

At some point, you may even do more than understand the model defined by the text editor — you *get* it. Here I use *get* in the colloquial sense to describe that leap of faith (or joy, or love) that comes into our lives from time to time, but probably never often enough. Once we get something, our relationship to it transcends reason. We believe, pure and simple.

The more important a thing is, the stronger our need to form this emotional attachment. It provides an important anchor when the sea of uncertainty develops whitecaps. It saves us the need to rethink basic decisions over and over. It becomes, in a real sense, a part of us.

Much of our lives as programmers involves controlling those invisible bytes scribbled on disks. Ours is an exacting trade. A single byte wrong can hold us hostages to frustration and boredom for days or weeks. We really need faith that we can control those bytes with some certainty.

That's why I see a text editor as the meeting ground between emotions and intellect for a programmer. It engages both our hearts and our brains. But that's not the end of it. We have to buy into a text editor in a third dimension as well.

Editing text is a mechanical operation. All that typing, pointing, and clicking takes more than simple intellectual understanding. It takes more than emotional conviction. It takes practice.

I'm certainly no expert on education. I have no teaching certificates, I've done no serious research on how people learn. Like most self-appointed teachers, I'm self-taught in the skills of teaching. That has not deterred me from studying the matter at least informally. And it has certainly not kept me from forming opinions. (Some would argue that no force on Earth could do so.) What I have observed is that there are (at least) three distinct ways that people learn:

We learn intellectually by accumulating experience. We read, we listen, we touch and feel. We make conjectures, perform experiments, and adjust our beliefs accordingly. Eventually, we build a sufficient base of long-term memories of salient facts. We also construct abstract models, as I described above, and accrete evidence that supports them. Our expertise comes from years of schooling and trial and error.

We learn emotionally in lurches. The process seems to require an accretion of experience, but the response is far from linear. (See **Essay 9: It's (Almost) Alive.**) We can learn some lessons from a single experience. Sometimes what we learn from that experience is demonstrably wrong, yet we cling to our convictions. We can be exposed to other lessons repeatedly and still not learn the obvious. This is what I call *getting it* earlier in this essay.

We learn kinesthetically only through repetition. Riding a bicycle, playing Bach on the piano, typing 30 words per minute — all are skills that take practice to master. To excel in this arena requires dedication. The best of the best shoot baskets hours a day. Or practice the violin, or sing scales. Nobody I know has found a shortcut to this form of learning.

The one consolation is that kinesthetic learning is as slow to fade as it is to be acquired. I have gone years without sitting a bicycle, only to ride off literally without a second thought. Whatever I learned is so far down my spinal cord that my brain is just a bystander. (It's like those stock pictures in company house organs of somebody being handed an award while the president "looks on.")

A quarter century ago, I mastered the dubious art of writing tape marks and rewinding tapes by flipping the keys on the console of an IBM 7090 data channel. To this day, I could still do it with my eyes closed. The skill has passed from the dubious to the arcane, but it's still there.

Every text editor I've met demands its dubious skills as well. Don't believe the bushwah you hear about intuitive operation. Nothing is really a single mouse click away. To run any text editor I've ever encountered, you've got to invest some time mastering its peculiarities. Some of those often border on the arcane.

Perhaps you can see where I'm heading. Text editors seem to be unique among the programs you use as a programmer. You have to invest a nontrivial amount of time mastering the underlying mapping between bytes in a file and marks on a display. You have to get that the editor is a safe tool for your varied needs. And you have to master an assortment of mechanical skills. That's quite an investment.

In my youth, I dabbled in the business of selling software. I sold compilers with reasonable success, to a broad assortment of customers. I sold operating systems with much more limited success. The assortment of customers I reached proved too narrow, at least for my ambitions. I have commented more than once on why I think this came to pass.

It's relatively easy for a techie or a front-line manager to decide to buy a compiler. You can tuck it in a corner, use it on a few projects, and ignore it on all the rest. It is a very discretionary product.

An operating system, on the other hand, requires a much greater commitment. The commitment extends well beyond individuals. It affects entire groups. That's because operating systems generally eat whole computers. They dictate the kind of software you can buy to run on those computers. I like to say that you don't simply buy an operating system — you marry one.

In that sense, picking a text editor is also much like getting married. You don't necessarily have to get a whole group to commit to the same text editor, to be sure. I've been in shops where there were almost as many different text editors as there were programmers. But each programmer must make a major commitment to learning how to live with a given editor. That commitment may start in the brain, but it extends to the heart and further down the spinal cord as well. It is not a cheap decision.

Many of us fall in love with the first text editor we use. I suspect the process resembles what newly hatched chicks go through when they fixate on a mother hen. We go through a similar process with our first programming language. Edsger Dijkstra has long maintained that a person weaned on FORTRAN is incurably damaged by the experience. I like to think that I am not, although I'm willing to concede that my development may have been retarded.

Certainly, I am still most comfortable with the first text editor I learned to depend on. It seems to me that earlier editors were too primitive. Later ones have too many whistles and bells, and they don't offer the close control I need.

I realize how much that sounds like the generic college valedictory address. *Ours was a generation of change. The college was a bit stuffy when we got here. We brought about needed improvements. But things have gone a bit radical for our tastes recently.* Sound familiar?

Nevertheless, I still have pretensions at professionalism in this, my chosen trade. That obliges me to at least try to change with the times. For that reason, I keep fiddling with new text editors as they come along. In some ways, they are distinctly better. In others, I feel they have lost ground. It could be that I am simply stodgy, but I don't think so. I'll recite my list of perceived pros and cons, then you can decide for yourself.

The best thing about newer text editors is that they offer a bigger window on the world. They have come a long way from those first text editors that popped up decades ago. The ones on mainframes mostly evolved from older batch update programs. You punched up a set of change-request cards and stuck them on the front of the deck you wanted to edit. The computer punched out a new deck with the edits incorporated.

When the editors went interactive, they retained the card-deck mentality. Maybe the deck to be updated came off a disk file, but the commands you typed sure looked like those change-request cards of yore.

More adventuresome were the programmers trying to tame the new breed of minicomputers In those days, memory was scarce and disks were practically nonexistent on minis. One of the earliest text-editor hits was a creature called TECO. It was modeled not on card decks but on paper tape. Editor commands let you yank in as much tape as would comfortably fit in the very limited memory, work on that chunk, then punch out the edited section.

Compared to existing paper-tape editing machines, TECO was much more flexible and powerful. Still, there was that notion of taking one pass over a sequential file of characters, mucking it over a section at a time. Commands were cryptic beyond belief. This was the days of Model 33 Teletypes running at 110 baud. The less you said that the computer had to echo the better. But the editing language was remarkably powerful. To this day, I still trip across the odd TECO devotee who mourns the good old days.

My career with TECO was mercifully short. Mostly, I got to play with a series of editors put up by the now famous Ken Thompson and Dennis Ritchie. You can still find their original work tucked in a dank corner of the **/bin** directory of nearly every UNIX system shipped. I refer, of course, to that venerable standby, the UNIX ed editor.

The design of ed profited, naturally, from earlier experiences with TECO. The terse input remained, but got moderately less cryptic. The UNIX version is actually a simplification of an earlier editor called qed. That beast was so powerful that you could actually write programs for it. Perhaps the worst thing I did to Bell Labs was write a relocating linker in qed, then describe the tricks I'd learned in a tutorial memo. I wouldn't be surprised if unmaintainable qed programs are still consuming enormous quantities of CPU time in backwaters of that organization.

I think the main conceptual advantage of ed over TECO came about because disks became more commonplace. That paper tape turned into a ring of text, all of which was quickly available to the editor commands you typed. You didn't feel quite so inhibited about taking multiple passes over a file.

A secondary advantage came from the UNIX host environment. UNIX standardized the representation of text streams inside the computer. The sequence of bytes inside the editor could be exactly the same as in the disk file, which was the same sequence you read and wrote. Any needed reformatting got pushed out to the edges of the system. That made it much easier for the editor to present an accurate representation of the underlying byte patterns.

Still, ed made you peer at the text a line or so at a time. It still carried the implicit conviction that the display device was a slow printer. When 9,600-baud CRT terminals appeared on the scene in quantity, a few folks grew impatient with ed.

That led to the development of vi and its ilk. These screen-oriented editors are still popular in many circles. They can work in character mode across serial links, yet they offer many new advantages. Most important, the conceptual model got friendlier. That paper-tape ring of characters has now widened into a ribbon of lines. You view the ribbon through a window that shows upwards of 2,000 characters at a time. You don't have to ask to see the effect of a command because you're always treated to a view of the current text that fits in the window.

Editors like vi have had to live with a vast range of character-oriented terminals. They need packages like curses and termcap to isolate them from the peculiarities of individual terminals. That restricts them to a set of screen-drawing primitives that comprises a lowest common denominator. If you only have to do battle with one flavor of screen, life can get easier.

And it did. The advent of the personal computer has brought the latest improvement in text-editor technology. Bit-mapped screens support multiple fonts. Fonts can vary in size and can have proportional spacing. Characters on the screen can be designated by a mouse as well as by keyboard commands. Even commands can be selected by mouse clicks on menus, so you have less to remember. The new conceptual model is often characterized by that overworked phrase, "What you see is what you get."

That's the good news. I can cheerfully report that I'm typing this text into one of those modern text editors. It uses windows, mouse, clipboard, menus, and all the other wonderful features you hear touted so aggressively today. Mostly I like it.

The bad news is that I couldn't do the whole job using just that editor. At least not comfortably. From time to time I put the file down with the new editor and picked it up with my ancient ed clone. Let me tell you why.

On one occasion, I had to drop a broad range of text lines. I first tried selecting the text by dragging the mouse across the entire range. The window neatly scrolled along as I dragged, for many many seconds. Then I goofed and bounced a mouse button at the wrong time. All gone. I started over from bottom to top. Many seconds later, I'd forgotten where the top was. Scrub the dragging and go looking for the right place again. You get the drift. Sometimes it's easier to just type a command than it is to point and click.

Here's a variation on that theme. Try a global search and replace with a menu-driven system. It's like filling in one of those landing cards they hand you when you take an international flight. Even if you get it right, you still have to outsmart the editor's helpful presumptions. No, I don't want a case-insensitive match, thank you. Yes, I would like to specify a match pattern with metacharacters, not just a match of letters and digits. Sometimes it's easier just to type a one-line command, no matter how cryptic it may appear.

I reserve my biggest gripe for the last. When I use a text editor, I want to edit text. I don't want to format a document. I don't want to fill in a form letter. I don't want to simulate a $600 typesetting package at a fraction of the cost.

People who write text editors these days are going off in the wrong direction, at least for my needs. They have confused "What you see is what you get" with "What you see is what you want." What I want is a display that helps me form an accurate mental model of the underlying bytes in the text file.

I don't want trailing spaces to disappear. Instead, give me some way to make them visible if they're there. I don't want long lines to fold automatically. I certainly don't want them to truncate. I want feedback and control.

Brian Kernighan deserves the last *bon mot* on this topic. He was touting the advantages of markup languages over the new breed of document formatters, but his point applies equally to this diatribe. You can suffer a major loss of information if you edit text with some of the newer user-over-friendly editors. If you're not careful, in fact, you will find that "What you see is *all* you get." □

Afterword: Text editors for programmers have become a hot marketplace lately. Some know the syntax of the programming language you're editing. Others try to be extremely flexible. I have tried several of them since I wrote this essay. I'm happy to see so much effort directed toward helping programmers. But I still haven't found an editor I like.

18 Approximating Functions

An amazing number of computer people are frightened of mathematics. Yes, I know that you don't have to know calculus to write a computer program. But both disciplines require a level of precision and a style of abstract thinking that are quite similar. You'd expect a familiarity with one would instill a level of comfort with the other. Nevertheless, I continually trip across folks in our profession who shy like a wounded stag at the sight of an unfettered cosine.

To be fair, I find equal numbers of mathematicians who view computer programming as only slightly above and to the right of plumbing. They gripe about the wages that both programmers and plumbers command, but feel moved to learn about neither trade. Suggest to such mathematicians that computer science may be at times a real discipline, that it may have occasional brushes with elegance, and they glaze over. It's like arguing the relative merits of acid-core versus rosin-core solder at a wine tasting.

Programmers averse to mathematics display an assortment of irrational behaviors. An extreme case is the occasional programmer who will do anything to avoid an operation more elaborate than add, subtract, divide, or multiply. I once ran across a FORTRAN program that contained a loop that looked something like:

```
      X = -1
      Y = 0
      DO 10 J = 1, N
      X = X + 2
   10 Y = Y + X
```

It took me a moment or so to realize what was going on. This code meticulously sums the first N terms of the series 1, 3, 5, 7, 9, ... You don't need to know a lot of mathematics to notice that the results for increasing N form the series 1, 4, 9, 16, 25, ... Those are just the squares of N.

I pointed this out to the programmer, an undergraduate liberal arts major. He blanched when I expressed the result of the loop in terms of the FORTRAN power operator — N^2. When I told him he could also write this as $N*N$, he brightened a bit. That he could understand. Then he looked sad. Seems he had spent a whole evening working out this method of obtaining the desired result. He was reluctant not to make use of his wondrous discovery.

ow that is a feeling that I can sympathize with. One of the beauties of mathematics is that it is a rich source of happy insights. Sure, it's nice when you can discover something before anybody else. Newton and Gauss must have led enviable inner lives. But even us pedestrian explorers can delight in our finds. As old as they may be to others, they are new to us. I have learned to savor each *aha!* however shopworn the discovery later proves to be.

On the other hand, sometimes you just have to get a job done. In that case, your travel budget may not cover safaris into well-explored territory. If you're working for others, as is often the case, they have a right to expect you to know the basics. Few customers willingly and knowingly pay your tuition.

More commonly, programmers averse to understanding mathematics treat formulas as incantations. Copy the stuff out of a book, they figure, and you can't go wrong. Somehow, the computer will turn all those exponentials and logarithms into elliptical integrals, or catenary curves, or whatever the problem at hand demands from the world of mathematics. The magic spell must work right because it came out of the Big Book.

It doesn't take much experience with floating-point arithmetic, however, to develop second-degree burns. As an approximation to the set of real numbers, floating-point numbers fall a bit short. They can represent very large and very small values, at least compared to integers in a computer, but at a price. That price is finite precision. You soon learn all the ways, subtle and not-so-subtle, that finite precision can curdle the result of a calculation that looks straightforward in the world of pure mathematics.

I find it interesting that programmers adapt quickly to the finite range of integer variables. Sure, the world is full of programs that overflow in stupid places. But by and large, programmers accept the fact that counting much past a billion is chancy. The good ones develop an assortment of techniques for living within that fairly narrow range.

The same bunch of programmers become quite incensed, however, when their floating-point calculations sink. In this arena, they don't want to have to think. They just want useful answers delivered up in response to the appropriate magic spell.

more sensible attitude toward using math, as always, lies somewhere in the middle. Opportunities abound for you to use simple math to advantage in many of your programs. Hide from those opportunities and they don't wait around — they pass you by. You are left to write a brain-damaged program, or to rediscover on your own the law of cosines. And most of the time you *can* use the functions in the math library as incantations. They summon up the appropriate demons for you and deliver the result you desire.

You have to be alert only when the machinery supplied with your favorite programming language doesn't deliver the goods. Sometimes the formula you copied is so ill-behaved with finite-precision (or finite-range) arithmetic that it is worthless. You need to find an alternate way to compute the function that is safer, at least over the limited range you care about. More often, the functions from the math library work fine, thank you, but they eat computer time like candy. They're busy computing 53 bits worth of precision when all you need, or have time for, is 16 bits.

For those reasons, and others, I have found it useful over the years to accrete an assortment of techniques for approximating mathematical functions on a computer. I presented some of them in earlier essays. (See **Essay 5: Safe Math** and **Essay 6: Do-It-Yourself Math Functions**.) As you may have guessed by now, I intend to revisit that ground and share a few more of these techniques with you. I think you'll be surprised how often you can bend one or more of them to your needs, even in programs that don't appear to have much of a mathematical slant.

Some of the techniques are remarkably simple, despite the mathematical trappings. Even so, I use them to produce production-quality functions to add to math libraries for general use. I also use them to make quick-and-clean approximations for specialized needs within a given program. (Please notice that I did *not* say quick-and-dirty. I don't know about you, but I don't have time to write programs that fast.)

You may recall that I am trained as a physicist. A chemist once introduced me to her fellow graduate students as "one of those guys who knows the math." Well, sort of. Unfortunately, I share with many experimental physicists a very utilitarian attitude toward mathematics. Like amateur carpenters, we will use a chisel as a screw driver if that happens to get the job done. So don't look for elegant proofs in what follows.

Let's say, for openers, that you have a function that you need to compute over a given domain of input values and to a given precision of output values. The nastiest case is when the domain spans all representable floating-point values and the precision is the maximum that the floating-point representation can retain. That's what I call *production quality*. Even that extreme is not as hard to achieve as it sounds. With careful analysis and simple hygiene, you can easily keep a function sane over its entire domain (the range of input values over which it is defined). You can also retain all but the least-significant one or two bits of precision.

More likely, however, you can get by with considerably less than the maximum range and precision. That's even true within production code. You compute many functions only over a small range, then apply various (computationally safe) identities to derive answers for the rest of the range. You begin many computations with a fairly coarse approximation, then iterate to improve precision.

The square root function is a classic example that I have used before. To review briefly, it is defined for all non-negative values of its argument (call it **X**). It is also defined for negative values of **X**, but that gets you into the world of complex numbers. I choose to avoid that world for the moment. For all positive values of **X** that you can represent in floating-point, you can also represent the value of the function. That's because **SQRT(X)** lies between **X** and 1 for all positive nonzero values of **X**.

There's a way to compute the square root that loosely resembles doing long division. I learned it in high school, many years ago, then forced myself to relearn it in college. I haven't used it since. Isaac Newton developed a much more powerful, and more general, approach while he was mucking about inventing calculus.

. Newton's Method is an iterative technique that converges like crazy to the right answer. You simply guess an answer (call it **Y**), divide it into **X**, and average the quotient with **Y** to obtain a better guess. If **Y** is correct to N bits of precision, the newer **Y** is correct to about $2*N+1$ bits. Start out with a guess accurate to only six bits — less than two decimal digits of precision — and you get 13 bits, then 27, then 55, and so on. The widely-used IEEE 754 Standard for floating-point arithmetic represents double precision to 53 bits, or over 16 decimal digits. That means you can compute a double-precision square root with only three iterations of Newton's method. *Wow.*

The obvious way to write **SQRT**, then, is something like:

```
SQRT(X):
    IF (X < 0)
        <despair>
    ELSE IF (X == 0)
        RETURN (0)
    ELSE
        Y = <guess>
        WHILE (2⁻⁵³ < |Y - X*X|)
            Y = (Y + X / Y) / 2
        RETURN (Y)
```

Nobody with any sense does so, however. That test for convergence is a nuisance to compute. It is also a bit perilous if you are too demanding — the code can end up looping forever for some values of **X**. Better you should know the quality of your guess. Then you can simply iterate a fixed number of times and return whatever you get. Keep the number of iterations small enough and you can write them out in line, thus eliminating the loop as well.

Say you want to do the job in three iterations. Then you need to approximate **SQRT** to within six bits on your initial guess. That sounds almost as hard as writing the function in the first place. Well, it can be, unless you first solve a more restrictive problem.

ou need to know most modern computers represent a nonzero float-ing-point value as a binary fraction times two raised to some integer power. You can write a floating-point value **X** as **FRAC*2^{EXP}**, where **FRAC** is in the half-open interval [1/2, 1). (In other words, **1/2 <= X AND X < 1**.) That's certainly true for IEEE 754 format. Older encodings, proprietary to various hardware vendors, look enough like this that the differences are usually unimportant.

If you rip **X** apart to get at **FRAC** and **EXP** separately, you have two smaller problems to solve. (The programming language C comes with a function called **frexp** that peels a floating-point number apart just so.) Find the square root of each part and multiply the two results to get the final answer. It's easy to take the square root of **2^{EXP}**. If **EXP** is even, the result is simply **2$^{\text{EXP}/2}$**. If **EXP** is odd, the result is **SQRT(2)*2$^{(\text{EXP}-1)/2}$**. All that remains is to take the square root of **FRAC**, which lies on a much smaller interval than the original **X**. As you shall soon see, it's fairly easy to contrive a six-bit approximation to the square root between 1/2 and 1.

This is why I consider **SQRT** to be such a classic example. There are several ways to compute the function, but the more obvious ones are computationally naive. A little knowledge of a function's behavior, and the properties of floating-point representations, can gain you considerable leverage. You can arrive at computationally stable, and efficient, algorithms with a minimum of effort.

Of course, **SQRT** is not a perfect example, as I have emphasized before. Of all the functions in a given math library, this is the one you are most likely to use unmodified. It is typically the cleanest, stablest, fastest function of the lot. You might replace it only if you need *much* less than full precision. Or you might want a fixed-point version — where you pretend, say, that a 32-bit integer has ten bits to the right of the binary point to represent a limited range of fractional values. Or you might have a need for a cube root function. The technique is basically the same, but the iteration is messier:

```
Y = (2 * Y + X / (Y * Y)) / 3
```

et's get back to approximating the fraction. We have reduced computing the square root to the problem of approximating the function between 1/2 and 1. We know that once we get six bits of precision, we are only three iterations away from a full-precision result. All the rest of the **SQRT** function is simply testing, cutting, and pasting.

A very simple approach, at this point, is to make a very simple guess for **Y**. We know that the function value ranges smoothly between **SQRT(1/2)**, about 0.7071, and **SQRT(1)**, exactly 1. What if we split the difference and guess 0.85 initially? The result is not bad. You have more than two bits of accuracy, so it only takes a couple of extra iterations to get full double-precision accuracy.

You can do better, however. The equation for a straight line is:

```
Y = M * X + B
```

A well-chosen straight line should track the square-root curve over this interval much better than the simple guess `Y = 0.85`. That guess, after all, is just a horizontal straight line. By picking good values for **M** and **B**, we ought to get a much better starting guess for only a little more computation. If that saves us two iterations, it is well worth it.

We have our criterion for "well-chosen" or "good." It's whatever values of **M** and **B** minimize the number of iterations. That's not easily expressed mathematically, however. (It can be done, but it leads to a lot of work.) What we want is some criterion that comes close to the best-possible choice, but that leads to a simpler computation of **M** and **B**.

There is such a criterion. At each point along the X-axis we can draw a vertical line between the square root curve and our straight line approximation. Sometimes the vertical lines go up and sometimes they go down as the curve wiggles about the line. We could add up all these line lengths algebraically and insist they sum to zero. Unfortunately, that allows big swings below the curve to cancel big swings above, with no penalty for badness of fit.

You can penalize a bad fit simply by squaring the lengths of all the verticals and adding them up. Now you can't hope to get a zero sum — all the contributions are positive. Only an exact fit gives a zero sum-of-squares. But you *can* minimize the sum-of-squares deviations between the straight line and the curve you want to approximate well. That leads to the formula:

$$SUMSQ = SUM((M * X + B - X^{1/2})^2)$$

In this case, we are fitting a smooth function whose mathematical formula we know. The proper way to compute **SUM** is to integrate its argument over the interval in question (between 1/2 and 1). It turns out that all the integrals you have to evaluate here are easy ones:

$$SUMSQ = \int_{1/2}^{1} (M * X + B - X^{1/2})^2 \; dX$$

I was able to do them without using a table of integrals, despite the fact that I haven't had a calculus course since sometime before Lyndon Johnson was president.

Sometimes the function is not so nice as the square root, however. Or you may not even have a function — just a set of sample points that you know the function passes through. In either case, you can evaluate **SUM** by summing over a finite set of (X, Y) pairs (the points). Either way, you still apply the least-squares criterion.

You want to choose the values of **M** and **B** that minimize **SUMSQ**. Differential calculus tells you to differentiate **SUMSQ** with respect to each parameter and set the result to zero. You end up with two equations in two unknowns. The solution gives you the best values for **M** and **B**. (Strictly speaking, the solution to these equations may not even exist. But, unless you try to fit a straight line through a single point, or something equally stupid, you'll get what you're looking for.)

What's nice about this approach is that the equations you get are *linear* in **M** and **B**. They're the sort of equations you can solve even if you don't remember how to spell determinant. In this particular case, you get:

$$\mathbf{M} * \int_{1/2}^{1} \mathbf{X}^2 \, d\mathbf{X} + \mathbf{B} * \int_{1/2}^{1} \mathbf{X}^1 \, d\mathbf{X} = \int_{1/2}^{1} \mathbf{X}^{3/2} \, d\mathbf{X}$$

$$\mathbf{M} * \int_{1/2}^{1} \mathbf{X}^1 \, d\mathbf{X} + \mathbf{B} * \int_{1/2}^{1} \mathbf{X}^0 \, d\mathbf{X} = \int_{1/2}^{1} \mathbf{X}^{1/2} \, d\mathbf{X}$$

I intentionally wrote the left sides in all their silly generality so that you can see the pattern it follows. Skipping lots of steps, I present the final equation for the straight-line approximation to **SQRT(X)** between 1/2 and 1:

```
Y = 0.5823 * X + 0.4252
```

It varies between 0.7164 (where you'd like 0.7071) to 1.0075 (where you'd like 1.0000). In between, the line dips below the curve by a similar amount.

The purpose of this exercise was not to encourage all programmers to write their own square root functions. Far from it. If you didn't know what was going on under the hood before, you should have a greater respect for math functions by now. You should know to use what's there whenever possible. Chances are, the author of the math library has already devoted more energy to getting right answers than you have time to divert from what you *should* be doing.

Rather, I wanted to illustrate several useful techniques for doing your own approximations when you must. These include ripping floating-point numbers apart, pasting results together from separately-computed pieces, developing simple approximations by least-squares, and precomputing precision rather than testing for convergence. I have a few more techniques in my bag of tools, but this is a good sampler to start with. □

fterword: This essay and the next are companion pieces. (See **Essay 19: Economizing Polynomials.***) Not all programmers care about numerical programming at this level of detail. Nor should they. But then, not all programmers should care about parsing theory as much as many schools think they should. I figure a working programmer should be exposed to the basic techniques of numerical programming. I find they come in handy at least as often as parsing theory.*

19 Economizing Polynomials

𝕴n the previous essay, I began a discussion of mathematical techniques in programming. (See **Essay 18: Approximating Functions**.) I used computing the square root as an example of several techniques for evaluating functions safely, robustly, and accurately. The techniques include dismantling floating-point numbers, working on their pieces, and gluing the answer together at the end. That often reduces the problem to a smaller range, where it is relatively easy to approximate the function with something easier to compute.

I showed how you can approximate a function (the square root in this case) over a small range by a polynomial (a straight line in this case). You minimize the sum of the squares of the differences between the function and the polynomial to determine the "best" coefficients of the polynomial. The advantage of this technique is that you get **N** linear equations in **N** unknowns for a polynomial of order **N-1**. You can get coefficients that give a slightly better fit by other means, but they often involve considerably more work. The minimum-sum-of-squares approach does remarkably well for being so easy.

I continue in this essay with a few more techniques for calculating functions on a computer. They are more goodies from the bag of tricks I have accreted over several decades of programming. I know that few readers of this column are in the business of writing professional math libraries. It is not my intention to train more people for that elite (and limited) profession. Most of the current practitioners know more than I about the topic anyway. Rather, I want to pass on an assortment of techniques that I have found generally useful. Math creeps into programming in many subtle ways. The more comfortable you are with how to deal with it wisely, the less likely it is to scare you, lead you astray, or bite.

𝕻olynomials are extremely important in approximating functions because they wiggle so nicely. Given enough coefficients, you can write a polynomial that approximates just about any smooth function as closely as you'd like. The more coefficients, the higher the order of the polynomial. The higher the order, the more control you have over the shape of the curve.

Polynomials are also important for another reason. You can compute a polynomial **P (X)** for any **X** by a series of multiplies and adds. Computers can compare, negate, add, subtract, divide, and multiply floating-point numbers. A few have hardware instructions that let you rip numbers apart and put them back together the way I did for **SQRT**. A very few have hardware instructions that compute **SQRT** or (pieces of) the fancier functions such as **SIN** or **EXP**. As a rule, however, you should expect to reduce all function computations to the basic arithmetic operations.

Horner's Rule leads to a compact loop for evaluating a polynomial of order **N-1**:

```
I = N-1
P = C[I]
WHILE (0 < I)
    I = I - 1
    P = P * X + C[N]
```

Here, the coefficients of the polynomial are stored in **C[0]** through **C[N-1]**, and **C[I]** is the coefficient of x^I.

The DEC VAX has a **POLY** instruction that performs a loop very much like this — you need to store the coefficients in the reverse order. Even machines that lack such a nifty instruction perform this loop quite rapidly. Horner's Rule is suboptimal, in fact, only for machines that can perform several multiplies and adds in parallel. Other ways of expressing the polynomial evaluation lead to higher degrees of parallelism.

I use a function with a name like **POLY** only to evaluate polynomials of reasonably high order. For smaller polynomials, I prefer to write the expression out in-line, as in:

```
P = ((C3 * X + C2) * X + C1) * X + C0
```

That avoids the cost of a function call, which can be a measurable part of total execution time for many functions. It also exposes the expression to anybody who feels moved to rewrite it for better operation on a parallel architecture.

Of course, few of the basic functions in mathematics look like polynomials. Part of the reason why we have **SQRT, SIN**, and **EXP** is that each wiggles in its own unique way. And none of them wiggle like a polynomial, over the long haul. Another reason why we have **SQRT, SIN**, and **EXP** is that so many other functions can be expressed in terms of these and a few of their buddies. We can often build what we want by combining the basic functions, and polynomials, in the expressions that constitute much of our programs.

But that approach breaks down sometimes. The mathematical formula that looks fine on paper may take too long to compute. Or it may lose precision because it is full of almost equal terms that cancel, but not before destroying the smaller terms that matter. Or it may involve instabilities that cancel out mathematically but blow up on a computer. Forman Acton gave me my first serious exposure to numerical computation while I was at

Princeton. I still remember his favorite dictum — if you're *near* a singularity mathematically, you're *at* a singularity computationally. (See **Act70**.)

Here's where polynomials come to the rescue. They may not track an arbitrary function over a wide domain. Over a narrow enough domain, however, they can do just what you need. They are, in the bargain, numerically stable and easy to compute.

𝒶 great source of polynomial approximations in this sense is various infinite series. Consider a function that you want to compute in an interval around **X = 0**, for example. Unless it is particularly perverse, you can usefully expand it as a Taylor series about the origin. This yields a polynomial in **X** that contains all possible powers. You don't want to compute that, of course. Even on a Cray 2, evaluating an infinite series eats too much computer time. But it does make a good starting point for determining an adequate approximation.

There is a value of **X** (call it **A**) that is the largest value for which you wish to compute the function. All you care about is getting good answers for, say, the interval **-A <= X <= A**. (You can also write this as [**-A, A**].) Finally, there is some limit to the precision you can retain (call it **N** bits), given the floating-point representation on the computer you're using. There is no point in generating more than **N** bits — the extras just get dropped when you store the result.

Now inspect the coefficients of the Taylor series. For high enough powers of **X**, they'd better start getting smaller. Otherwise, the series describes a function that blows up rather impressively. Some functions do, the arctangent being a classic example. If that is the case, you're probably better off with a continued-fraction approximation or a ratio of polynomials. Nothing matches a function that blows up better than an approximation that flirts with division by zero.

For now, let's stick with tamer functions. You should know the value **YMAX**, which is the largest magnitude value that the function **Y** attains over [**-A, A**]. (Often it is **Y(A)**.) You need to identify the largest power of **X** that you need to keep to generate a respectable approximation to **Y(X)**. Discard all higher-order terms and you have a finite polynomial in **X**. If you have chosen your cutoff point wisely, you will obtain the same answers as the infinite series, only much sooner.

A simple technique usually gives a good-enough answer. Inspect higher-order terms in succession until their contributions to the sum begin to drop off. Then look for the first term that is small compared to the value of the function. By small, I mean:

$$LOG_2 (C[M] * X^M) - LOG_2 (YMAX) < -N$$

In English, the **M**-th term doesn't contribute to the high-order **N** bits of **YMAX**. If a term is right on the edge, you may want to keep it. Also, be particularly wary of a series whose successive terms alternate signs. (There are many of these.) You may have to consider pairs of adjacent terms to choose a wise cutoff point.

Let's revisit a concrete example. (See **Essay 6: Do-It-Yourself Math Functions**.) Say you want to compute the sine function, **SIN**. Yes, I know it's another questionable example, just like **SQRT**. Of all the functions you're likely to tackle, these two are very low on the list. You're almost invariably better off using a version written by a pro. Still, it is a function that many people know. And it nicely illustrates many useful principles.

The series representation we care about for sine starts out as:

$$Y = X - X^3/3! + X^5/5! - X^7/7! + \ldots$$

Those factorials in the denominators do a wonderful job of getting big fast. It's never long before they swamp out the growing powers of **X**, however big **X** gets. In this particular case, the news is even better. The largest value of **X** that you absolutely have to compute is $\pi/4$, or about 0.7854. Since that is less than one, higher powers of **X** also get steadily smaller. You can see why the sine is such a nifty candidate for a polynomial approximation based on its series expansions.

The trick, of course, is to avoid computing **SIN(X)** for $|X| > \pi/4$. Remember that sine and cosine are aptly named *circular* functions. They cycle through the same set of values repeatedly as **X** changes by 2π. And even over one cycle, both of these functions have additional symmetries. If you are also willing to compute **COS(X)** for $|X| < \pi/4$, it is easy to construct either **SIN** or **COS** for any **X**. (The series for **COS** is similar to that for **SIN**.) The result is always **SIN(X)** or **COS(X)**, possibly negated, for **X** reduced to this smaller angle.

The obvious way to reduce the angle is to subtract some multiple of $\pi/4$ from **X**. All but the low two bits of the multiplier are useless — they just count how many times **X** went around the circle. The low two bits determine the quadrant that **X** inhabits. Hence, it selects whether to compute **SIN** or **COS** and whether to negate the result. I won't bother to show the logic here. Unfortunately, the obvious way to reduce the angle is not the best way. Every time you add 2π to **X**, you push some fraction bits off the end. **SIN(X)** gets "grainier" as $|X|$ gets larger. For large enough $|X|$, no information remains about where you are within a quadrant, or possibly even around the circle. You'd think, therefore, that subtracting those multiples of 2π can't make matters any worse. But it can.

Unless you do a careful job of extracting the reduced angle, the function gets jerky as well as grainy. That can lead to surprising artifacts when you're computing lots of sines and cosines for related angles. I won't discuss the matter further here. I just wanted to warn you about a problem that people often overlook.

$\mathfrak{B}$ack to the series representation of **SIN(X)**. The largest value is assumes over the interval we care about is **SQRT(1/2)**, about 0.7071, at **SIN(π/4)**. The X^{15} term contributes at about bit 45, X^{17} contributes at about bit 54, and X^{19} contributes at about bit 63. If we want to compute a double-precision result on a modern computer that adheres to the IEEE 754 Standard, we need 53 bits of precision. We can certainly drop the last of these and all the terms that follow. The middle term is iffy. We certainly want to keep the X^{15} term.

We can, and should, rewrite the polynomial as **X*P(X^2)** to get rid of all those zero coefficients for even-powered terms. We then need an eighth-order polynomial in X^2 to get full precision over the entire range of interest. What's sad is that the last term or two are needed only for the largest argument values. The approximation is superb near the origin. All the error is concentrated out at the ends.

As you might expect, this is not the best way to approximate a function. The ideal is to pick an approximation that wiggles back and forth around the curve you want to fit. All wiggles should deviate by about the same (small) amount. There are techniques for finding such a curve that is ideal or nearly so. They can take a lot of work. It's too bad that the truncated power series does such a poor job because it takes so little work. Wouldn't it be nice if you could split the difference? Do just a little more work and get a more economical approximation.

You can. A technique called *economizing* starts with an adequate approximation to a function. It tells you how to eliminate one or more of the high-order terms and still keep an adequately precise fit. You basically smear the contribution of each of these higher-order terms over the lower-order ones. And you do so in a way that also smears the big error at the ends into smaller errors along the curve.

The trick is to express the polynomial in terms of Chebychev polynomials. (You can find several alternate spellings of Chebychev, depending on how folks translate Cyrillic letters to Roman. Tchebychev is one of them, which explains the common use of **T** to designate his polynomials.) The first few Chebychev polynomials, written T_i, are:

```
T₀ = 1
T₁ = X
T₂ = 2*X² - 1
T₃ = 4*X³ - 3*X
```

They have several important properties. First, they are orthogonal. You can express a polynomial of order **N** as a linear combination of the T_i up through T_N. Second, they wiggle nicely, at least over the interval [–1, 1]. T_N, in fact, passes through zero **N** times over that interval. Between zero crossings, every wiggle tops out at +1 or bottoms out at –1.

So let's see what we can do with the approximation to **SIN**. First, transform it to the interval $[-1, 1]$. Introduce the new variable $Z = (4/\pi) * X$. Then Z ranges over $[-1, 1]$ as X ranges over $[-\pi/4, \pi/4]$. The polynomial in X replaces each $1/N!$ with $(4/\pi)^N/N!$. Now we have entered the world of Chebychev polynomials.

Next, express the polynomial in Z is a linear combination of Chebychev polynomials. The first few powers of X are:

```
X⁰ = T₀
X¹ = T₁
X² = (T₀ + T₂)/2
X³ = (3*T₁ + T₃)/4
X⁴ = (3*T₀ + 4*T₂ + T₄)/8
```

For more on this topic, see R.W. Hamming's, *Numerical Methods for Scientists and Engineers*, (**Ham62**). Many authors endeavor to explain Chebychev polynomials. I've yet to find one that beats this master explainer at his best. He shows you how to construct all the tables you need to economize polynomials of any order.

You now have a set of coefficients for the various T_i. Those powers of two in the denominators above ensure that the high-order coefficients drop off rapidly. It turns out, in fact, that you can approximate **SIN** to our self-inflicted standards with just the polynomials through T_5. You can translate that back to a polynomial in X over the interval $[-\pi/4, \pi/4]$. You end up with a fifth-order polynomial that is an adequate approximation to the eighth-order one we started out with.

That's only part of the good news. Think what happens when you drop that linear combination of T_6 through T_8. Each of the T is a curve that wiggles uniformly about zero. Multiply it by a small coefficient and it represents a small but uniform wiggle about zero. The terms that you drop represent the error between the initial and final approximations. So the error you introduce in discarding the higher-order contributions is a small error that wiggles roughly uniformly about the desired curve. That was what we were looking for.

The errors are not perfectly uniform, of course. We made a transformation of coordinates and threw away more than one term. Both introduce small distortions in the wiggles. But the solution is quite good, thank you. It is almost as good as the best job you can do with considerably more work.

For the record, here are the coefficients of the polynomial approximation to **SIN** over the interval $[-\pi/4, \pi/4]$:

```
C[0] =  0.99999 99999 99999 99953
C[1] = -0.16666 66666 66671 27453
C[2] =  0.00833 33333 33333 37205
C[3] = -0.00019 84126 98315 81921
```

```
C[4]  =   0.00000 27557 31921 88977
C[5]  =  -0.00000 00250 52617 59934
C[6]  =   0.00000 00001 60592 57791
```

These coefficients differ only slightly from $1/N!$ for odd values of **N**. That small differences makes all the difference, however. I computed these by writing a script for the UNIX utility dc. It is not a program. It contains no loops or tests. I simply constructed all the keystrokes needed to get dc to compute these coefficients to 20 decimal places.

It was an easy matter to edit the script to do the same job for **COS**. I put the whole works together and verified that the approximation is indeed adequate even at multiples of $\pi/4$.

I conclude with my repeated reminder. I don't encourage you to write your own **SIN** and **COS** functions. Use the ones in the library of your favorite programming language. If you find the need for a polynomial approximation, however, you can see the steps involved. Find a series approximation that converges. Determine where it's safe to truncate the series. Then economize it to get a smaller polynomial with better error properties.

I can't say it's a breeze, but it certainly isn't very hard. For some of us, it's almost fun. □

Afterword: I confess to an ulterior motive in writing this essay and the previous one. It took me a long time to gather the information presented here. It took even longer to understand it well enough to use it. I wanted to see if I could explain it in such a way that someone else could pick up the material much faster. For those with a pragmatic bent (like me), I think I succeeded. For those with more of a mathematical bent, however, I suspect that this presentation is annoyingly and hopelessly colloquial.

I had an additional motivation. When I wrote The Standard C Library *(Pla92), I needed approximations to a number of math functions. I was distressed to learn that not all publishers were quick to grant the rights I needed to coefficients listed in their books. At the eleventh hour, I found myself generating my own, using the techniques outlined here. Sometimes economics is more fundamental than mathematics.*

20 Technical Writing

I like to explain things. That much should be obvious by now. Over the past five years, I have written a couple of books and well over a hundred essays like this one for various trade publications. I have been known to give the odd seminar as well.

Fortunately for me, my technical passions have come into vogue these past few years. Not only do I get to prattle about topics I love, I get decent compensation for my efforts. That encourages me to write and speak still more. I even make a point of picking up a new fact from time to time, to avoid being completely repetitious.

I understand that not all technical types like to explain things. I have known programmers who bravely face a 250-kilobyte core image at three in the morning. They don't flinch at chasing an intermittent bug, while armed only with a hexadecimal calculator and a cup of coffee. Yet those same programmers blanch when told to write two paragraphs describing how a module works.

The problem is partly one of practice. Many of the technical types I have hired over the years — and even more of the non-technical ones — could barely paste sentences together. They were bright, or I wouldn't have hired them. Forced to write regular reports and odd bits of documentation, most of these people got steadily better. A few hundred more hours of writing assignments in high school and college would have made all the difference.

I don't pretend that writing is easy. I became a writer because I love to *have written*. Doing the actual writing often comes hard, even after the million-odd words I've published since leaving school. Occasionally I get caught up in a topic. Several hours and several thousand words later, I notice that I missed lunch. Such moments of passionate engagement are a delight, but sadly rare. Writing is easier than digging coal, at least to me, but it is no snap.

This essay could easily degenerate into a harangue about the state of education in America. I believe that education can and should be better for a host of reasons. But I do not believe that we can train masses of people to write with ease. We can teach grammar, discipline, and critical thought. Writing gets better with practice, but not necessarily easier. For many of us, it never gets close to effortless.

My concern for now is somewhat narrower. I want to address the business of technical documentation. That is a fairly stylized genre that is well within the reach of anyone with a technical education. Or at least it should be. I'm not talking Pulitzer Prize material here. I'm talking about the straightforward narration needed to describe a technical topic simply and clearly.

I confess to a vested interest in improving this form of literacy. For one thing, I edit about a hundred articles a year for one publication or another. It sure would be nice if the techies who write those articles stopped making the same mistakes over and over. My fellow copy editors and I would welcome even a decrease in the frequency of barbarisms.

For another thing, I buy software and textbooks along with all the rest of you out there. Don't think I'm any better than you are at re-hanging a dangling participle to resolve an ambiguity. Particularly not when I'm trying to figure out how to rescue three-hours' work before I dare turn off the machine. I thrive on simple explanations and clear directions.

I also confess to having committed my share of sins against the English language. I look back at my earlier writing and occasionally cringe. As my own best fan, I delight in much of it. But as my own worst critic, I see all sorts of places where it could and should have been made clearer.

Several years ago, my company got a contract from IBM to overhaul one of our compilers to their specifications. I took on the task of rewriting the documentation. They presented us with this style guide that I found absolutely asinine. It called for prose written to an eighth-grade reading level. It disallowed parenthetic remarks, passive voice, phrases that begin with "e.g." or "i.e.", and numerous other useful constructs.

I tackled the job with teeth clenched. I'd show them that I could write that way, however silly the final product. I shipped off the first 50 pages and got it back dripping with copy corrections. Seems I had missed the intent of some of the rules. A few iterations later, I learned the art of sliding stuff past the IBM copy editors. Eventually, I finished the rewrite.

Along the way, however, something magical happened. I began to *appreciate* most of the silly rules laid down by IBM. They began to make sense. My writing got less highfalutin and easier to read. Even more surprising, the resultant manual was the most usable one I had produced to date. I could actually *find* things in it on the first try, and understand those things on the first reading. (Yes, I use my own manuals and textbooks for reference. I can't remember everything.)

As a writer with a success or two under my belt, I did not take kindly to criticism, constructive or otherwise. As a confirmed gadfly, I still do not like to concede that corporate dogma can ever be a good thing. As a speaker/entertainer, I get more mileage out of zinging IBM than praising such a big and bright blue target. Please don't spread it around too much that I found an occasion when they were right.

I said earlier that a lack of practice was *part* of the reason for bad writing, technical or otherwise. With technical documentation, another factor looms at least as large. Seems most of us were actively taught in school to write badly.

If it's clear writing, there must be something wrong with it. Make a direct statement and you're more likely to be challenged. Never use first person, lest you be accused of bragging or not sharing credit properly.

Believe those rules (and their inevitable companions) and you will write verbal Jello. It will be shapeless and semi-opaque. Try to pin it down and it will quiver. Seek nourishment in it and you will surely hunger within the hour. Anything substantial you mix in gets lost, like the tasty bits in an aspic.

Having worked that metaphor to death, I will now essay some positive advice. What follows is my personal guide to writing clearer technical documentation. As is my custom, I present the material in terms of a handful of principles. Most of them rehash what everybody else says, but with critical differences. As is also my custom, I put a top spin on each. The trick, of course, is to rescue the principles from being mere platitudes. And to encourage you to keep your eye on the ball.

Principle: **Qualify your writing, not your audience.** Everybody tells you to begin a technical document by outlining the qualifications you expect of your audience. That's basically the right idea. You need to make clear what prerequisites you assume on the part of the reader. You need to define some starting point. You can't begin every document assuming that the Earth is without form, and void. (The writer who did that first has *much* better credentials than you or I.)

What you have to be on the alert for is condescension. A reader may not know the intricacies of a given technical field and still be quite intelligent. Assume that is the case. Avoid smiley faces and stick figures inserting diskettes in the drive right way 'round. (Show the diskette properly oriented, ditch the stick figure.) Never confuse ignorance with stupidity, lest you be shown up as the stupid one.

Beginners may not be stupid but they are often insecure. That means you must be alert for obscure jargon and incomplete explanations. Try to remember *everything* you do when performing a given operation. Spell it out. Let an innocent test drive your documentation. (That only works once with a given subject, sadly. Such is the fleeting nature of innocence.) Nothing reassures better than clear and complete instructions.

I state the qualification principle backwards for another reason as well. You can expect people of all levels of ability to read what you write. Tell them where you're coming from and they can adapt. The unqualified will more quickly forgive when you aim over their heads. The overqualified will be more patient of your detailed explanations.

Fail to qualify your writing properly, however, and you win no sympathy. Each reader calibrates you by a separate set of standards. Only those whom you reach at just the right point in their personal development will be happy. That's a narrow audience to count on.

Principle: **Build a skeleton for your presentation, not just an outline.** Your high-school English teacher probably taught you to outline everything before you write it. If you're like me, you probably wrote the outline to hand in *after* you wrote the essay. In extremis, you outline an occasional large document. Most of the time you wing it.

Well, I'm here to confess that I outline more and more as I get older. Any serious technical document has to have a clear notion of where it's going and how it's going to get there. If that is not clear from the table of contents and the introduction, expect your readers to get lost frequently.

I make one major concession to my intrinsic laziness. I outline absolutely no more than I must in order to stay on track. For this essay, I got everything on one of those little yellow Post It notes. (How did the pioneers ever cross the plains without them?) For a heavyweight manual or book, I write an outline that varies between two and six levels deep. (Some subtopics lend themselves to structuring much better than others.)

Another concession I make is to deviate from pure outline form whenever I choose. Like block-structured code, a neatly indented outline has a seductive order about it. But both disciplines break down from time time to time. You should be ready to adopt other forms when that happens.

One of my favorites is the two-dimensional grid. If I want to say the same sorts of things about a list of related topics, I've got the grid labeled right off the bat. An example is my book, *The Standard C Library* (**Pla92**). It contains a separate chapter for each of the fifteen standard headers in C, plus an introductory overview. Each chapter has the same subsections: background, quotes from the C Standard, advice on usage, code to implement the functions in the header, how to test the code, references, and exercises. The chapters vary from eight to over 100 pages, but the structure works fine for all of them.

Another good structure is the spiral. You can introduce a difficult topic by first touching all its aspects in broad overview. Then revisit these aspects in greater detail. Then revisit them again in all their intricate glory. Each time around the spiral you climb one level of sophistication. A good tutorial often follows such a path.

Whatever structure you use, make it sufficiently visible to serve as a guide both to you and the reader. You are building a skeleton, the bones on which to hang all the meat. Do it right and you know exactly where to put each concept. Each has one right place. Not only that, your reader knows where to look to find each concept. That beats a 40-page index every time.

Principle: **Define your jargon early, then stick with it.** Here is a rare place where the poets cause more trouble than the pedants. We all know how boring it is to say the same thing the same way over and over again. We are all taught to vary our sentence structure, our word order, our choice of phrasing. That's fine if your goal is to entertain with the written word. If your goal is to write good technical prose, it stinks.

One of the few things that distinguishes technical writing is the need for exquisite precision. You don't say it almost right, you say it *exactly* right. Elegance and precision both demand that you define an economy of terms and use them religiously. Variety is best left to fashion magazines.

People assume that jargon is the bane of technical writing. Not so. That caveat applies only to *obscure* jargon. Your goal is to develop an appropriate jargon for whatever you write. Define it clearly. Then reinforce each definition by using your terms repeatedly and consistently.

When I write about high-level languages, for example, I tune my jargon to the particular topic. If I am describing a particular compiler, then I consistently talk about "compiling source files and linking them with the library to produce an executable file." If I am describing the same language in general terms, then I talk about "translating source to executable form." You will find no mention of generic source in the former, no mention of source files in the latter. Get the idea?

This is often an iterative process. You start out writing from one human being to another. Hit a concept with subtle technical implications and the techie takes over. Create a term for the concept. Define that term precisely and use it ever after. If you find a need to refine the term, go back and look at every use of the term you have indulged in so far. Push the refinement back as early as you can. Make sure that all uses agree with your refined meaning.

For a large enough document, don't hesitate to build a glossary. Use it yourself to stay consistent. Publish it as part of the document if you can. Omit it only if it appears wholly inappropriate.

Principle: **Use the active voice to give blame where blame is due.** Everybody tells you to write in the active voice. Such writing, those anonymous bodies say, is more direct and forceful. While I have no quarrel with that sentiment, I can't endorse it as a justification for hamstringing your technical writing style. You need a more compelling reason.

We all know why the passive voice has been adopted. It obscures what was done by whoever it was who may have done it. It leaves nobody to blame for whatever has been said.

I prefer to commit sins of omission. I will tell you that I did something even if it annoys you that I claim credit for it. I will even avoid secondary passives as much as possible. Look at the previous paragraph. Every sentence apparently begins with a subject and a strong verb. Yet every sentence contains a passive construct. Blame me for the ambiguity.

There's an even more important reason to avoid passive constructs. Just as you need jargon in technical writing, you need active agents. Who writes the program? Who translates it to executable code? Who executes that code? If you say the program is written, then translated, and then gets executed, how is the poor novice ever to guess?

Now introduce a few active agents. You write the program. The compiler translates the program to executable form. The computer executes your program (or the program executes). Now we know whom to blame at each stage. Find a passive construct and ask yourself whodunit. Rewrite the passive with the agent as the subject of an active verb and your descriptions suddenly get clearer.

I still indulge in the passive voice from time to time (just as I can't resist an occasional parenthetic remark). I use it when I really do want to obscure the active agent. Perhaps one of three different agents can be acting. I said so earlier and you probably still remember what I said. I don't want to repeat the list of three agents for precision. So I just let the action happen. Still, I try not to be vague by accident.

Principle: **Write to be understood, not admired.** Some people write like English majors. Some people write like newspaper reporters. I was fortunate. At the tender age of 17, I was taught to write like a chameleon. Between the Princeton English department and the Princeton University Press Club, I was forced to master a dozen different writing styles. Between my penchant for partying and New Jersey weather, I was forced to write quickly, even while hung over, even in the rain.

As a result, my heroes are the writers who express themselves clearly with an economy of prose. They include Ernest Hemingway (fiction), Isaac Asimov (nonfiction), and C.S. Forester (both). I can admire Roger Zelazny for his erudition and verbal gymnastics, but I have little desire to emulate him. (Well, maybe just a little.)

My experience with technical writing reinforces that early training. You are trying to communicate ideas that are often complex and subtle. You don't want the words to stand between the ideas and the reader. Rather, you want to write what is called *transparent prose.* You don't see the words slide by until well after the ideas have lodged firmly in your brain.

One way to achieve transparent prose is to imitate spoken language. In graduate school, I somehow developed the reputation as the writing consultant in residence to my fellow graduate students. (Maybe it was the gracious arrogance that I affected so demurely.) People would repeatedly come to me for help in phrasing a sentence properly.

Every time I would ask, "What is it you want to say?" Every time they would tell me in words simple and to the point. Every time I would reply, "Then why don't you write down what you just said?" Every time my reply came as a mini revelation.

Naturally, I use this technique on myself. On those rare occasions where it draws a blank, I fall back on the surest technique of all. I get angry (at myself, in this case). Ever notice how eloquent you become when you're really teed off? You can hold your focus and make your points with undeflectable zeal. Harness this energy and you can say anything.

The hardest application of this principle I save for last. Every once in awhile, you emit a phrase or a paragraph that seems to have a life of its own. It has just that mix of aptness and cleverness you wish you could pull off all the time. When you write stuff like that, swallow hard and throw it away. Two months later, you will recognize it for the irrelevant purple prose it really is.

Principle: **Use writing-analysis software, but don't trust it.** I'm always on the lookout for software that will really help me as a writer. I was once a good speller and an adequate typist, but the liters of gin and tonic have taken their toll. Now when I get a word wrong in my head, it sticks there for years on end. (My current bugaboos are *concensus* for spelling and *funciton* for typing.) I have thus learned to be more accepting of spelling checkers.

I also buy almost every grammar and style checker that comes along. Sometimes they give good advice. Sometimes they are off the wall. I figure they are always worth a check to see how I stack up against the more popular rules of the trade. After all, I do fancy myself a professional writer these days.

But I have one final confession to make. I run all these programs repeatedly and ignore most of what they have to say. Spelling checkers catch about one error in ten thousand words for me. They produce about fifty "false positives" in the same stretch of code. It's tedious to wade through the trash for that one gem of genuine garbage.

I also refuse to trust that these programs tell me everything. Use the wrong word (spelled properly) and they won't notice. Mistype one word to look like another and they are equally blind. Don't forget to check for the "false negatives" as well.

Similarly, grammar checkers mostly tell me when I'm being colloquial or when I've written a sentence fragment. My usual response is, "Thanks for sharing, but I already knew that." What I watch the closest is the various measures of reading level and complexity. If my sentences start getting too long, the numbers go up. I go back and chop until the metrics come down.

I intentionally favor a style with many short sentences. It seems to help get points across.

If you share my overweening pride and self-confidence, you can treat such software the same way. If, on the other hand, you find writing more of a chore, listen to what they have to say. Like those silly IBM guidelines, much of their advice seems artificial and pedantic, but it does help. Once you find yourself repeatedly saying "Thanks for sharing," you know they've inadvertently taught you how to write better technical prose. □

Afterword: This was one of my more successful essays. More than one person has told me that it has become an informal writing guide within some technical enterprise or other. I also enjoyed writing it. A final confession, however. I produce spelling errors at a much higher rate now than I reported here. Either I was deluding myself then or my brain has decayed further in the interim. I suspect that both conjectures are true. At any rate, I now use spell checkers and other writing aids religiously.

21 All I Want to Do Is

They say that necessity is the mother of invention. That may be so, but I know who the father is. He's the guy who begins some conversation with those fateful words, "Look, all I want to do is ..."

No, I'm not talking about disingenuous seduction. That's the stuff of novels and short stories. The fictitious guy I'm describing here has his mind elsewhere. He has some problem he wants solved. He also has some partially baked notion about how to solve it. He is trying to rally assistance in implementing his solution.

Why is he rallying assistance? Probably because the thing he needs changed is too big for him to change by himself. Or it is a thing that is used by others who must also consent to the change. In our business, that "thing" is often a large piece of software. Or it may be a standard specification for a programming language or an operating system.

All I want to do is add this one small feature. I know just how I want to use it. I don't care if it does anything else useful at all. How about it, folks?

The trouble with that approach is that it is single minded. Tinker with a complex system and you introduce all sorts of surprises. The less concerned you are with the secondary ramifications of a change, the more likely those ramifications will be disastrous.

There's a difference between "all I want to do" and "all I have to do." The latter finishes the job. It deals with important concerns such as orthogonality, completeness, and consistency. It addresses that elusive concept called elegance.

One small change probably won't break a system, however poorly it is integrated into the whole. Keep adding such small changes, however, and they soon add up. You get a system that surprises at every turn. It gets progressively harder to make each new change. It suffers a form of hardening of the arteries.

A particularly atherosclerotic system is the nroff/troff typesetting package that grew up under UNIX. It is still a powerful workhorse, in use at sites all over the world. But it can be a challenge to use, chock full of surprises.

My colleague and office mate when I was at the University of New South Wales was Professor John Lions. He's the bloke who turned the source code of the UNIX V6 kernel into a readable study guide. He actually taught an operating systems course by exposing students to a real, working operating system. Even in 1977, he had this to say about the document-formatting software that came with UNIX:

The co-operation of the nroff program must also be mentioned. Without it, these notes could never have been produced in this form. However, it has yielded some of its more enigmatic secrets so reluctantly, that the author's gratitude is indeed mixed. Certainly nroff itself must provide a fertile field for future practitioners of the program documenter's art.

I know some programmers who would have put that less politely.

It was such a beautiful baby. Brian Kernighan, I am told, conceived the first runoff program while in graduate school at Princeton. He began by saying, "All I want to do is punch text on computer cards in free form. The computer should be able to reformat that input to look good on the printed page."

Thus was born roff, the granddaddy of many modern document formatters. Of course, Brian couldn't do exactly what he purportedly said in the previous paragraph. In those days, common keypunches punched only upper case letters. The program had to guess where each sentence started. It would leave the first letter upper case, then force remaining letters to lower case. Brian had to add special escape sequences to signal exceptions to this rule.

He also had to add additional markup. There's more to formatting a document than squaring up the right sides of paragraphs. Brian wired in an assortment of formatting commands, each signaled by a line beginning with a funny character. (Traditionally, it is a dot.) To the best of my knowledge, Kernighan invented the concept of a document markup language. If he didn't, he refined the concept better than anybody else I know.

It was Joe Osanna at Bell Labs who decided to soup up roff for UNIX. He liked the markup notation but found it too restrictive. He said, "All I want to do is make it possible for people to define their own markup commands in terms of the existing ones." That meant adding macros to roff to make a "new roff." Hence nroff.

It's easy enough to add macros, providing you're not too ambitious. Add a command that names the macro and signals the start of its definition. Add another that signals the end of the definition. Everything in between gets memorized. Name the macro later and the definition gets played back.

But what if you want macros that accept arguments like some of the existing formatting commands? Then you have to invent a set of escape sequences to name the arguments within the definition. Each escape sequence gets replaced by its argument definition when the definition is played back.

But then what happens if an argument can contain macros that need expanding? You need rules for when the expansion occurs. It can happen once, before the definition starts playing back. It can happen each time the corresponding escape sequence pops up during play back. Whichever way you decide can make sense. But you get different languages, with quite different properties, depending on how you choose.

If you're ambitious (and Joe always was), you'll want to add conditional expressions. Depending on how a test turns out, the playback includes different chunks of definition. That leads to some pretty powerful macros. If you also allow recursive calls on the same macro, you have most of the trappings of a serious programming language. It's not always very readable, but it's potential power is impressive. Given enough aspirin, you can rule the world.

Joe did all this and one thing more. He added the capability to divert the output of the formatter into a macro definition. I suspect someone came to him and said, "Look, all I want to do is write my footnotes directly in line. When you get to the bottom of the page, dump 'em out." Sounds neat. Until you deal with footnotes formatted by different rules than the running text. And footnotes that don't all fit on the current page. And so forth, and so forth.

I have no idea how many mortals have written footnote processors for nroff. I happen to be one of them. Getting all that nonsense to come out right is a real challenge. It also invokes a heck of a lot more machinery than Brian Kernighan ever stuffed into roff.

And it leads to further design decisions. You can find yourself writing macros that define macros. Great. Then how do you include an argument escape sequence within such a nested definition? You need to escape escapes. Guess wrong on the notation and you have a programming nightmare. An early text editor written by Dennis Ritchie had powers comparable to nroff. But you had to write 2^{N-1} escapes to defer processing of an escape sequence $N-1$ times. I wrote editor scripts that sometimes had fifteen escape sequences in a row!

Joe got that part mostly right. The biggest problem with macros in nroff was the power they accreted over the years. Combine terse notation with the power to cloud people's minds and you have a debugger's nightmare. Imagine staying up half the night finding bugs in a program transliterated, without comments, from APL to C. Get the idea?

The second biggest problem with nroff was the irregularity that is intrinsic to document formatting. For example, most of the time you want to suppress any blank lines that occur at the top of a page. Except when you don't. I never did figure out a reliable recipe for telling nroff when to keep such space. And that is one of perhaps two dozen such issues.

Mike Lesk and a few others eventually hammered out a set of standard macros that tamed nroff. Mostly. You could hide behind them and avoid the raw power of the underlying machinery. We were just getting comfortable with using them, in fact, when the world of computer typesetting dawned.

Naturally, somebody said something like, "Look, all I want to do is take my nroff documents and typeset them unchanged." And naturally, Joe Osanna rose to the challenge. Thus was born the "typesetting roff," or troff. (Eventually, these two distinct programs were brought back together. The current instantiation, written in C, is called nroff/troff, among other things.)

After a decade of ten-point Courier, the switch to ten-point Times Roman was a real improvement. It was a proportionately spaced font that gave documents a real typeset look. And many existing nroff documents did, indeed, typeset well unchanged. The biggest problem was the occasional table whose layout depended upon all characters having the same width. Smarter tab stops fixed that.

But of course, that was *not* all we wanted to do. Even the earliest typesetters held multiple type faces. You could display them in multiple font sizes. Everybody wanted to produce documents that used more than one font.

Most of the machinery was already in nroff. Joe added a richer set of escape sequences to specify fonts and funny characters. He wired in an nroff/troff switch that let you write smart macros. You could have the same macro mean one thing when speaking nroff to a conventional printer. It meant something similar, but smarter, when speaking troff to a typesetter. People became wise in the ways of writing documents that both printed and typeset well.

Still, that machinery began to strain in many small ways. Remember the underlying model. You feed in mostly free-form text. The program makes various intelligent guesses about how to rewrite it to print prettier. You intersperse occasional markup. The program executes builtin commands and defined macros to augment the intelligent guesses. You also divert occasional chunks of formatted text from the printer into macro definitions. Later, the program is expected to eat this refried text and like it.

In the case of nroff, refried text differs little from the original. Printers eat much the same characters that terminals produce and consume. The set may be a bit richer, but it still fits in an eight-bit byte. The text may also take its interspersed white space more seriously. But that is not such a big difference either. Occasionally, you tell nroff to honor the spacing in the input text anyway. (This is "no fill" mode.)

In the case of troff, however, the output is much richer than the input. Each character has an associated type face and point size. The spacing between characters is no longer some integral number of space characters. This is not the sort of thing you want to divert into a macro for later reconsideration.

Whatever the program diverts into a macro, it must be palatable as typed input. It must also capture various aspects of how it should appear when emitted to a typesetter. That leads to some nasty encoding decisions within nroff/troff. Those decisions shine through to the user in various ways. They determine the conceptual model that you must understand to program macros correctly.

It is a tribute to Joe Osanna that he got this beast working at all. It is a greater tribute that he improved it over a period of years to make it useful for an ever-growing constituency. Brian Kernighan and I typeset our first few books using troff. As pioneers, we relied heavily on Joe's responsiveness. We weren't disappointed.

When Joe died, Brian inherited nroff/troff for a spell. What he found inside that program was a classic case of hardening of the arteries. Too much had been done for too many different reasons over too long a period.

Here is an example. One of the neat things that a good type face gives you is a set of ligatures. These are groups of letters mushed together to look prettier. Common ligatures are "fi," "fl," and "ffl." You will find them more often in the older type faces than in the newer ones. (Such is progress.) Naturally, Joe taught troff how to look for ligatures automatically in text to be typeset. The program replaces each one with a funny internal code that typesets appropriately. You can, of course, turn this machinery off if you are a Philistine.

The tough design decision is where in the processing of text to introduce ligatures. Do it too early and you corrupt text that might not be destined for the printed page. Do it too late and you might miss opportunities to recognize ligatures. It's a hard enough decision to make to a newly specified program. Retrofitting it to existing code is much harder.

What Brian found inside nroff/troff was revealing. The main loop for processing markup commands had some funny code in it. First it memorized the current state of ligature processing. Then it turned such processing off. Only then did it eat a line and process it as a command. When it was done, it reverted ligature processing to the appropriate state. (That state might change as a result of executing the command, of course.)

You can guess why. The ligature filter was obviously inserted upstream from the command processor. A "fill" command, written as `.fi`, gets turned into a ligature before it can be recognized. The machinery has to be temporarily shut down for each command.

I don't pretend that this state of affairs is anything less than horrid. I used to cite it as a classic case of bad program design. That was years ago, before I watched some of my own code silt up. Now I'm more understanding. Bad as it is to process ligatures in the wrong place, I can forgive Joe for doing so. He knew better than anybody what sort of compromises were necessary to do the job at all. Everyone around him was busy starting sentences with, "Look, Joe, all I want to do is ..." Few cared what he had to do to make it work.

Kernighan once said, "Look, all I want to do is typeset equations simply. Let me describe what they look like instead of trying to parse what mathematicians insist on saying about them." He went on to invent the eqn language, which was an instant and lasting hit. Ventura Publisher has adopted it almost intact for their equation-setting markup. (I've yet to find any credit given to Brian in any of their documentation, however.)

Brian's implementation of eqn was as a preprocessor that filters troff input. It spots equations, eats them, and spits out the most astonishing troff-ish critters you are likely ever to see. Seeing all those macro expansions squirming about in eqn output is like lifting a rock in moist soil. Again, it is a tribute to the willing beast called troff that it will eat such worms. Just to make life easier for those of us who must typeset the occasional equation.

Mike Lesk did a similar thing for typesetting tables. I'm sure that tbl also evolved from somebody saying, "All I want to do is typeset tables without a lot of hassle." It too utters troff obscenities behind your back to get the job done. And table formatting has also become one of those specialized add-ons to modern typesetting packages.

Those modern typesetting packages are pretty impressive. They have menu-driven command input, WYSIWYG displays, and output drivers for a gazillion different printers. They are generally easier to use than nroff/troff, with fewer surprises. (Note: I said *generally.*) But they are also weaker than nroff/troff in important ways. Few endeavor to provide the powerful macro capabilities that gave the older package its flexibility. Instead, the newer packages wire in the successful machinery built atop nroff/troff. What you don't see, you can't get.

I have rambled back and forth between history (as I saw it) and design issues. In case the critical points got lost, let me summarize:

- Users tend to be single-minded in asking for what they want. They are indifferent to the need for elegance — until they later get bitten by its lack.
- Programs silt up with change. The cleaner you make them up front, the longer they last. Even the best of programs eventually loses its elasticity, however.

■ The people who write the programs that are popular today love to chortle over the errors made by their predecessors. They quietly imitate their successes. But don't worry about the apparent lack of justice. Their day will come. □

Afterword: My original intentions in writing this essay were much more ambitious. I was going to start with nroff/troff, then go on to various aspects of programming-language design. I soon found, however, that I had more than enough to say just about document formatting. I also felt it important to recite in one place the history of these programs. Both Kernighan and Osanna have been slighted more than once by the very people who have profited most from their pioneering work in this area.

The overarching lesson here is one of caution. By all means, listen to your customers. But don't think you can simply give them what they want. Wherever possible, give them what they need instead.

22 Programming for the Billions

$\mathfrak{I}$ have been fretting about portability almost since the day I began programming computers. In the early 1960s, computers tended to be large, expensive, and manufactured by IBM. I often found it necessary to run the same FORTRAN programs on several different machines, if only to dodge the regular operators and do what I wanted. I quickly saw the advantage of producing card decks that could move unchanged from one IBM FORTRAN environment to another.

Nevertheless, I couldn't succeed in producing a universal card deck. I won't repeat all the reasons why. See my essay, "Standard C: Evolution of the C I/O Model," in *The C Users Journal* (**Pla89**) if you care. That goes into the gory details a bit more.

Portability was hardly a big market issue in those days. Quite the contrary. Each major computer vendor did its best to lock you into its particular flavor of hardware and software. Those were the days of FORTRAN IV PLUS, FORTRAN V, Extended FORTRAN, and other contrived dialects. It was hard to avoid the trap of using the cute little extras. It was harder still to climb out of the trap when a different vendor came along with faster and cheaper hardware.

UNIX and C were born in the early 1970s. Both have done more to support portable software than any other single factor I can name. Nevertheless, neither was put forth originally as an aid to portability. Each solved some neat little design issues on DEC minicomputers. Each was a boon to serious programmers. That UNIX and C both surpassed their particular origins is a tribute to the insights of Ken Thompson and Dennis Ritchie. It was not in their original business plan.

I started my company, Whitesmiths, Ltd., in the late 1970s. I did so because I believed in UNIX and C as vehicles for hosting and writing more broadly usable code. At the time, AT&T was limited in its ability to sell commercial software. For a time, interest and opportunity merged for me. I spent a decade with Whitesmiths writing and selling numerous C compilers and the occasional Idris (UNIX-compatible) operating system.

I was almost fanatical about writing portable code. Exactly the same C source files went into the software we sold to run on a Z80 or a DEC VAX. We had layered libraries, the bulk written in portable C. Under that came system-specific functions, usually written in nonportable C. At the bottom lay an irreducible minimum of assembly language for each target system.

We could thus move the C compiler, or even the Idris operating system, with remarkably little work.

A small fraction of our customer base appreciated this support for machine-independent programming. They had products that had to run on two or more platforms. They were happy they could buy compatible products from a single vendor. They were willing to code for the common denominator to get a greater degree of portability.

Most of our customers, however, were at best indifferent. They wanted our products on their favorite system. If we could keep the price down by moving portable code, fine. If we kept the features down by avoiding nonportable code, not so fine. They wanted access to the peculiar features of their favorite system.

Eventually, we lost the focus on portability. Versions proliferated internally as we chased each different market opportunity. It costs money (read: internal time and effort with no immediate payback) to keep code portable. Whitesmiths was never as much fun for me once that happened.

And that leads me to several important points. Portability is as much a statement about economics as it is about technology. **A program is portable when it is cheaper to move it between platforms than to rewrite it for the new platform.**

Thus, portability is not a Boolean attribute for each program. It is a figure of merit, a cost. A program may be portable in one context and not portable in another. Or it may not be portable enough to warrant the investment. **It costs more to write and maintain a portable program than one tailored for a specific environment.**

Finally, it is cheaper to write a program with portability in mind than to retrofit portability. That is also true of correctness, robustness, testability, and several other virtues. Unlike those virtues, however, you are not assured of a payoff. Unless you actually move the program between platforms one day, you lose the investment. **Writing portable code involves an up-front risk that you can seldom afford to defer.**

The last few years have seen an upsurge in interest in portability. International standards are now all the rage. Trade groups are forming "de facto" standards where the formal bodies can't move fast enough. The ads for compilers and support libraries tout platform independence.

Most of the people who care about portability occupy fairly small market niches. If you sell only a few hundred packages a year, you care about every single sale. You can't stay on just one UNIX platform, the market is too diverse. You can't even afford to stay on just PC compatibles, not if your typical customer needs workstation power. So you write in portable C to lower the cost of moving to several platforms.

Traditionally, the big hitters have been able to afford code that is less portable. Lotus could tailor 1-2-3 for each new platform because they could prorate the support and development costs over a large number of units. In fact, they couldn't afford *not* to tailor. The competition has long been too fierce in each arena.

But even the large-market vendors are starting to feel the pinch. Today's major products involve megabytes of code, not kilobytes. You need to ship that much complexity to be competitive in many areas. The cost of parallel support and development is expensive enough for the bits that must be tailored. Nobody wants to pay two to five times over for the common core. So even products with significant nonportable components are developing significant portable foundations.

The large-market vendors are also facing their own problems with proliferating versions. An area of significant growth for American companies is overseas sales. That often outpaces the growth of domestic markets. Traditional American insularity is succumbing to the need for ever more sales prospects.

The historic changes in Eastern Europe and Russia will eventually accelerate that trend. These new kids on the block may be broke now, but they are determined to develop their economies. They recognize the need to use computers to maximum advantage. So if you want to make a buck in the software business, be prepared to collect in marks, rubles, or dinars.

You'd also better be prepared to make your software speak German, Russian, or Croatian. Programmers are accustomed to learning English to use program-development software. That's not a major added burden, since English is an important second language for many professionals. But you don't get major market penetration with word processors and spreadsheets that speak only English.

I'm not just talking about spelling checkers and hyphenation algorithms. *Every* nontrivial application needs some degree of cultural adaptability. You can get a lot of mileage (kilometrage?) out of icons, to be sure. The highways of Europe demonstrate that. But you also need to utter an occasional error message. Or prompt, or date, or monetary amount, or some other culture-dependent utterance.

What software vendors want to do is produce a single product in a shrink-wrap package for dealers' shelves. (PC compatibles and Macintoshes are thus desirable platforms. There are so many of the little critters out there.) If the French marketplace requires a different version, however, you can't adopt that simple approach. You must develop, package, and ship a special French version. The market size is smaller and your parts count is larger. Thus, your costs go up and so does the package price.

I learned that you can drown in packages. For many years, Whitesmiths created every package we were capable of producing. With success came a geometric increase in package varieties. Soon, it was taking as long to produce all the packages as it did to develop each release. Portability notwithstanding. We learned to prepackage only the most popular combinations. Any other flavor we sold at a premium.

What the world now needs is a way to deal with the combinatoric explosion of cultural marketplaces. It's sad that the smallest and newest markets are the ones that cost the most to service. Better we address the economic problems from a technical perspective. We need to factor out as many cultural specifics as possible to keep the parts count down. We want one market that numbers in the billions, not thousands that number in the millions.

Similar problems have been solved well in the past. We take for granted that computers come in varied sizes, speeds, and configurations. Do you know who manufactured your diskette or hard disk drives? Do you care? I can assure you that you don't want to *have* to care.

An important role for an operating system is to smooth over broad differences among computers. An application can read and write all disk files through a standard set of system calls. It can use memories of various sizes and displays of various flavors with similar ease. Ambitious applications can play the CGA/EGA/VGA alphabet game, to be sure. But most don't have to.

To solve the cultural problem, then, you need similar machinery:

- The machinery must be standardized across platforms.
- Actual cultural support must be tailorable separately for each user's machine.
- The information about a given culture must be decoupled from each application.

None of this is news. People have been working on various aspects of cultural adaptability for years. You will often find useful stuff tucked away in the more popular operating systems. All you have to do is look for it and make a point of using it.

UNIX, for example, has long been helpful about time zones. Each user can log in from a different time zone. Dates, times, and the names of time zones all print properly. The system records all times in universal form (UTC), so no confusion exists between users.

More recently, various groups have been working to make UNIX more of a cultural chameleon. Several companies now have versions of UNIX that speak Japanese. Standards groups such as POSIX and X/Open have been hammering out how to specify character sets and collating sequences that vary among (and even within) language groups.

PC compatibles and Macintoshes fret about a variety of cultural issues. You can adapt keyboards for those funny characters with accents that exist in every language but English, Hawaiian, and Swahili. You can exercise some control over date formats. You can sometimes stir up an occasional error message in German.

None of these facilities are uniform across many platforms, however. It helps if you can isolate the cultural dependencies in your code. But you still must write bespoke code for each platform to obtain the information you need and smuggle it into the code. To eliminate such difficulties requires a new level of standardization.

That level of standardization now exists, or at least a good beginning for it. You will find it in the new ANSI/ISO Standard for the C programming language. C is the first language to make a serious stab at supporting programs that want to adapt to varied cultures. It even worries about cultures with very large character sets, such as Japanese, Chinese, and Arabic.

X3J11 is the ANSI-authorized committee that developed the C Standard. From the outset, in 1983, the membership expressed a strong desire to assist programmers in writing portable C programs. Character-set independence was also an early and oft-stated goal. (The IBM representative kept reminding us that EBCDIC was also an important character set, not just ASCII.) That made it easier to accommodate the various ISO 646 variants of ASCII used with different European languages.

Rather late in the standardization process, the Europeans expressed a strong desire to add cultural adaptability to C. They were unhappy that so many Americanisms were wired into the C library. At the least, they wanted some way to circumvent such wired-in behavior. At the most, they wanted to be able to rewire the library on the fly to adapt to different cultures. They got both, in the form of a facility dubbed *locales*.

Very late in the standardization process, the Japanese expressed a very strong desire for language support for manipulating large character sets in C. ISO adopted a Japanese motion that all future programming language standards support such operations. C could have been the last language *not* to include large character set support. Instead, it became the *first* standard language to do so.

Locales and large character sets form a significant new component to the C language. Together, they represent the internationalization of C. (That's such a big word that most people write it as *I18N*. The 18 stands for the 18 omitted letters.) Let's look at each of the pieces separately.

A locale is a collection of conventions peculiar to a given cultural group. At first blush, you might think that "locale" and "language" are synonymous. If you travel between America, England, and Australia, however, you soon learn better. It is no joke that the English-speaking world is often divided by a common language. I still misread dates in Australia because the locals insist on writing numeric dates backwards from the way I was taught to read them. At best, language is but one component of a locale.

Even within a given country, you will find varying locales. Most civilians write negative numbers with a leading minus sign. Accountants often favor surrounding parentheses instead. Or they write a trailing **DB**, for example.

You may think you know how to sort text. Look up words in a dictionary and you know to ignore case distinctions. Look up names in a telephone book and watch out for funny rules about ordering McIntyre and MacWilliams. Neither of those documents match the default output you're likely to get from your favorite computer sort utility. See what I mean about subcultures?

A locale involves useful lore about character sets, collating sequences, date formats, and currency formats. It certainly doesn't cover *all* the differences that exist between cultures, but it includes many important aspects. You can write many application programs that avoid text messages. A judicious use of icons can go a long way. But it's hard to avoid displaying the odd date, currency amount, or sorted name list. That's what many people use computers to manipulate. So that's what is included in a C locale.

The set of locales is open-ended. The C Standard doesn't say how many there are. All it requires is a "C" locale that behaves like the C language and library of yore. It also defines a *native* locale, named by the empty string " ". The native locale is presumably the locale favored by the locals for a given computer system.

Beyond that, an implementation can specify as few or as many locales as it chooses. It can also name them as it sees fit. Nor does the C Standard say how an implementation must specify a locale. The Standard only says that it must.

That may not sound like much of a standard, but it is more useful than you might think. The best analogy is to files and file systems. The C Standard imposes quite a few requirements on the properties of files. That way, programs can read and write files on a broad assortment of computers. But the standard says little about how you *name* files. And it lets an implementation provide many other file services as well.

Support for large character sets is a similar combination of the specific and the general. X3J11 introduced the concepts of *multibyte character* and *wide character*. Those are the two popular ways of representing large character sets:

- A multibyte character is a sequence of one or more characters that represents one character from a large character set. It can occur in a string that includes locking shift sequences. Thus, the interpretation of a given byte can depend on what has gone before. Multibyte characters are most useful for sending large character sets along single-byte pathways — serial communication lines and text files on diskettes and hard disks.

- A wide character is a fixed-size integer, typically 16- to 32-bits wide, that holds a distinct code for each member of a large character set. Wide characters are most useful for manipulating text within a program.

Both forms have their uses.

The C Standard lets you put funny characters in comments and character strings within C source code. These take the form of multibyte character sequences. It provides additional library functions for converting between multibyte and wide character forms and for manipulating these new creatures at run time. It specifies how you can switch among coding schemes (within limits) by using the locale machinery. That seems to be the irreducible minimum that must be standardized to permit uniform handling of large character sets.

X3J11 refused to mandate a specific encoding for conventional one-byte character sets. (The committee could have done so — Ada is defined in terms of ASCII.) It is hardly surprising, then, that the committee refused to mandate a specific encoding for large character sets. Thus, the C Standard imposes several constraints on how you can encode large character sets, but it permits various encodings.

In fact, all the popular encodings of Kanji fit this scheme. Some are multibyte codes without shift states, some are multibyte codes with shift states, and some are wide-character codes. The proposed ISO 10646 universal character set works as a wide-character code. So too does Unicode, from which ISO 10646 was derived. You get in trouble only if you try to use an encoding for the wrong choice of representations.

The major weakness with the Standard C approach to internationalization is a lack of practical experience. Some prior art exists for each component, to be sure. But nobody has proved that this particular combination of ingredients will truly enhance portability.

I decided to address the issue by implementing all this stuff. I have just published a book, *The Standard C Library* (**Pla92**). It includes a complete implementation of locales and support for large character sets. You can get the machine-readable code, compile it, and link it into applications without paying a royalty. My hope is that this will stimulate wider experimentation with coding for the international marketplace.

Of course, I had to make up a few things as I went along. I defined a format for a "locale file." You can use a conventional text editor to specify as many locales as your heart desires. If a program asks to change locales, the library reads this file to find the required information. Such a scheme is indeed open-ended. But it may not be as efficient as necessary for some applications. And it may not fit well with culture-specific support provided by other vendors and standards groups.

It's still too early to judge the success of the C Standard, this implementation, or any serious applications in the area of cultural adaptability. I am optimistic that the C Standard takes basically the right approach. I like to think that my implementation is a good one. But until we get feedback from the writers of applications — and their users — we can't pass final judgment. Stay tuned. □

𝔞fterword: Since I wrote this essay, standards activity has increased dramatically in the area of internationalization. Countries and companies, large and small, now look to such standards to ensure the proverbial "level playing field." As a result, I believe that too much is going on now. We still need to analyze what the world needs, even as pressure mounts to synthesize new standards right away. Fifteen years ago, some of us worried about portability among machines. Now we worry about portability among cultures. The issues are similar, but the market forces have become much stronger.

This is the first of three essays on writing culture-dependent code. (See **Essay 23: All Sorts of Sorts** *and* **Essay 24: Transforming Strings**.*)*

23 All Sorts of Sorts

$\mathcal{S}$orting once dominated computing. In the days when mainframes ruled, I am told that the largest single task occupying many of the big machines was sorting. All night long, operators mounted multi-reel data sets a reel at a time on multiple tape drives. They sorted the day's transactions and applied them (via a merge) to gigantic data bases. The result was a new set of tapes for processing the next night.

We now live in an era where "gigabyte" is a common noun. Most of those multi-reel data sets have migrated to online disk files. Many of them now live on departmental, or even personal, computers. The very large data sets now inhabit optical jukeboxes and other modern approximations to infinite storage. You can access in milliseconds what once took a day or more to read from archival storage.

Sorting has not gone away, however. It gets smeared out across all those accesses. The data base is kept in sort by some criterion. So each access knows how to cut corners to find the record in question. (This corner-cutting is called *searching*.) Insertions and deletions must maintain the sort criteria, of course.

The algorithms for sorting and searching are a fascinating topic. For an encyclopedic reference, see Donald Knuth, *The Art of Computer Programming*, Volume 3, "Sorting and Searching" (**Knu73**). Much as I love to explore that topic, however, I sidestep it for now. My concern at the moment is a different aspect of sorting and searching.

At the heart of every sort or search is a function that determines the ordering criterion. The function compares two items to be ordered and yields a three-valued result. The first item is either less than, equal to, or greater than the second item. Clever algorithms may minimize the number of comparisons they make. In the end, however, they depend on a comparison function to define the sort order.

That function must play fair. It cannot, for example, cop out and return "I don't know." That can be a reasonable response for certain comparisons in other contexts. An IEEE 754 floating-point value can be a code that represents "not a number" or NaN. Compare a NaN with a finite value, such as 3.2, and the answer is, "I can't say how these two values are ordered."

In a sort or search, however, the result must be augmented. It may make sense to sort a NaN before any finite value. Or it may make sense to sort a

177

NaN after all other values. It may also make sense to have all NaNs compare equal, regardless of their codes. So long as the comparison function returns one of three answers, as above, the sort or search can proceed.

The answer had better be reproducible as well. Every time you call the comparison function with a given pair of items, it must yield the same answer. Much of the cleverness in sorting and searching algorithms depends on this property. Even a pedantic algorithm that repeatedly compares pairs of items can get testy if the sort order changes under foot.

$\mathcal{F}$inally, the answer had better be consistent with all other answers. That means, for example, that comparisons must be transitive. If *A* is less than *B* and *B* is less than *C*, then *A* must be less than *C*. Seem obvious? Then consider the ancient game of scissors, paper, and rock: scissors cut paper, paper covers rock, rock smashes scissors. The dominance is circular. Try to sort by dominance with this function and most algorithms will produce fruity results. I suspect that some may even loop forever.

I am amazed at how seldom these properties are spelled out for comparison functions. I suppose they are sufficiently obvious to most programmers that they are hard to see as important semantic constraints. It's only when you violate one or more, and spend three days debugging a program, that you are reminded of their importance.

A classic failure is to change ordering functions in the middle of the stream. For example, the Standard C library has a function called **bsearch**. You specify an array that is in sort, an item to look up, and a comparison function. The **bsearch** function returns a pointer to an array element that compares equal, or a null pointer if it can find none. As the **b** in the name implies, **bsearch** presumably speeds its search by performing a binary chop. Thus, it can search an array with 1,000 elements with at most ten comparisons.

The binary-chop algorithm assumes that the array is sorted by the same criterion as is enforced by the comparison function you specify on the call to **bsearch**. You can use another Standard C library function called **qsort** to ensure that this is so. One argument to **qsort** is a comparison function that behaves much like the one for **bsearch**. The arguments to both are nearly identical. With a bit of care, you can ensure that both functions use exactly the same comparison function.

What many people do, however, is initialize the search table statically, right in the C source code. They sort the initializers for each element by hand. Or they use a sort utility that comes with their development system of choice. Usually, that works fine. Probably, the sort utility and your comparison function specify the same ordering. The "key" is often just a text string that sorts in one obvious way. Right?

Move the code to a machine with a different character set and you can be surprised. Character data in sort on the original host no longer sorts the same on the new target. The comparison function yields answers inconsistent with the ordering of the table. Disaster ensues.

I have learned to be wary of arrays whose order depends on character codes. I still initialize them statically, but I no longer make them constant. Instead, I sort such tables at program startup, using the same comparison function that I use for later searches. (I also comment each such table clearly so that future maintainers retain this discipline.) That saves all sorts of nasty surprises.

You find similar problems among the UNIX utilities. The *sort* command lets you specify all kinds of special options for the comparison function. You can specify multiple keys, or ordering criteria. (Later keys are tested only when earlier ones compare equal.) Each key can specify a different subfield of the text lines to be sorted. Each subfield can be interpreted in different ways. The main thing wrong with all this flexibility is its complexity. It usually takes me between ten minutes and an hour of experimentation to get all the keys right for a specialized sort.

There is another thing wrong, however. Several other UNIX utilities also require a comparison function. For example, you drop duplicate adjacent lines from a file by piping the sorted file through *uniq*. And you identify lines common to two files (or unique to just one of them) by sorting both files and passing them through *comm*. Both uniq and comm have some notion of "before" and "equal" when comparing two text lines. If that differs from the notion imposed by the earlier sort, these utilities often misbehave.

My knowledge of UNIX is admittedly out of date. But the last time I looked, the utilities uniq and comm lacked all the ordering options of sort. I have slammed into that incompatibility with annoying regularity over the years. That inspired me many years ago to write library functions for parsing sort keys and using them in comparisons. I still have versions of sort, uniq, and comm that can agree on fairly ornate sort criteria. They have proved their worth many times over.

In summary, the comparison functions you use with sorts and searches are critical pieces of code. They tailor standard algorithms for particular applications. Coded properly, comparison functions help you order data sets efficiently and robustly. Done wrong, they cause all sorts of pernicious errors.

The set of all useful comparison functions is very large. I have used dozens of distinct ordering criteria with various sort utilities over the years. I would gladly have used more, had the sort options been more flexible. I have written more comparison functions in C than I care to count. It is clearly hard to guess the parameters you need for a flexible parametric comparison function. It is also onerous to require users to specify comparison functions by writing C code.

Both of those problems came back to haunt me recently. As I mentioned in the previous essay, my latest magnum opus is a book on the Standard C library (**Pla92**). (See **Essay 22: Programming for the Billions**.) One of the interesting features added to C is the concept of locale-dependent collation. In other words, you can specify how to compare two text strings using ordering rules that vary across cultures (and subcultures).

The workhorse function is called **strcoll**. You call it with pointers to two null-terminated strings. It returns the usual three-way value you need to order strings by pairwise comparisons. If you expect to repeat such comparisons often, another function can speed the process. You call **strxfrm** to translate a string into an alternate form. Byte-by-byte comparison of two such transformed strings yields the same ordering as calling **strcoll** with the untransformed strings.

The C Standard says that an implementation must contain the functions **strcoll** and **strxfrm**. It says that changing the locale category **LC_COL-LATE** can change the behavior of these functions. But that's all it says. It gives no hints about:

- how to specify various "collations"
- what names to give them
- how to implement the functions
- how to change their behavior when the locale changes

Those were the issues I tackled when I chose to implement a complete version of the Standard C library.

My approach to locales was to introduce a *locale file*. This is a text file that you can prepare with your favorite text editor. You use it to describe one or more locales. Each specifies a number of culture-dependent parameters. For example, here is a sensible locale entry for Australia:

```
LOCALE              AUSTRALIA
currency_symbol     "$"
decimal_point       "."
grouping        "3"
int_curr_symbol     "AUD "
mon_decimal_point   "."
mon_grouping    "3"
mon_thousands_sep   ","
nega tive_sign      "-"
positive_sign       "+"
thousands_sep       ","
frac_digits         2
int_frac_digits     2
n_cs_precedes       1
```

```
n_sep_by_space       0
n_sign_posn          4
p_cs_precedes        1
p_sep_by_space       0
p_sign_posn          4
dst_rules       ":010 100:042802:102702"
time_zone       ":AST:ADT:-540"
time_formats "|%d %b %H:%M:%S %Y|%d/%b/%Y|%H:%M:%S"
LOCALE          end
```

Some of these fields speak for themselves. Some are downright cryptic. I don't pretend that casual users can or should learn the mysteries of locale files. More likely, a system administrator or programmer would modify an existing locale file for each peculiar need. The point is that you can capture many of the peculiarities of a given culture with just a few hundred bytes of text.

A program can read this file at program startup and adapt in several critical ways to the preferences of the locals. Or it can adapt repeatedly to various locales as it runs, if it is more ambitious. Or it can tailor a specialized locale by choosing French dates, say, and accountants' conventions for formatting monetary values. A program that is shared in a multiprocessing system, such as UNIX, can even adapt simultaneously in different ways to different users.

This example specifies how the locals prefer to format monetary and non-monetary amounts, and how they write their dates. That's probably the information of widest interest to programmers writing adaptable applications. The locale file can also specify:

- additions to various character classes, such as letters with accent marks or additional punctuation characters
- the encoding of multibyte character strings and their corresponding wide-character codes, for large character sets
- the ordering rules for **strcoll** and **strxfrm**

It is this last item that I wish to focus on for now.

Despite what I said earlier, **strcoll** is *not* the fundamental function. You can write **strcoll** in terms of **strxfrm**, but not the other way around. Each ordering rule is thus defined in terms of a string transformation. How the transformed strings sort determines the behavior of the ordering rule. So you want some flexible way to specify string transformations.

Perhaps you can see the quandary I faced. I want people to be able to specify a large assortment of ordering rules by adding text to a locale file. That rules out writing a predetermined set of functions. Each may be very fast at enforcing a given ordering rule, but it is also limited. Choosing among a finite set of ordering rules is not a happy solution.

I have already described my frustration at using parametric sort packages. And I can't say I've done any better than others with my own designs. The sort-key parser that I wrote was nice, but it was hardly more flexible than the UNIX sort utility. Unless the locale-file reader includes a C compiler, it is hard to provide adequate flexibility. And having written the odd C compiler over the years, I knew better than to try anything *that* ambitious.

Nevertheless, I did design and write several parametric versions of **strcoll** and **strxfrm**. Each worked for an interesting subset of cases. Each foundered on the shoals of cultural diversity. The problem was that I knew too much about what people wanted, but I didn't know enough about how to deliver. What I knew was courtesy of IBM and the POSIX subcommittee on internationalization. Both of those organizations have studied collation rules used around the world. Both have a stake in helping computer users implement those rules. Let me give you a few examples.

The easiest collation rule to implement is one where **strxfrm** transforms each string unchanged. That makes **strcoll** equivalent to the old war-horse C function **strcmp**. The ordering is determined by the codes assigned to the execution character set. I chose that behavior for the **"C"** locale you get at program startup. I figured it was most culturally neutral.

A rule almost as simple is to make letter comparisons case insensitive. You get this behavior by translating all upper-case letters to lower case (or the other way around). The mapping still produces one character for each character in the input string.

That leaves you one step away from a *dictionary* sort. Such an ordering rule is case insensitive, but it also ignores any punctuation. In the extreme version of a dictionary sort, you discard all characters other than letters. Thus, "can't" and "cant" sort equal, and "cane" sorts before "can't" regardless of the values assigned punctuation codes. (I assume that letters sort in alphabetical order.)

On a visit to Stockholm, I discovered a peculiarity with Swedish telephone directories. Seems they treat "i" and "j" as equivalent in determining sort order. You can handle such rules by an obvious variation on the dictionary sort. Simply map equivalent characters to the same character in the transformed string.

Most languages other than English have characters with accent marks. Occasionally, these are encoded as a sequence of two characters — an accent mark followed by the letter. That derives from the days of mechanical typewriters with *dead keys* for the accent marks. The carriage spaced only after you struck the letter following. The modern trend, however, is to define separate character codes for each combination of letter and accent. Display a binary file on your terminal screen and you will probably see some of them.

The ordering rules for accented characters (and other funny characters) strain the bounds of creativity. Some simply sort the same as their unaccented cousins. That's easy to deal with. Some sort as if they were *some other* combination of letters. (The German "ß" often sorts as if it were "ss.") That's still not bad.

Where life gets exciting is when you get to the disambiguating rules. Seems some cultures are happy to order accented characters the same as unaccented, *provided the rest of the two strings differ.* If they prove to be equal, then one form of the letter precedes the other. That's somewhat messier to capture in a transformed string.

What you have to do is transform the string more than once. Take one pass over the string replacing each character with its sorting equivalent. Then tack a distinctive marker on the end. Then take a second pass over the string adding characters only for each one that may have to be disambiguated.

 ere is an example that you can read. Let's say that you want to order strings by dictionary order as above. That means ignoring case distinctions among letters and effectively discarding non-letters. But you also want distinct strings to compare unequal. Effectively, you want to take a second look at strings that sort equal by the dictionary rule. On the second pass, you want to perform a comparison of the original text.

One way to do so is:

- change all upper case letters to lower case
- append a period to this string
- append the original string following the period

Thus, the string "Can't Happen" becomes "canthappen.Can't Happen" as a sort key. It sorts very close to "can't happen" (which becomes "canthappen.can't happen") but doesn't compare equal to it.

The reports I read from IBM and POSIX go on for pages. Every time you think you know all possible sorting rules, some central European country throws you another breaking fast ball. It's fun reading, if you're perverse.

My final solution was almost as extreme as allowing C code in locale files. I went back to the simplest programmable system that is also powerful, fast, and flexible. I coded **strcoll** and **strxfrm** in terms of a table-driven, finite-state machine. What you put in the locale file is the specifications for the code tables. Here, for example, is how you specify the modified dictionary sort I showed above:

```
collate[0, 0      ] '.'            $0 $I $1
collate[0, 1:$#    ]                  $I $0
collate[0, 'a':'z'] $@             $0 $I $0
collate[0, 'A':'Z'] $@+'a'-'A'     $0 $I $0
collate[1, 0:$#    ] $@            $0 $I $1
```

Again, I don't pretend that this is readable. I won't even try to interpret it for you at present. That's my topic for the next essay.

All I will say for now is that this approach has proved fruitful. I have been able to encode a wide variety of comparison rules with this (albeit cryptic) scheme. It is satisfyingly terse, so as not to bulk up a locale file. And I think it is even reasonably efficient. □

Afterword: As I warned in this essay, there seems to be no end to complexities in collation rules. I have since learned that sorting French text requires an added refinement. You ignore any accents on the first pass. Then you consider any accents in reverse *order. The rationale I've heard is that accents near the end of a word often change its meaning dramatically. Those near the beginning merely change its pronunciation. It is clear that we have much to learn about the needs of various constituencies in sorting text.*

24 Transforming Strings

$\mathfrak{I}$n the last two essays, I have been describing some of the features added to Standard C to adapt programs to different cultures. (See **Essay 22: Programming for the Billions** and **Essay 23: All Sorts of Sorts**.) My interest in that topic has driven me to implement the Standard C library and flesh out support for locales and large character sets. (See **Pla92**.)

I ended the last essay by sketching the way I chose to specify a wide variety of collation sequences. I implemented the critical functions **strcoll** and **strxfrm** in terms of a table-driven finite-state machine. You specify the tables as part of a locale in a text file. If a C program changes locales, it scans this file and encodes the relevant locale to alter the behavior of various library functions.

Here is a brief review of the problem. You specify a collation as a transformation of one string to another. The function **strxfrm** performs this transformation for you. Its behavior can change when you change locale. Compare two transformed strings byte by byte and you get the desired ordering of the untransformed strings. The function **strcoll** will transform two strings and compare them all at once, if you prefer.

Ordering rules vary greatly among cultures around the world. In many cases, you can nevertheless capture the local ordering rule with a character-by-character mapping of the input string to the transformed string. In some cases, however, you must rescan the input string to produce a suffix for the transformed string. This suffix defines the order when, say, two strings differ only in an accent mark on one of the letters. The accent mark matters only if the character sequences *following* the accented character are identical. Yup, that's right.

To perform these transformations, I defined a simple machine with up to sixteen states. At any given moment the state determines which table of actions to use. The next (eight-bit) input character serves as an index to select which table entry to use. A table entry consists of an eight-bit translation value, a four-bit successor state, and four one-bit action flags:

- **$F** — Fold the translation value into the 16-bit accumulator.
- **$I** — Consume the Input character.
- **$O** — Output a character (the translation value if it is nonzero, otherwise the less-significant byte of the accumulator).
- **$R** — Rotate the accumulator left eight bits.

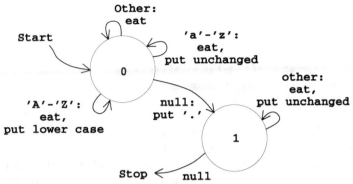

Figure 24.1: *State-transition diagram for simple dictionary sort.*

Consuming the terminating null character starts a rescan of the input string. Outputting a null character stops the translation normally. An invalid transformation or silly table entry terminates the transformation with extreme prejudice. The machine starts in state 0 with a 0 accumulator.

$\mathfrak{H}$ere once again is the ordering rule I showed in the last essay. It sorts strings by dictionary order — ignoring case distinctions between letters and discarding non-letters. Two strings that compare equal by this rule are then compared byte-by-byte. Figure 24.1 shows a state-transition diagram for this ordering rule. What you write in the locale file is:

```
collate[0, 0        ] '.'          $O $I $1
collate[0, 1:$#     ]                 $I $O
collate[0, 'a':'z'] $@            $O $I $O
collate[0, 'A':'Z'] $@+'a'-'A'   $O $I $O
collate[1, 0:$#     ] $@          $O $I $1
```

The first line sets the collation rule for state 0, character code 0 to consume the null input character (**$I**) put out a period in its place (**' . '** and **$O**), then enter state 1 (**$1**). Consuming the null input character starts a rescan of the input string.

The second line sets the collation rules for all nonzero character codes (1 through **$#**, which is 255) in state 0. The action is to consume the input (**$I**) without producing any output and remain in state 0 (**$O**).

The third line rewrites the entries for the lower-case letters. The action is to transform the character to itself (**$@**), output this transformed value (**$O**), consume the input (**$I**), and remain in state 0 (**$O**). Of course, this notation works properly only if the lower-case letters have adjacent codes, as in ASCII.

The fourth line rewrites the entries for the upper-case letters. The action is to transform the character to its lower case equivalent (**$@+'a'-'A'**) then consume and put the letter as immediately above. The last line sets all collation rules for state 1. The action is to put the character unchanged,

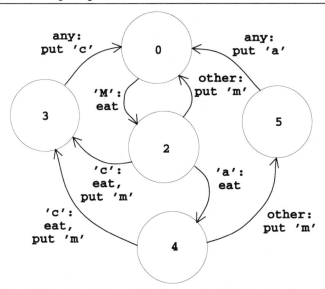

Figure 24.2: *Additions to state-transition diagram for* **Mc/Mac** *equivalence.*

consume it, and stay in state 1. Emitting the terminating null ends the transformation.

I wrote the rules in a slightly illogical order to keep them shorter. It is easier to flood a state table with the "otherwise" case, then go back and overwrite the special cases. Note that this particular transformation makes no use of the accumulator. Some messier transformations need it to retain a character code or two and reduce the number of distinct states.

$\mathcal{F}$or a more complex example, we can add a Celtic flavor. Many phone books sort names beginning with **Mac** interchangeably with those beginning with **Mc**. Thus, **McIntyre** sorts *before* **MacWilliams**, not after. That makes it easier for most of us to find such names when we're not sure of the exact spelling.

Figure 24.2 shows what you have to *add* to the state-transition diagram in Figure 24.1. Note that half the added complexity lies in undoing the damage for names such as **Mallory**. Here are the lines you have to *add* to the earlier ones in the locale file to define this ordering rule:

```
collate[0, 'M'     ]                    $I  $2
collate[2, 0:$#    ] 'm'                    $0
collate[2, 'c'     ]                    $I  $3
collate[2, 'a'     ]                    $I  $4
collate[3, 0:$#    ] 'c'         $0     $0
collate[4, 0:$#    ] 'm'         $0     $5
collate[4, 'c'     ] 'm'         $0 $I  $3
collate[5, 0:$#    ] 'a'         $0     $0
```

A little arithmetic will tell you that this set of state tables occupies over 3,000 bytes of storage. Half of that is used simply to emit the letters **m**, **a**, and **c**. I'm sure that you can write a comparison function that is *much* smaller than this, and doubtless considerably faster. I know that I could.

But why should you? If you have an application that applies this sort rule all the time, it may be worth coding in C. That will give you improved performance, if that matters. It also will let you tailor the comparison more than a mere 16 states allows.

Otherwise, you are better off coding in this higher-level language. It still requires programmer-type skills. But you can sit at a keyboard for ten minutes with a suitable test harness and beat on it until it works. That's the same sort of investment I make in getting the command line right for a hairy UNIX sort. And you can use it, just like a shell script that drives a sort, with programs available only as executable binaries. No need to compile and link-in chunks of code.

You can stockpile dozens, or even hundreds, of ordering rules such as this. Give each a mnemonic name and a descriptive comment line or two. Put the most-used ones in your standard locale file. Keep the rest handy in a directory of files you can scan with grep. Add them to your active locale file as needed. That, to me, is a sensible way to deal with the telephone directories of Europe.

Another important addition to C is support for large character sets. The Japanese, Chinese, and Arab cultures all have character sets that number in the thousands. They have become, or are becoming, major new markets for applications software.

The C Standard lets you encode large character sets two different ways. *Multibyte characters* are sequences of one or more bytes, each typically eight bits. Each sequence specifies one character in the larger character set. *Wide characters* are fixed-size integers, each typically 16 to 32 bits, that can represent all the characters in the large character set as distinct codes.

The Standard C library provides the functions **mbtowc** and **mbstowc** to translate from multibyte to wide-character forms. The first delivers a single wide character. The second translates an entire null-terminated multibyte string to a null-terminated wide-character string. The library also provides the functions **wctomb** and **wcstombs** to translate the other way.

None of these functions has to worry about rescanning a string, as **strcoll** and **strxfrm** must. But they face a different nasty problem. Some encodings of Kanji, the large set of Chinese characters used by the Japanese, employ multibyte strings with *locking shift states*.

Some of you may have encountered a similar encoding used on ASR 37 Teletypes and equivalent terminals. The ASCII control code *shift out* (SO) puts the terminal in an alternate shift state. Type a letter **b** and you get a

Greek β instead, for example. The terminal continues to speak Greek until you send it the control code *shift in* (SI). It then reverts to its *initial shift state,* speaking the approximation to English favored by programmers.

Not all popular encodings of Kanji (or other large character sets) use locking shift states. For the rest, each multibyte sequence is self determining. As you inspect each character starting with the first of a sequence, you know:

■ whether it is a valid character
■ whether an additional character follows

And given a valid multibyte sequence, you know its corresponding wide-character code.

The C Standard offers several additional anchors in this sea of varied character sets. It specifies that multibyte strings within a program (such as comments and format strings) begin in the initial shift state. In the initial shift state, the common characters such as **a** are the one-byte codes you know and love. And most important, the null character (code value zero) can never occur as part of a multibyte code. It always stands for a one-byte null character.

Still, there are problems. Large character sets abound, as I keep emphasizing. Major vendors have, in recent years, adopted Kanji encodings across much of their product lines. They thus have a stake in supporting their particular encoding very well. Sadly, differences often exist between vendors.

I chose to implement the Standard C library without choosing a particular large character set. That put me in the position of having to support (potentially) all the more popular encodings. I couldn't ignore codes with locking shift states. Nor could I assume they would always be present. I thus had to write **mbtowc**, **mbstowcs**, **wctomb**, and **wcstombs** to be as general as possible.

As with the collation functions, I mucked about for awhile with different ways to parametrize these transformations. And as with the collation functions, I found myself repeatedly thwarted by cultural diversity. I couldn't easily encode all the ways that European cultures have chosen to sort text. Nor could I encompass all the ways that Japanese programmers have contrived to encode Kanji.

My solution, once again, was to introduce two more table-driven finite-state machines. One translates a multibyte sequence to its equivalent wide-character code. The other does the reverse. Both have to fret about state memory, in case the multibyte code involves locking shift states. And, of course, both must be defined together. You want to translate back and forth between multibyte sequences and wide characters with some degree of consistency and sanity.

I find it sad that I ended up with three different finite-state machine drivers. Perhaps if I were smarter, I would have found some way to combine them into one. All are similar enough to use the same notation in their locale-file specification. But each differs enough from the others to warrant separate treatment. Consider:

- The collation functions map a string of characters to another string of characters.

- The multibyte functions map a string of characters to a string of wide characters.

- The wide-character functions map a string of wide characters to a string of characters.

I suppose that's difference enough to warrant three distinct sets of functions. Two particular differences are:

- The multibyte functions output an entire wide character.

- The wide-character functions copy each input wide-character to the accumulator, then index into the current state table using the less-significant byte of the accumulator.

The drivers for the three sets of functions also differ in how they return control part way through a transformation. But that involves low-level programming details that I choose not to address here.

Here is a practical example. One popular Kanji multibyte encoding is called *Shift JIS:*

- A character code in the interval [0x81, 0x9F] or [0xE0, 0xFC] signals the first of a two-character sequence. Any other code is a single character.

- The second character must be in the interval [0x40, 0xFC].

A variety of wide-character codes for Kanji also exist. The string transformations supported by this implementation are, of course, limited. I thus endeavor to define a wide-character code set that is adequate and within the capabilities of table-driven finite-state machines. In this case, I chose:

- The wide-character code for a two-character sequence is the first byte shifted left eight bits and ORed with the second byte.

- The wide-character code for a single character is that character code with high-order bits zero.

This encoding meets two important constraints that the C Standard imposes on wide-character codes:

- The wide-character code for a common character such as **a** (written **L'a'** in C source code) equals the one-byte code **'a'**.

- The wide-character code for the null character is zero.

Figure 24.3 shows the state-transition diagram for the multibyte functions. Figure 24.4 shows the corresponding state-transition diagram for the wide-character functions. Each requires three states, and each reports an

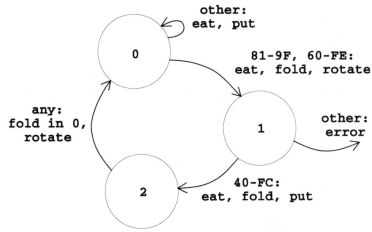

Figure 24.3: *State-transition diagram for translating Shift JIS to wide character.*

error for any invalid codes. What you write in the locale file to implement these string transformations is shown in Figure 24.5.

The entry **mb_cur_max** defines the current value of a macro accessible to the C programmer. It promises that no multibyte sequence in this locale need be longer than two bytes. That can be invaluable in allocating buffers for assembling and disassembling multibyte sequences.

The only other peculiarity I will explain here is the symbol **X**. I use it to mark those table entries that report an erroneous transformation when executed. Beyond that, I leave it to your new-found knowledge to interpret what's going on (assuming, of course, that you still care).

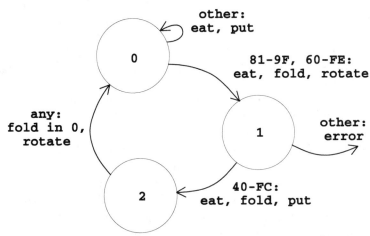

Figure 24.4: *State-transition diagram for translating wide character to Shift JIS.*

```
NOTE JIS codes with 0x81-0x9F or 0xE0-0xFC
NOTE           followed by 0x40-0xFC
SET A 0x81
SET B 0x9f
SET C 0xe0
SET D 0xfc
SET M 0x40
SET N 0xfc
SET X 0
mb_cur_max 2
mbtowc[0, 0:$#]  $@ $F      $O $I $0
mbtowc[0, A:B ]  $@ $F $R      $I $1
mbtowc[0, C:D ]  $@ $F $R      $I $1
mbtowc[1, 0:$#]     X
mbtowc[1, M:N ]  $@ $F      $O $I $2
mbtowc[2, 0:$#]   0 $F $R         $0
wctomb[0, 0:$#]        $R         $1
wctomb[1, 0:$#]     X
wctomb[1, 0   ]        $R $O $I $0
wctomb[1, A:B ]  $@    $R $O    $2
wctomb[1, C:D ]  $@    $R $O    $2
wctomb[2, 0:$#]     X
wctomb[2, M:N ]           $O $I $0
```

Figure 24.5: *Locale file for translating shift JIS.*

I have developed locale specifications for two other popular Kanji encodings:

- *Extended UNIX Code* (or EUC) is a variant of Shift JIS, at least in its simplest form. It also requires two three-state machines.
- *JIS* is an older encoding with locking shift states. It requires six- and nine-state machines.

I won't bother to show you either of these additional locales. The points I emphasize are the same as for the collation functions. You can certainly write code that is smaller and faster for any given encoding of a large character set. The machinery I have implemented can do the job, however, often with adequate efficiency in space and time. If you need the flexibility, this may be the only way to fly.

I conclude with a brief polemic. It seems that ISO is finally getting serious about standardizing a "universal" large character set. It is intended to provide a unique code to every glyph scrawled by humankind since graffiti first appeared on the walls of caves. Basically, I agree that this is a good idea.

An early effort along these lines was tentatively dubbed ISO 10646. It represents the widely-used Latin alphabet in four characters, as three spaces plus the usual single character. Standard C, in its current form, can tolerate this provided we can also represent the common characters as single-character forms. As a 32-bit wide-character encoding, it can be made to work with similar additions.

ISO 10646 appears to be losing out, however, to an alternate scheme called Unicode. Unicode represents Latin as three null characters plus the usual single character. As a 32-bit wide-character encoding, that's just fine for Standard C. Unfortunately, it is being put forth as a multibyte code. That leads to character sequences with embedded null characters.

C programmers have learned over the years that null is well worth reserving as a string terminator. It is certainly not essential, but it is often convenient. Our protests, however, have fallen on deaf ears within ISO. Their attitude is basically that C is a twenty-year-old language, and just one of many. We will have to grow up and learn to use whatever the character-set experts devise for us.

My attitude is rather different. I believe that C is the quintessential language for manipulating text. Look what's been accomplished in the past two decades with C and UNIX. We have experience that is well worth listening to. And we have a culture that is broad and deep enough to truckle to with any new standard.

Every one of the constraints on character sets that I've outlined here has been challenged, at one time or another, by other standards bodies. My experience implementing the Standard C library only reinforces my prejudice that we chose those constraints wisely.

As far as I know, the ISO large character set encoding is still not frozen. I only hope that the C community gets a proper hearing before that happens. □

𝒜fterword: I can now report that ISO 10646 is frozen. It corresponds closely to UNICODE. And it meets the rules of C for forming sets of wide-characters. Mostly. A few problems remain to be reconciled between ISO 10646 and various programming-language standards (including C). But I have hopes now that the marriage will be fruitful.

The software technology outlined in this essay is another matter. It seems that the POSIX Standard takes a somewhat different approach to specifying locales. I am still investigating how to reconcile these differences. The rapid evolution of other standards on internationalization only adds to the confusion. You may not care about all this activity now, but I suspect that within a few years many of you will.

25 Books for Our Times

April first marks the beginning of my fiscal year, morally speaking at least. It's the time when I take stock of the previous twelve-month. I pay my taxes by atoning for any excess hubris. I plan the year to come with all the humility I can muster. I also indulge in a bit of noise making and fireworks, to avoid an excess of sobriety.

In short, April Fool's Day combines the best of New Year's Day, Rosh Hashanah, and Chinese New Year. To me at least. It has the added advantage that hotels and restaurants are less crowded. And I figure I'm better off in the company of a few fellow fools.

Books are heavy on my mind this time around. I've spent much of the past couple of years churning out technical books on the business of computer programming (**P&B89**, **P&B92**, **Pla92**). I still have a backlog of several more. Ten years of running a software company kind of got in the way of this particular passion. I have a lot of catching up to do.

It's easy to lose perspective, however. We book authors do considerable churning for each book we get out. When we're not home writing, we're off giving lectures. We talk to fellow authors and lecturers about the latest ideas and techniques. We work hard to stay at the cutting edge.

We tend to forget about all the poor programmers who must live well back from the cutting edge. They work with inadequate tools and spotty training. They have goals that are shapeless and shifting at best, impossible at worst. For many, programming is not a creative attempt to bind ever greater complexity with ever greater reliability. It's more like being an accountant for a mediocre chain of restaurants in the middle of a deep recession.

It's about time somebody started writing books that tell the truth. No point in discussing data-flow diagrams when most programmers can't even find all the data they're supposed to be processing. Why teach CASE tools to people who don't even have access to all the source code and compilers they need? Forget reliability measures if survival is the principal measure of success.

What follows is a list of book proposals. They are aimed at the beleaguered masses, for a change. Software engineers need not apply. Look them over. If you see some that you might like to buy, let me know. I'll pass the most popular ones on to my publishers. Who knows, they just might end up on my future projects list.

By the way, some of the themes may seem familiar to you. You may have run across a book with a similar title in the past. Don't think I'm stealing other people's bright ideas, however. Remember that all great minds think alike.

Proposed title: **Algorithms – Data Structures = Assembly Language.** The problem with most programming languages is they get in the way. They insist that you commit to some data type for each area of storage that you set aside. That's fine if you want to treat pointers as pointers all the time, or floating point as floating point. It's a real nuisance if you want to fiddle bits to your heart's content.

Data structures cause even more problems. Your typical compiler insists on leaving holes between some members where you might not want them. It insists that you add bogus elements to put holes where you really want them. It makes you create unions wherever you use storage more than one way. You can't just make a list of byte and bit offsets on the back of a napkin, the way you really want.

This book teaches you how to implement algorithms with code that is as compact and speedy as possible. It shows you how to avoid the silly preoccupation with data structure that is costing the industry so many megabytes and microseconds. It de-emphasizes readability and maintainability in favor of truly important goals. The title says it all — assembly language is the key to ignoring data type and structure.

For the advanced student, you will also find discussions of:

- writing self-modifying code
- protecting trade secrets through obscure names and comments
- job security in an uncertain marketplace

The book contains numerous untested code fragments. About 500 pages. No illustrations.

Proposed title: **The Programming of Art's Computer.** Why is it that 80 per cent of all software project managers, and essentially all purchasers of contract software, have names like Art, Mike, or Susan? And why is it that Art (or Mike or Susan) always picks the hardware before talking to any software types? The reasons are shrouded in mystery. The fact remains that most programmers work on projects that are doomed from the outset. We don't get to pick tools and equipment that suit the job. Instead, we spend nearly all our time programming Art's computer.

I envision this as a multi-volume series, to be produced over a number of years. The topic is simply too vast to cover in a single book. Programming the wrong equipment goes to the very heart of what many of us do for a living. I haven't had time to work out the entire series, but here are the first three offerings:

- **Fundamental Aggravations** that you have to put up with in getting the hardware to work at all
- **Semiliterate Auditors** and how to keep them at bay while you're struggling to get the job done
- **Sorting and Searching** through documentation to get hints about how to make the hardware work right

All code in the series is presented in an artificial assembly language for a nonexistent machine. Unsupported assemblers and interpreters are available from various third parties for a wide assortment of prices. No correlation exists between price and reliability of this software. The idea is to model your normal work environment as accurately as possible.

The first volume will consist of about 400 pages. The second edition of the third volume will be released just after the third edition of the second volume.

Proposed title: **Strictured Design.** Nobody likes to talk about the real constraints on designing computer software. We hide behind Pert charts and reliability measures. We talk glibly about cohesive modules and performance guarantees. What we really care about, however, are the practicalities. Let's face it, nobody is going to let you write programs if you tell the bald truth.

The trick is to concoct prices and delivery schedules that are at once believable and easily disposed of. You need to get the decision makers to commit, naturally. Then you have to string them along until you can really get the job done.

Being a bald-faced liar is a help, but it's not enough in these competitive times. You have to learn enough technical mumbo jumbo to avoid paying penalties when the project comes in late. (Notice that I did not say *if* the project comes in late.) That's what this book is about.

Strictured Design discusses the real-world strictures that plague any well-meaning effort to deliver the software goods. It ignores the mundane details of actually writing the code — you know how to crank out a few thousand lines of code, for heaven's sake. Instead, it emphasizes those interpersonal skills that many programmers learn too poorly or too late. You learn, for example:

- **back-to-front scheduling** — "I want it in six months. When can I have it?"
- **capacity planning** — "My brother-in-law sold me this machine. Is it big enough?"
- **creative equivocation** — "These specs seem a little vague here. Can you tighten them up?"

Maybe 300 to 600 pages. Possibly with illustrations. Expected delivery, fourth quarter of the fiscal year.

Proposed title: **Disciplining Programmers.** For those of you who have made it to the ranks of management, this book is for you. You know from first-hand experience just how unmanageable programmers can be. They'll spend all their time playing Tetris and flaming each other via e-mail if you don't keep them in line. They certainly don't believe in the project, the schedule, or the company style guidelines. (Why should they? You don't either.)

Nevertheless, there are ways to keep them in line. To paraphrase Mohandis Gandhi:

- The best leaders are those who get the programmers to say, "We messed it up ourselves."
- The next best are those who get them to say, "We love our boss regardless of who messed up."
- The next best are those who rule by hatred or fear.

Third best is generally good enough for most programming projects. Thus, this book focuses on ways to control a programming staff by playing to their basic hatreds and fears. Emphasis is on generalities, naturally. Nevertheless, the book can't help but give an occasional piece of concrete advice.

A central theme is boredom as a management tool. Some programmers actually fear for their jobs, particularly in these hard economic times. But all programmers detest boredom. Consider, for example, **Chapter One: Bringing Your Staff to Heel**. It describes how to escalate meetings and progress reports until even the burnt-out cases beg for mercy. **Appendix A: Dealing with Smart-Asses**, shows several more subtle ways to inflict boredom on individual trouble makers.

You will find no space wasted here on conventional management wisdom. None of that Harvard Biz School hoity-toity nonsense. Instead, emphasis is consistently on ruling the unruly while avoiding blame for the inevitable failures. If you wanted an easy job, you'd be an accountant for a mediocre chain of restaurants.

Six hundred pages, including 150 pages of useless forms with wide margins as an appendix.

Proposed title: **Sin and the Maintenance of Art's Motorcycle.** Here's the surreal member of the set. The idea is to teach the realities of software maintenance through allegory.

The protagonist in this philosophical narrative is recovering from a nervous breakdown after five years of managing failed software projects. She is working her way back up the ranks by performing telephone customer support for the products she helped develop. (It's the latest thing from California — a combination of tough love and aversion therapy.)

Meanwhile, our protagonist (call her Hydra) is also working on her long-standing fear of hardware. She is moonlighting at a nearby garage doing tune-ups and rotating tires. Then fate takes a double-helical twist. The chief mechanic puts her in charge of maintaining the vintage Harley driven by her boss, the notorious Art. (See above.)

Christian guilt wars with her natural desire for revenge. Should she loosen an occasional bolt? Set the timing off by five degrees? Hide his 9/16-inch wrench? All would serve him right for the way he treats his staff. (See immediately above.)

But Hydra also realizes that vengeance, like inadequate maintenance, is a never-ending cycle (no pun intended). She moralizes at length about the duties of the mechanic, and the programmer, to do a proper job. Students of Japanese manufacturing practices will enjoy her droll comparisons between Harleys and Kawasakis.

The climax comes when Art discovers Hydra's dual role in his life. He's still struggling with the teleological implications even as Hydra quits both jobs. With several friends, she buys a mediocre restaurant from a failing chain and turns it around. It becomes the most successful vegetarian taco place in town. The only male employee is the dishwasher, who was once the accountant for the restaurant chain.

That rather obscures the points made earlier in the book, but feminists will love it. Three hundred pages, paperback only. □

Afterword: This is the last of my April Fool's essays in this collections. It is also the most off-the-wall. In case you missed the point, this essay spoofs a handful of the more popular books in our field. (See if you can recognize all the originals.) Unfortunately, several readers agreed that a number of these books are truly needed. The most votes went to The Programming of Art's Computer. *I don't know whether to laugh or cry.*

26 Through the Grapevine

I finally installed a network at home. That's an exercise I've put off repeatedly. You can only deal with so many pockets of complexity at any one time. No point in adding new ones until the need is clear and present.

For me, the need became clear and present with surprising suddenness. I found myself the owner of an assortment of computers. All are PC compatibles, of various shapes and sizes. Each assumes a different support role for me and other members of my household. All seem to need to exchange great quantities of data every day. You can only run from computer to computer with stacks of diskettes for so long. Then you start thinking about the problems you wanted to solve with computers in the first place. When the putative solution starts taking more time than the original problem, it's time to shift gears.

Like many of you, I center my working life around a computer. First thing in the morning and last thing at night, I use a Compaq laptop to collect my Internet electronic mail. Filing mail, composing responses, and noting action items can take anywhere from ten minutes to an hour. Part of my day often goes into typing in essays like this one. I send them to magazines via e-mail and get the galleys faxed back to me on a Compaq desktop computer. I also use e-mail and fax to review proposals and edit articles for *The C Users Journal*.

I typeset all the textbooks I write using Ventura Publisher. Quick proofs go to a Hewlett-Packard DeskJet 500C. Serious PostScript goes to a NEC laser printer. Production quality output goes onto diskettes and down to a service bureau in Cambridge. The same machinery produces listings, letters, and illustrations. (My son Geoffrey does most of the latter, in both color and gray scale.)

What I write about is computer programming. Years ago, I adopted the silly constraint that I should stay experienced in what I write about. (Yes, we can all name several experts who earn far more than I, partly by wasting little time on such frivolities. I didn't say I was smart.) That self-imposed discipline means that I keep writing code and testing it. And that means that I keep buying compilers, installing them, and using them.

I really shouldn't call them compilers. What people sell these days are *program development systems*. They combine compilers with source-code control, text editing, interactive debugging, on-line help systems, and libraries galore. You have heard me gripe on several occasions about the tens of megabytes of disk capacity that each of these wondrous packages commandeers. I should also gripe about the computer power they need to perform adequately. I had to buy a 50 MHz 486 from Gateway just to store and run all these packages. Still, many of them do happen to perform minor miracles of code generation as a useful side effect.

My wife, Tana, and I also keep checkbooks, budgets, and tax records online. Then there's telephone numbers, calendars, lists of things to do, and so forth. Last and hardly least come computer games. I use them to procrastinate, when the adult in me says "write" and the child says "no." For Geoffrey, they are simply a way of life. (See "Programming on Purpose: Piled Higher and Deeper," *Computer Language*, September 1992.)

Perhaps our household is a bit more computer centered than average. As a high-tech enterprise, however, it is hardly unique. Many an office or work group faces similar problems. Multiple people need access to multiple computers and printers to access multiple data files for multiple reasons. Sometimes they cooperate, sometimes they compete for limited resources. In all cases, they want to do their jobs with a minimum of running around and knocking into things.

Once upon a time, large companies bought mainframes to solve this problem. Nobody else owned computers. Later on, smaller companies and departments bought minicomputers with multi-user operating systems. The answer today is to buy lots of single-use computers for individuals. That minimizes conflicts, but at the cost of isolation.

To overcome the isolation between computers, you have to hook them together somehow. I have gotten by for years with a powerful product called Laplink. It comes with a cable that ties two machines together by either their serial or parallel ports. Fire it up on both machines and it lets you shovel data reliably back and forth at prodigious rates. So long as the need is occasional and one machine is portable, it's hard to want more than what Laplink provides.

Many people find that their principal need for interconnection is to share printers. Where that is the case, you can cut corners all sorts of ways. Oodles of gadgets exist for multiplexing printers across two or more computers. Some do a serious amount of buffering for you. Most are pretty good at resolving conflicts safely and automatically. All are typically much cheaper than a full-bore network. (Nevertheless, my friends tell me that many an office has laid out $10,000 or more for a network that only shares a laser printer among multiple PCs.)

As an erstwhile computer expert, I am supposed to know all sorts of stuff. Nevertheless, I have managed to stay remarkably ignorant about certain pockets of our broad and turbulent field. Not even my penchant for soaking up trivia has led me to peer inside a few of those pockets. One pocket of ignorance I confess to is data-base technology. Another, until very recently, has been networking.

Once I committed to installing a network, I began reading voraciously. The trade magazines, surprisingly enough, were not of much help. They are aimed primarily at network managers. These folk want to be reassured that their jobs are indeed thankless. Or they want to know about the latest in boards, boxes, and software packages that help them spy on legitimate users of the network. Or they want detailed rationales for upgrading from version 2.x to 3.x of whatever network they're running on. (Have you noticed lately that two thirds of all software products have just introduced version 3.x?)

I did find a trade book that fit my needs remarkably well. It's *PC Magazine Guide to Connectivity* by Frank J. Derfler, Jr. (**Der91**). The author assumes that you know nothing about networks, but that you're not stupid. He takes you from a standing start to where you can talk sagely about PC networks at a cocktail party. And he feeds you considerable data from *PC Magazine*'s thorough product reviews.

I learned that Novell's NetWare dominates the market for server-based networks. Such networks require that you dedicate one machine to running the network. Typically, that machine serves as a central repository for lots of files. You put your big disks, and maybe your printers as well, on the server. All the other machines on the network are clients. They can get away with little or no disk storage of their own. Transfers over the network are fast enough that clients don't mind using the server's disks. That, of course, also eliminates duplication of resources. And it makes it easier to control access to shared resources.

Novell is hardly alone in this important field. Microsoft's LAN Manager and Banyan's VINES are two tough competitors. The payoff for us consumers, as usual, is twofold. Prices are held in check and the products keep improving at a rapid rate.

But I didn't want to dedicate one of my computers to running a network. That would over stretch an already strained equipment budget. What I wanted was a peer-to-peer network. Such a network lets any of the machines on the network behave as a client, a server, or both. All machines still behave mostly as standalone PCs. Occasionally, a server gets boggy when someone else pokes at one of its files or printers. Otherwise, being a server just costs you a little of your precious RAM.

The most important thing I learned about from Derfler's book was Artisoft's LANtastic. It's a peer-to-peer network for PCs that has consistently earned top marks from *PC Magazine*'s product reviews. It has good performance and reliability, and it makes fairly modest demands on memory, even for servers.

So I knew I wanted to install LANtastic. You'd think I'd be home free. Nothing is easier than convincing someone in the computer business to sell you hardware or software. The only trouble is, I didn't know exactly what to buy.

A network is a devil's brew of hardware and software. You need wires to ship the data around. You need boards and boxes to send signals along the wires. Each computer needs a device driver that talks to its particular network board or box. Then you need several layers of software atop those drivers to make the network hum.

Boards and boxes are boring to software types. Derfler wasted little space describing such critters. Even the literature I got from Artisoft was remarkably unspecific. Hardware designers have performed minor miracles with these network boards. Now nobody wants to look twice at them. They are part of the wallpaper.

If you've ever stuck a board inside a PC, you understand some of the issues. Does it need an 8- or a 16-bit slot? Does it occupy address space in the upper 384 kilobytes of RAM? What choices do you get for setting IRQ and I/O port addresses? Get a board that's too rigid or too demanding and you'll never get it to work right in a heavily loaded PC.

Networks add a further complexity. Even after I settled on Ethernet, I found I still had decisions to make. You can wire Ethernet three different ways. The original "frozen yellow garden hose" has evolved to *thick Ethernet* — a multi-wire cable. You can also use *thin Ethernet* — a coaxial cable similar to TV cable (but different, naturally). And the newest option is to use *10BaseT* — a group of four twisted-pair telephone wires.

As usual, there are gazillions of tradeoffs among these choices. I soon determined, however, that any of them would meet my modest needs. So naturally I leaned toward the cheapest and easiest of these wiring schemes. With computers spread all over the house, I didn't want to have to tear up too many walls to run the network wiring.

Our house is an early Victorian monster that dates back to 1850. We renovated it extensively when we sold Whitesmiths. Part of the improvement was to replace a clunky old ITT phone system with a sleek new AT&T Merlin system. All those 25-pair cables disappeared, along with their fat telco connectors poking out of holes in the floor. They got replaced by demure wall-mounted phone jacks.

By some uncanny stroke of good fortune, I had the sense to demand two phone jacks in most rooms (to the utter confusion of our Yankee electricians). Merlin requires RJ45 4-pair jacks. That wiring also happens to support Ethernet 10BaseT. So the worst part of installing a network was already solved. We wouldn't have to butcher the walls to run still more wires.

The next worst part was buying the right boards and boxes. Artisoft will sell you several different "starter kits." These include two driver boards, a length of cable, and all the software you need. But I needed to hook up a laptop. And I was running machines in several rooms. For these and other reasons, their 10BaseT starter kit just didn't meet my needs. So I got one of their fancier starter kits that also happened to support 10BaseT.

I also bought a neat box called the Artisoft Central Station. I connect the parallel port of my laptop to the Central Station, which connects in turn to the network. I can also drive my printer through the Central Station as if it were directly connected to the laptop. Artisoft also promises to do all sorts of neat things with the extra connectors on the back, one of these days. The Central Station has something else that is invaluable to us programmer types. It provides lots of flashing lights on the front panel. That way I can convince myself that the network is actually doing something.

The last box I needed connected everything together. It's called a 10BaseT hub and it squats in the basement where all the RJ45 cables come together. It used to hang by a couple of Velcro strips, but I gave up on them. Twice the network went down — literally — when the adhesive on the strips failed.

I accumulated all this stuff over a period of weeks and slowly pasted it together. (Misco supplied the paste in the form of various RJ45 cables and connectors.) I'd like to say that it worked right off the mark, but it didn't. The first Central Station was DOA. Artisoft replaced it practically over-night. I had to take the Compaq desktop apart and rebuild it from scratch to eliminate various hardware conflicts. That was probably good hygiene anyway.

The LANtastic software came right up, but with an assortment of idio-syncrasies. One by one, I chased them down by repeated scans of the manuals and **READ_ME** files. Still, the various printers behaved erratically over the network. In the end, I spent 40 minutes on the phone with a patient techie from Artisoft. Since then (months ago) the network has been mostly invisible. And that, to me, is high praise.

What I have now is remarkably close to what I wanted. Each computer can use any of the printers on the network with little or no perform-ance penalty. Each can treat disks on another computer as extra disks of its own. Sloshing data around is nearly as fast as reading and writing the local disks.

It's not perfect. I still haven't packed all the network software into the upper 384 kilobytes on some of the machines. I like to back up files with Laplink, but it refuses to talk over the network. A few other bits of software seem to be similarly "network half-aware." Aborting a printout is fraught with peril, particularly for the H-P DeskJet. I have learned that it is often easier to waste paper than to try to save time. And about once a week, I find it easier to reboot all the computers than to disentangle a perplexed network. It gets broody when it's upset. Still, it's mostly a friendly ghost.

I didn't install my own network to save money. Nor should you. Part of the exercise was to advance my education. If there's a network in your immediate future, you face two choices. Either start learning about the technology now, to spread your tuition payments, or get help. Configuring and installing computer networks is an active subindustry. Many are eager to take your money and some are competent. Most are more competent than you are likely to be. Think of it this way — buying a network for your office is no worse than buying aluminum siding for your home. And no better. □

Afterword: My journey through network land continues. The network keeps getting better, but never quite settles down. There's always some reason to perturb it, or to try something new with it. And you know what that means with any complex system.

Looking back over these essays, I see any number of continuing journeys. I still muck about with computer arithmetic, encryption, human interfaces, international standards, and a dozen other topics I've yet to write about. The glory of our business is that it offers such a rich mixture of problems at once pragmatic and theoretical. For someone who never really wanted to leave college, it's a great way to stay in school — without the bane of student wages.

The buggy whip is a common symbol of obsolete technology. Those who worked to improve that mundane tool doubtless mourned its passing. Some, I'm sure, passed from the commercial scene along with the whips they made. Others found something new to make, and to make better. You can make whips or you can make hand-held implements. You can sell carriages or be in the transportation business. All it takes to change with the times is a willingness to learn new things. Continuously.

This collection is intended as a sampler, to stimulate thought. I don't pretend that it's a coherent body of knowledge. It has no niche in the ACM Curriculum. But it does give a flavor of several interesting topics in computer software. And it might stimulate a few new journeys.

Appendix A   List of Columns

The following list gives the publication date, destination, and title of each installment of "Programming on Purpose" published in *Computer Language* through December 1992. For example, the entry

Jul 1986   Design   1   Which Tool is Best?

tells you that the essay "Programming on Purpose: Which Tool is Best?" was first published in the July 1986 edition of *Computer Language*. You can also find it as Essay 1 in the collection *Programming on Purpose: Essays on Software Design*, Prentice-Hall, 1993. The other two collections are *Essays on Software People* and *Essays on Software Technology*.

Date	Collection	#	Title
Jul 1986	Design	1	Which Tool is Best?
Aug 1986	Design	2	Writing Predicates
Sep 1986	Design	3	Generating Data
Oct 1986	Design	4	Finite-State Machines
Nov 1986	Design	5	Recognizing Input
Dec 1986	Design	5	Recognizing Input, Part 2
Jan 1987	Design	6	Handling Exceptions
Feb 1987	Design	7	Which Tool is Next?
Mar 1987	Design	8	Order Out of Chaos
Apr 1987	Technology	1	You Must Be Joking
May 1987	Design	9	Marrying Data Structures
Jun 1987	Design	10	Divorcing Data Structures
Jul 1987	Design	11	Who's the Boss?
Aug 1987	Design	12	By Any Other Name
Sep 1987	People	1	Honestly, Now
Oct 1987	Design	13	Searching
Nov 1987	Design	14	Synchronization
Dec 1987	Design	14	Synchronization, Part 2

Date	Collection	#	Title
Jan 1988	Design	15	Which Tool is Last?
Feb 1988	Technology	2	Computer Arithmetic
Mar 1988	Technology	3	Floating-Point Arithmetic
Apr 1988	Technology	4	The Central Folly
May 1988	Technology	5	Safe Math
Jun 1988	Technology	6	Do-It-Yourself Math Functions
Jul 1988	Design	16	A Designer's Bibliography
Aug 1988	Design	17	A Designer's Reference Shelf
Sep 1988	People	2	You Can't Do That
Oct 1988	Technology	7	Locking the Barn Door
Nov 1988	Technology	8	Half a Secret
Dec 1988	People	3	Protecting Intellectual Property
Jan 1989	People	4	What and How
Feb 1989	People	5	Skin and Bones
Mar 1989	Technology	9	It's (Almost) Alive
Apr 1989	Technology	10	The (Almost) Right Stuff
May 1989	People	6	Product Reviews
Jun 1989	People	7	Awaiting Reply
Jul 1989	Design	18	A Preoccupation with Time
Aug 1989	Design	19	Structuring Time
Sep 1989	People	8	Soup or Art?
Oct 1989	People	9	The Seven Warning Signs
Nov 1989	Design	20	Abstract It
Dec 1989	Design	21	Encapsulate It
Jan 1990	Design	22	Inherit It
Feb 1990	People	10	The Politics of Standards
Mar 1990	People	11	Setting the Standard
Apr 1990	Technology	11	Instant Lies
May 1990	People	12	All the Standard Reasons
Jun 1990	People	13	The Physicist as Programmer
Jul 1990	Technology	12	What Meets the Eye
Aug 1990	Technology	13	Technicolor and Cinemascope
Sep 1990	Technology	14	What Meets the Ear
Oct 1990	Technology	15	Warm Fuzzies
Nov 1990	People	14	Shelfware
Dec 1990	People	15	It's Not My Fault

Date	Collection	#	Title
Jan 1991	People	16	Customer Service
Feb 1991	Design	23	Heresies of Software Design
Mar 1991	People	17	Heresies of Software Management
Apr 1991	Technology	16	Font Follies
May 1991	Technology	17	Text Editors
Jun 1991	Technology	18	Approximating Functions
Jul 1991	Technology	19	Economizing Polynomials
Aug 1991	People	18	Watching the Watchers
Sep 1991	People	19	Washing the Watchers
Oct 1991	Technology	20	Technical Documentation
Nov 1991	Technology	21	All I Want to Do Is
Dec 1991	Technology	22	Programming for the Billions
Jan 1992	Technology	23	All Sorts of Sorts
Feb 1992	Technology	24	Transforming Strings
Mar 1992	Design	24	Remedial Software Engineering
Apr 1992	Technology	25	Books for Our Times
May 1992	People	20	Who's Always Right?
Jun 1992	People	21	The Cycle of Complexity
Jul 1992	People	22	Pity the Typist
Aug 1992	People	23	Criticism
Sep 1992	People	24	Piled Higher and Deeper
Oct 1992	Technology	26	Through the Grapevine
Nov 1992	People	25	Lawyers
Dec 1992	People	26	Bankers

Appendix B Bibliography

The references that follow are all cited in the essays in this collection. I do not include references to "Programming on Purpose" — Appendix A summarizes all of those essays.

A&S65 — M. Abramowitz and I. Stegun, *Handbook of Mathematical Functions,* Dover Publications, Inc., 1965 (and later).

Act70 — F. Acton, *Numerical Methods that Work,* Harper and Rowe, 1970.

Bro75 — F. Brooks, *The Mythical Man-Month,* Addison-Wesley, 1975.

D&H76 — W. Diffie and M. Hellman, "New Directions in Cryptography," IEEE Transactions on Information Theory IT-22, p. 644, November 1976.

Der91 — F. Derfler, Jr., *PC Magazine Guide to Connectivity,* Ziff-Davis Press, 1991.

Elk88 — T. Elkins, "Safe and Sound," *Computer Language,* p. 36, September 1988.)

Ham62 — R. Hamming, *Numerical Methods for Scientists and Engineers,* McGraw-Hill, 1962.

Har78 — J. Hart, E. Cheney, C. Lawson, H. Maehly, C. Mesztenyi, J. Rice, H. Thatcher, Jr., and C. Witzgall, *Computer Approximations,* Robert E. Krieger Publishing Co., 1978.

Hel79 — M. Hellman, "The Mathematics of Public-Key Cryptography," *Scientific American,* August 1979 (reprised in *Scientific American Trends in Computing, Special Issue, Vol. 1,* 1988).

Hoa81 — C. Hoare, "The Emperor's Old Clothes," *Communications of the ACM* 24:2, p. 75, February 1981.

IEE85 — *IEEE Standard for Binary Floating-Point Arithmetic,* Institute of Electrical and Electronics Engineers, 1985.

Knu68 — D. Knuth, *The Art of Computer Programming, Volume 1: Fundamental Algorithms* Addison-Wesley, 1968.

Knu73 — D. Knuth, *The Art of Computer Programming, Volume 3: Sorting and Searching,* Addison-Wesley, 1973.

Mas88 — J. Massey, "An Introduction to Contemporary Cryptography," *Proceedings of the IEEE,* p. 533, May 1988.)

NBS77 — National Bureau of Standards, *Data Encryption Standard,* FIPS Publications 46, 74, and 81, NTIS, Springfield VA, 1977.

P&B89 — P. Plauger and J. Brodie, *Standard C,* Microsoft Press, 1989.

P&B92 — P. Plauger and J. Brodie, *ANSI and ISO Standard C,* Microsoft Press, 1992.

Pla87 — P. Plauger, "Son of PC Meets the C Monster," *Computer Language,* p. 41, February 1987.

Pla89 — P. Plauger, "Standard C: Evolution of the C I/O Model," *The C Users Journal,* August 1989.

Pla91 — P. Plauger, "State of the Art: Floating-Point Arithmetic," *Embedded Systems Programming,* August 1991.

Pla92 — P. Plauger, *The Standard C Library,* Prentice-Hall, 1992.

RSA76 — R. Rivest, A. Shamir, and L. Adleman, "A Method for Obtaining Digital Signatures and Public-Key Cryptosystems," *Communications of the ACM* 21:2, p. 120, February 1976.

Sim88 — G. Simmons, "How to Insure that Data Acquired to Verify Treaty Compliance are Trustworthy," *Proceedings of the IEEE,* p. 621, May 1988.)

Ste72 — P. Sterbenz, *Floating-Point Computation,* Prentice-Hall, 1972.

Sto88 — C. Stoll, "Stalking the Wily Hacker," *Communications of the ACM* 31:5, p. 484, May 1988.

Tho84 — K. Thompson, "Reflections on Trusting Trust," *Communications of the ACM* 27:8, p. 761, August 1984.

Index